Reading Marx

Books by B.N. Ray

Tradition and Innovation in Indian Political Thought
Political Theory : Interrogations and Interventions
Critical Theory : The Marx-Marcuse Encounter
Liberalism and the Communitarian Challenge
John Rawls and the Agenda of Social Justice
C.B. Macpherson and Liberalism
Contemporary Political Thinking
Nietzsche After Hundred Years
Citizenship in a Globalising World
Gandhigiri
Reading Gandhi
Political Theory and Thought
Indian Political Thought
Foundations of Western Political Thought
Political Philosophy
The Radical Monk: Social and Political Philosophy of Swami Vivekanand

Reading Marx

B.N. Ray

Kaveri Books

New Delhi - 110 002

First Published in 2018

ISBN: 978-81-7479-211-2

Published by

Kaveri Books

4832/24, Ansari Road

New Delhi-110002 (India)

Tel: 011-23288140, 23245799

E-mail : kaveribooks@vsnl.com

kaveribooks@gmail.com

Website: www.kaveribooks.com

Typeset at

Delta Book World, New Delhi - 110 002.

PRINTED IN INDIA

In Honour of

Dr. Achyuta Samanta

the Founder of KISS and KIIT

which have completed 25 years of glorious journey endeavouring to give voice to the voiceless and power to the powerless through education.

Preface

This is the kind of anthology that indefatatigable Marx scholar Hal Drapers calls a 'bits and pieces collection' – passages drawn across Marx's writings, arranged by theme. The dangers of this sort of collection are many and obvious. Marx's thought can be easily misrepresented by quotation out of context; by selection of generalizing, summary or aphoristic material at the expense of the dense and the complex; by imposition, through the choice of themes and ordering of the material, of priorities that were not his own. I have done my utmost to avoid these pitfalls. In particular, I have restricted any temptation to force Marx's thought into the categorical frameworks of later sociology. Readers will not find separate chapters on 'class'or 'alienntion'; such themes are treated as they occur in Marx, as integral parts of his overall analysis of bourgeois society. On the other hand, a 'bits and pieces' collection has advantages other formats often lack. It can give wider currency to passages buried in works that none but specialists would normally read, and thereby shake up simplistic ideas of Marx gleaned from textbooks or a cursory reading of the Communist Manifesto. It permits comparison of Marx's ideas on particular topics across a range of texts. Most importantly of all, it allows the many who do not have the time to plough through Capital, or even a hefty standard anthology like McLellan's selected writings, the opportunity nonetheless to get a flavor of Marx himself.

I have minimized commentary in order to increase room for Marx's own writings. I do, however, provide a brief introduction, which endeavours to say something about the nature of Marx's literary legacy, and the interpretive problems it poses. This seemed to me essential in a book of this kind.

Thanks are due also to my editor for his painstaking copy-editing. But since I am presuming to present a selection of somebody else's writings and in the case of Marx such an enterprise has often enough struck me as simply ludicrous, given their magnitude, it is more than conventionally necessary to stress that the responsibility for whatever defects this book might have is mine alone.

Marx, wrote an enormous amount (the Marx/Engels works will amount on to more than one hundred fat volumes), over a period of some forty years. This textual legacy is as varied as it is vast. Marx's writing do not form a unified as canonically equivalent. Book licks the first volume of Capital, finalized for the press and revised through several edition, form the smaller journal articles. Twice he did this as editor of his own paper, though in the first case under conditions of censorship, and he also wrote occasionally for the socialist press. But much of this journalism was done on a paid basis, mainly for the New York Daily Tribune (1852-62). These newspaper articales were often wtitten in haste, and sometime on subjects that Marx had by no means researched in the same depth as he did, say, Capital. His own view of his 'newspaper muck' was that 'in the final analysis (it) is nothing (...) Purely scientific works are something completely different'.

Many of what would now be accepted as amongst Marx's major writings, were not polised for publication, but were drafts left in various stages of completion. Amongst these are the bulk of his so-called 'early works', including the Critique of hegels,el's Rechtsphilosophie (1843b), the Economic and Philosophical Manuscripts of 1844 (1844c), and the German Ideology (with Engels, 1845-6)(1846a). The publication of these writings, half a century after Marx's death, was a bombshell, playing havoc with received ideas of what he stood for. Their status in his legacy has been acrimoniously debated ever since. Some see the early writings as mere juvenilia, others hail them as providing the 'humanist' key to Marx's entire oeuvre. The German Ideology (1846a), which is generally acknowledged as (at least) a major 'transitional' work in Marx's intellectual development, provides the fullest account anywhere in his writings of the overall 'premises' of his viewpoint. It also nicely illustrates the difficulties of assessing drafts. For it was abandoned by its authors to 'the gnawing criticism of the mice', how in whilst Friedrich Engels, unearthing the manuscript forty years later, commented that it showed 'only incomplete our knowledge of economic history was at that time'.

Such difficulties extend to the very heart of Marx's work. Of his immense 'economics' – the several 'pamphlets' he proposed in the Preface to the 1844 Manuscripts, which grew to become his 'dramatically incomplete' life-work – only the 1859 Critique and Capital 1 were prepared for the press. The 'first draft' of capital, the mighty Grundrisse (1857-8), was not. It was only effectively published in 1953, while as late as 1968 Martin Nicolaus, its eventual English translator (1973), could write an article on his text with the thoroughly accurate title 'The unknown Marx'. Even volumes 2 and 3 of Capital were issued by Engels after Marx's death (1885-1894b). He wove together volume 2 from eight separate manuscripts, written between 1865 and 1878, and edited volume 3 mainly from Marx's incomplete and often very scrappy first draft of 1864-5 a text compiled before volume 1 was revised for press. The three volumes of Theories of Surplus Value, which Marx had also intended as an integral part of his 'economics' were left in draft from too in 1861-63. Theories was first published in full a century after it was written. There are other smaller manuscripts that are also associated with the 'economics', of various dates: of particular note is one known as 'Results of the immediate process of production', dating from sometime between 1863 and 1866. Other drafts of Marx's, which are today seen as important because they are fuller and more revealing than final texts, include those of The civil War in France (1871) and the letter to Vera Zasulich of March 1881.

Much of this material was unknown both to the generations that gave Marxism its shape and form, and to Marx's classical critics. Yet these provide the interpretive grid through which he is so often still read today. The 'young Marx' was unknown to Kautsky, Plekhanov, Labriola, and Lenin, the Grundrisse to Gramsci, Lukacs, and Korsch, too, hastily written off by successive biographers as a period of 'slow death'. In many ways, arguably, Marx still remains 'unknown'. The problem now is less the availability of texts, than the blinkers imposed by past interpretations the tradition of all the dead generations weighs like a nightmare on the minds of the living.

Other categories of Marx's writing pose different problems. He penned a lot in the context of his political activity, notably as a founding member of the General Council of the International Working Men's Association (1864-72). Much of this sort of material is of little interest save to Marx specialists or to idolators: for instance his scurrilous portraits of political opponents in 'Great Men of the Exile' (with Engels, 1852), or his tedious polemic (on which he wasted eighteen months) against Karl Vogt. But even the more enduring writings of this kind pose difficult questions of context and interpretation. Marx was sometimes constrained, for instance, by the pressures of organizational politics. His 'toning-down' of The Civil War in France from drafts to final text may be explained by this factor, although this is mere conjecture.

The circumstances of Marx's more directly 'political' texts need always to be borne in mind when their content is at issue, whether it is a matter of the grand rolling simplicities of the Manifesto – it was after all precisely that, a call to arms in the heady revolutionary year or 1848, not a reasoned discourse on social theory – or the noncommittal reply Marx eventually sent in 1881 to Vera Zasulich, a member of a Russian revolutionary sect he had very little time for, on the vexatious question of the destiny of the Russian peasant commune. The issue of whether or not the commune could be a possible basis for a distinctive kind of socialism bitterly divided the Russian revolutionary movement, then and later. Concern as to the uses to which his words might be put, rather than a change of mind on Marx's part, is the most plausible reason for his own excision from the final text of the very detailed (and eminently 'unorthodox') analysis present in his initial three drafts. The point about context also holds more generally. In seeking to interpret the famous Preface to the 1859 Critique, for instance, a text that has been repeatedly used to legitimate scientific, deterministic readings of Marx, we should perhaps remember that Marx wrote this with a eye on the Prussian state censor. He was concerned to portray the Critique as a work of empirical science rather than of political agitation – and to get it published.

Throughout his life, Marx had the habit of taking copious notes and excerpts from other writers, that he would annotate with his own comments. Indeed, the degree to which Marx developed his analysis of capitalism through a critique of its theorists, the political economists, rather than through empirical investigation, is worth underlining. Engles, by contrast, had first–hand acquaintance with factory production, and in his Condition of the

Working Class in England in 1844 produced a pioneering classic of empirical sociology. Some of Marx's notes and excerpts (like the 1844 notes on James Mill, the 1874 comments on Bakunin's Statism and Anarchy, and the 1880 marginal notes on Adolph Wangner) are now relatively well known; but amongst the most interesting are the so-called Ethnological Notebooks of 1879-80, on Lewis Henry Morgan and others published in Holland in 1972 and still awaiting English translation. Much has still to be published, at least in the West. In the early 1880s, for example, Marx compiled a massive chronology of world history from the first century BC to the 17th century, which runs to some 1500 pages in print. Apparently it focuses, amongst other, on the rise of the modern nation state, the early development of capitalism, and the importance for both of the Reformation – topics on which Marx's views have been extensively debated. So far the only published text is in Russian. Generally, Marx's notebooks are valuable for the light they shed on his sources, his working methods, and areas of his thought not developed in published writings. This is true in particular of his last decade, in which he read prodigiously and published little. The notebooks also illustrate the breadth of Marx's interests. Like many another Victorian, he was an amateur of the natural sciences, attending lectures on chemistry for 'a Sunday amusement'. Amongst his notebooks are ones that deal at length with geology complete with drawing of fossils, the uses of electricity, and even with calculus.

Similar things can be said of Marx's correspondence, which was copious. Not only is this of evident biographical interest. Letters, like drafts an notebooks, illuminate the development of his thought – we can watch him wrestling with problems – and its many byways. And at times, they provide brilliantly succinct summaries. The letter to Annenkov of December 1846 is as good a précis as any of Marx's general outlook at the time. One of the clearest formulations of his theory of value is to be found in a letter of the late 1870s to the editorial board of the Russian periodical puts it in black and white that Capital does not legitimate extrapolation of the trajectory of capitalist developed in Western Europe into a 'universal path' all peoples are fated to tread.

I have not yet mentioned Marx's youthful literary ventures, or the three volumes of poetry he dedicated, as a student, to his future wife Jenny von Westphalen. These may perhaps be passed over, without too much contention, as amongst his least enduring creations. But they do, at least, have the virtue of revealing the man behind the myths. This anthology begins in this vein, with Marx's so-called 'Confessions', his answers to questions put to him as part of a parlour game by his daughters Jenny and Laura, sometime in the 1860s. Here we learn, among other things, that Marx's 'favourite heroes' were Spartacus and Kepler, his 'favourite poets' Shakespeare, Goethe and Aeschylus and his 'idea of misery' submission. It is salutary to find that his 'favourite motto' was 'De omnibus dubitandum' (doubt everything). His 'favourite virtue in man' was strength. In women, however, it was 'weakness'; and his 'favourite heroine' was not a Boadicea or a Joan of Arc, but Goethe's fictional Gretchen. Marx may, of course, simply have been teasing his female children; but he was, amongst many other things, a very Victorian, if Bohemian, paterfamilias. Such ephemera serve to remind us that this was not the only respect in which Marx was a man of his time and place.

Like most other Victorians, Marx thought both 'race' and family natural categories even if subject to some 'historical modification', and had little trouble in distinguishing between 'civilization' (which for him was white, western, and modern) and 'barbarism'. His views on the beneficial results of European colonialism would embarrass many twentieth-century Marxists, notwithstanding his denunciations of the violence of its means, and the sharp intimations of what has since come to be called the 'development of underdevelopment' that are occasionally to be found in his work. Marx was, at best, ambivalent on claims to national self-determination, particularly where Slavic peoples were concerned; and his assessment of peasantry was not one that anticipated the peasant wars of the twentieth century, often led by Marxist parties. Peasant revolutions have been an enduring feature of the modern global landscape: they are a striking illustration of the way the course of history has declined to conform to Marx's expectations. There are others. What he might have made of 'Marxist-feminism' is anyone's guess; but his notes on the split in the American section of the International (1872) dismiss the American feminist Victoria C. Woodhull as 'a banker's woman, free-lover, and general humbug', and he had her section summarily expelled in August 1869, might appear somewhat naïve to Marxists.

Marx's assertions that nothing could be introduced either in primary or higher schools that admitted of party or class interpretation. Only subjects such as the physical sciences, grammar, etc..., were fit matter for schools. The rules of grammar, for instance, could not differ, whether explained by a religious Tory or a free thinker. Subjects that admitted of different conclusions must be excluded and left for the adults.

None of this is intended to diminish Marx. To criticize him for failing to transcend all the prejudices and preconceptions of his era, makes just about as much sense as berating Aristotle for omitting to invent the steam-engine – or defending slavery. But it is all well to be aware, in a world that has seen Marx's work transformed into exactly the kind of theological master-key to history he himself so emphatically spurned, that his writings are products of a time and place, which are steadily receding into the past. Capital might have been a very different book had it been written a hundred years later; Marx was not in the habit of deducing the world from his own writings.

Marx's legacy would be different enough to interpret, even if it had not been caught up in the tribulations of the bloodiest century in human history, and hopelessly mythologized by his foes and friends alike. What weight, for example, should be given to 'early' works as against later the 'humanist' Marx of the 1844 Manuscripts as against the 'scientific' Marx of Capital? How are we to balance the always difficult, sometimes confused, but often brilliant Grundrisse against the polished masterpiece of world literature that is volume 1 of Capital? What are we to make of Marx's most widely read text, the Communist Manifesto, knowing both that he painted a very much complex picture of 'the history of all hitherto existing society' elsewhere, and that he later on explicitly dissociated himself from the political 'programme' of this work – still regularly reproduced in undergraduate texts – in the light, of the experience of the Paris Commune of 1871?

The short answer is: in all of it – inclusive of the many uncertainties, ambiguities, hesitations, changes of mind, and, on occasion, downright inconsistencies – and in none of it, if what is expected is a single, authoritative, talismanic statement of doctrine. 'The authentic Marx' is as chimerical a figure as the definitive production of Hamlet. It is often possible to show that he did not hold views often ascribed to him; and it is also clear what he was against – injustice, oppression, and exploitation. That said, his textual legacy is still capable of legitimately sustaining a variety of interpretations, all of which can find some backing in his writings, and none of which are beyond 'refutation' by selective quotation – that favourite Marxological device – from some other part of the canon. This is not to say that Marx was in any way an incoherent thinker, but – simply that he was human. 'Marxism' did not spring fully armed from his brain, one fine day in 1845, like Athene from the head of Zeus; nor is it the offspring of some mysterious entelechy, smoothly unfolding itself from the Paris Manuscripts of 1844 to Capital. There were false starts, dead ends, chance encounters – like with the rebellious young son of a pious Barmen industrialist, who at the stage of the game, knew far more of the modern world than he. It is the translation of Marx's writings into scriptures, texts deserving of reverential exegesis rather than than critical confrontation, that makes authenticity an issue in the first place. Behind its self-appointed arbiters stands the gulag.

I do not, then, intend to tell readers how Marx should be read, beyond suggesting the merits of an awareness of historical contexts – both the contexts in which Marx himself wrote, and those in which he has been variously appropriated. We must 'doubt everything' his favourite motto.

This anthology focuses on what would nowadays be called Marx's sociology: it does not pretend to illustrate all his concerns equally. Neither Marx's political activities, nor the more technical reaches of his economics, are much addressed in this page. Within this rubric, I have ranged pretty widely across the various categories of his output discussed previously in the belief that a decent selection should reflect Marx's writing in its diversity. Readers will, of course, find many well-know passages.

It remains to say only that this anthology, like any other, is a personal selection. Others would doubtless have chosen very differently, and produced equally good collections. But that, in a way, is itself a testimony to the continuing fecundity of Marx's thought. To transform his texts into sacred tablets is to make a mockery of the critical spirit that animates everything he wrote. Nonetheless, when all is said and done, Marx remains, for all his Victorian prejudices, our contemporary. The study of modern society still begins with his work, even if it cannot and should not end there.

The book will equip us to approach a key thinker's original texts by explaining his key ideas, putting him into context and, perhaps most importantly, showing you why this thinker is considered to be significant. The emphasis is on concise, clearly written guides which do not presuppose specialist knowledge. Although it focuses on particular Marx, it stresses that no critical thinker ever existed in a vacuum but, instead, emerged from a broader intellectual, cultural and social history. Finally, this book will act as a bridge between you and the thinker's original texts: not replacing them but rather complementing what he wrote. This book is necessary for a number of reasons.

There is still a need for authoritative and intelligible introductions. But this reflects a different world from the 1960s. New thinkers have emerged and the reputations of others have risen and fallen, as new research has developed. New methodologies and challenging ideas have spread through the arts and humanities. The study of literature is no longer – if it ever was – simply the study and evaluation of poems, novels and plays. It is also the study of the ideas, issues and difficulties which arise in any literary text and in its interpretation. Other arts and humanities subjects have changed in analogous ways.

With these changes, new problems have emerged. The ideas and issues behind these radical changes in the humanities are often presented without reference to wider contexts or as theories which you can simply 'add on' to the texts you read. Certainly, there is nothing wrong with picking out selected ideas or using what comes to hand – indeed, some thinkers have argued that this is, in fact, all we can do. However, it is sometimes forgotten that each new idea comes from the pattern and development of somebody's thought and it is important to study the range and context of their ideas. Against theories 'floating in space', the critical theory places key thinkers and their ideas firmly back in their contexts.

More than this, these books reflect the need to go back to the thinker's own texts and ideas. Every interpretation of an idea, even the most seemingly innocent one, offers its own 'spin', implicitly or explicitly. To read only books on a thinker, rather than texts by that thinker, is to deny yourself a chance of making up your own mind. The purpose of these books is to give you a 'way in' by offering an accessible overview of a these thinkers' ideas and works and by guiding your further reading, starting with each thinker's own texts. To use a metaphor from the philosopher Ludwig Wittgenstein, these books are ladders, to be thrown away after you have climbed to the next level. Not only, then, do they equip you to approach new ideas, but also they empower you, by leading you back to a theorist's own texts and encouraging you to develop your own informed opinions.

Finally, this reader is necessary because, just as intellectual needs have changed, the education systems around the world – the contexts in which introductory books are usually read – have changed radically, too. What was suitable for the minority higher education system of the 1960s is not suitable for the larger, wider, more diverse, high technology education systems of the twenty-first century. These changes call not just for new, up-to-date, introductions but new methods of presentation. Thus reader has been developed with today's students in mind.

Karl Marx is 'critical' for three reasons. First, he is examined in the light of subjects which involve criticism: principally literary studies or English and cultural studies, but also other disciplines which rely on the criticism of books, ideas, theories and unquestioned assumptions. Second, studying his work will provide us with a 'tool kit' for informed critical reading and thought, which will heighten our own criticism. Third, he is critical because he is crucially important: he deals with ideas and questions which can overturn conventional understandings of the world, of texts, of everything we take for granted, leaving us with a deeper understanding of what we already knew and with new ideas.

No introduction can tell you everything. However, by offering a way into critical thinking, this book hopes to begin to engage us in an activity which is productive, constructive and potentially life changing.

B N Ray
Higher Education Campus-3
KISS University
Bhubaneswar, Odisha

Diwali 2017

Contents

1

Life and Times

Karl Marx (1818-1883) is arguably the most controversial figure in the long history of political philosophy. Intellectual and activist, journalist, pamphleteer, revolutionary organizer and essayist, public figure and fugitive, he was author or coauthor of some fifty volumes of both scholarly and political writings. He was an opponent of much of the past, even while appreciating how that past served as a foundation of a more desirable future. A complex thinker, sharp-tempered, and an articulate speaker, debater, and critic of various contemporaries, he clashed with many people during his life.

In addition to the immeasurable effects of his work on world events, Marx profoundly affected a number of scholarly disciplines beyond political philosophy, most importantly economics and sociology but also art and literature. Because of the wide reach of his theories and their many implications, it is hard to imagine an important aspect of study or life that has been immune to his influence. This simply suggests the multiple ways that thinking individuals have understood the tremendous output of this literary giant. Entering into the field of Marx studies is like embarking on an intellectual adventure relatively few other authors or books can offer. The questions he raised, the insights he had, and the solutions he proposed deal with the most significant issues facing humanity. Interpreters have found in Marx mine of ideas that they believe can be applied to such concerns as poverty, peace, feminism, discrimination, ecology, and, ultimately, human survival. Given his vast output, and that of commentators on his work, there are many paths one can use to approach his writings. Any single route has its supporters and no one choice fully satisfies every critic.

Einstein, Freud, Jesus, and Karl Marx have been listed as the most important figures in history. Of course, the followers of Marx probably outnumber even the followers of Jesus. Some people, moreover, regard themselves as both Marxists and Christians. Marx was the son of a Jewish lawyer who converted to Lutheranism despite having descended from generations of rabbis; Marx was thus raised as a Protestant. He studied at German universities in Bonn, Berlin, and Jena, first in law and then in philosophy. His PhD at Jena (received when he was only twenty-three) was based on a completely ordinary dissertation on Democritus and Epicurus. While in Berlin, Marx had come under the sway of Hegelianism and a group of radical Hegelians. But later, strongly influenced by the philosophy of Ludwig Feuerbach, he rejected idealism for materialism and his own theory of history as the outworking of economic factors.

Marx's radical views prevented him from occupying an academic post. In 1842 he became editor of a Cologne newspaper that during his tenure became much too radical for the authorities and was suppressed. The twenty-five-year-old Marx then went to Paris, where he mingled with many famous radicals and established another radical periodical. In Paris he also met his future collaborator, Friedrich Engels. In about a year Marx was expelled from Paris, and from 1845 to 1848 he lived in Brussels. While there, he helped form a worker's union that, together with other similar groups, became known as the Communist League. It was for this organization that he and Engles wrote their famous and stirring *Communist Manifesto* (1848). Marx spent a brief period again in Paris and then in Cologne, participating in both the French and the German revolutions of 1848. He was, however, expelled once again from both countries. In 1849 he went to London and stayed there for the rest of his life.

Grief at Edgar's death was intensified by privation. There was, as ever, a domestic cash crisis. Jenny visited the 'pop-house', as she called the pawnbrokers, so often that she called the amiable local Soho pawnbroker Uncle. 'Pop Goes the Weasel', the nursery rhyme about a shoemaker pawning his tools, was an early favourite of Tussy's. Not that she had a nursery: her bedroom and playroom were the multifunctional twin boxes of the little Soho flat squeezed into by the three grown-ups and her rapidly growing elder sisters. Borrowing against her better linens, wedding silver and the family's clothes, Jenny kept the domestic economy circulating whilst her husband busied himself with the inaugural meetings of the International Working Men's Association and burned the midnight oil to catch up on his overdue articles. Jenny and Lenchen were perennially short on crockery, glasses and sufficient food for the flow of friends and guests to their home, constant as the tide.

Tussy arrived into a family of political radicals under constant surveillance. In 1850 a German newspaper editor calling himself Schmidt arrivcd in London, purportedly to visit the Great Exhibition. In fact, Schmidt was Agent Wilhelm Stieber, briefed by the Prussian Minister of the Interior to spy on Marx and his associates. Stieber infiltrated German communist, meetings and the homes of people connected with the worker and democratic movements, observing in detail the dwelling of its most prominent leader:

Marx lives in one of the worst and hence cheapest quarters of London. He has two rooms, the one with the view of the street being the drawing—room, behind it the bedroom. There is not one piece of good, solid furniture in the entire flat. Everything is broken, tattered and torn, finger-thick dust everywhere, and everything in the greatest disorder. A large, old-fashioned table, covered with waxcloth, stands in the middle of the drawing-room, on it lie manuscripts, books, newspapers, then the children's toys, bits and pieces from 'his wife's sewing basket, next to it a few teacups with broken rims, dirty spoons, knives, forks, candlesticks, inkpot, glasses, Dutch clay pipes, tobacco-ash; in a word all kinds of trash, and everything on one table; a junk dealer would he ashamed of it. When you enter the Marx flat your sight is dimmed by coal and tobacco smoke so that you grope around at first as if you were in a cave, until your eyes get used to these fumes. Everything is dirty, everything covered with dust. It is dangerous to sit down. Here is a chair with only three legs, there the 'children play kitchen on another chair that happens to be whole; true – it is off ed to the visitor, but the children's kitchen is not removed; if you sit on it you risk a pair of trousers. But nothing of this embarrasses Marx or his wife in the least; you are received in the friendliest manner, are cordially offered a pipe, tobacco and whatever else there is; a spirited conversation makes up for the domestic defects and in the end you become reconciled because of the company, find it interesting, even original. This is the faithful portrait of the family life of the Communist leader Marx.

In London, Marx required financial help from Engels, for just as some are addicted to gambling, Marx was addicted to reading and writing, and these activities did not produce much of an income. Despite Engels help and the small amount of money he received for articles he wrote for the New York *Tribune*, he lived in poverty, illness, and – when his children and wife died one by one – immense sadness.

During this period Marx wrote the *Critique of Political Economy* (1859) and, more important, the work destined to become the primary document of international communism, *Capital* (vol. 1, 1867; vols. 2 and 3, edited by Enegls, 1885 and 1894). In 1864 he helped create the International Workingmen's Association (the so-called First International), which he later led. A famous clash between Marx and the anarchist Mikhail Bakunin, however, led to its dissolution within about ten years. Marx died of pleurisy in London when he was sixty-five.

The utilitarians pursed social and political reform. Karl Marx went even further. Marx wanted not merely to reform society but to transform it. Marx, who is famous for his remark that philosophers have tried only to interpret the world, whereas the real point is to change it, did not regard his work as philosophy. Marx offers a description and analysis of the human social and political condition, but he did not himself present this understanding as the absolute and final truth. For Marx the ideal society has no economic classes, no wages, no money, no private property, and no exploitation. Each person will not only be provided a fully adequate material existence but will also be given the opportunity to develop freely and completely all physical and mental faculties. The alienation of the individual from the surrounding world will be minimal.

Humans, Marx believed, are social animals with physical needs, needs that are satisfied when we develop the means to satisfy them. These means of producing the satisfaction of needs are called the means or forces of production. The utilization of any one set of means of production leads to fresh needs and therefore to further means of production. For example, the invention of iron tools (a new means of production) for the cultivation of crops leads to still a newer need – for iron – and therewith to the means for satisfying this newer need. Thus, human history consists of successive stages of development of various means of production. Furthermore, the utilization of any given means of production, whether it is a simple iron tool or a complex machine, necessarily involves certain social relationships, especially those involving property. These social relationships are called the productive relations. Thus, the social relationships (the productive relations) depend on the stage of evolution of the forces of production.

The forces of production at a given stage, however, develop to the point where they come into conflict with the existing social relationships, which are then destroyed and replaced by new social relationships. For example, the need at the end of the Middle Ages to supply the new markets in the Far East and the colonies in the New World required new methods of manufacture and commerce, which brought with their development societal changes incompatible with the feudal social structure of the Middle Ages.

The new social relationships then endure until new needs arise and a new stage is reached in the evolution of the forces of production. This dialectical process repeats itself over and over again and is the history of people, economics, and society. To put this another way, history is the result of productive activity in interplay with social relationships. According to Marx, this interplay accounts not only for all socio economic – political situations but also for morality, law, religion, and, to a greater or lesser extent, even philosophy and art. According to Marx the critical social relationships involve property. With the advent of private property, society became divided into two classes: those with property and those without.

Hostility between the two classes was, and is, inevitable, Marx said. Those with property, of course, are the dominant class, and government and morality are always the instruments of the dominant class. When the forces of production create conflict with the existing social relationships, class struggle becomes acute, revolution results, and a new dominant class seizes control of the organs of state and imposes its ethic. The dialectical process repeats itself until private property and the division of society into opposed classes disappears In modern capitalist societies, what has happened, according to Marx, is that the means of production are primarily concentrated in large factories and workshops in which a group of individual workers cooperatively produces a product. They collectively "mix their labor with the product", as Locke would say. But the product they mix their labor with is not owned by them. Rather, it is appropriated by the owners of the factories, who thus in effect also own the workers. Out of this circumstance comes the fundamental conflict of capitalist society: production is socialized, but ownership is not. Furthermore, Marx argued, capitalists obviously must sell what their workers produce for more than they pay the workers to make it. The laborers thus produce goods that are worth more than their wages. This exploitation of the workers is inevitable as long as the conflict between socialized means of production and non-socialized ownerships continues. It is a necessary part of the capitalist system and is not a result of wickedness or inhumanity on the part of the capitalist.

There are two further unavoidable consequences of continuing capitalism, in Marx's opinion. First, the longer the capitalist system continues, the smaller and wealthier the possessing class becomes. This is simply the result of the fact that the surplus value of products – that is, the value of a product less its "true" cost, which is the cost of the labor put into it- continues to accrue to the capitalists. Further, as smaller capitalists cannot compete, and as a result fail in their enterprise and sink into the ranks of the workers, society's wealth becomes increasingly concentrated: fewer and fewer people control more and more of it.

The second consequence of continued capitalism, according to Marx, is the increasing alienation of the workers. The more wealth the workers produce, the poorer they become, relatively speaking, for it is not they who retain this wealth. So the result of increased productivity for the workers is; paradoxically but inevitably, their devaluation in their own eyes and in fact. They have become mere commodities.

In addition because workers produce through their labor, the worker's labor nor are the products they make their own. Both labor and products are as alien things that dominate them. Thus, workers feel at home with themselves only during their leisure time and in eating, drinking, and having sex. Worker's presence at work is not voluntary but imposed and, whenever possible, avoided. Because they have put their lives into what belongs to others, workers are abject, debased, physically exhausted, and overcome with malaise. And because the relation of people to themselves in first realized and expressed in the relationship between each person and another, workers are alienated from their fellows.

The situation Marx describes is, in his view, self-liquidating. The capitalist system of property ownership is incompatible with the socialized conditions of production and ultimately destined to failure. Inevitable overproduction will result in economic crises, a falling rate of profit, and increased exploitation of the working class, which will increasingly become conscious of itself and its own intolerable condition, the inadequacy of capitalism, and the inevitability of history. The revolution of the proletariat leading to a dictatorship of the proletariat, will follow. In this instance, however, the overturning of the existing social order will eventually result in the classless society just described, for property, as well as the means of production, will have become socialized. The disappearance of classes will mark the end of class struggle and also, therefore, the end of political power because the sole function of political power is the suppression of one class at the expense of another.

By the end of the nineteenth century, most European socialist parties were committed to Marxism, but a split developed between the revolutions, those who believed that a violent revolution was necessary to set in the place the collective ownership of the means of production and distribution of goods, and the revisionists or evolutionary socialists, those who thought that these ends could be achieved through peaceful and piecemeal reform.

Although evolutionary socialism became strong in Great Britain and survives in the socialist parties of many nations to the present day, the revolution gained ascendancy in the Second International, the successor to the First International. Under the leadership of Lenin, the revolutionist Bolsheviks came to control the Russian Social Democratic Labor Party and seized control of Russia itself in the Revolution of 1917, becoming in 1918 the Communist Party of the USSR.

Although the Russian Communists withdrew from the Second International and founded Third International or Comintern in 1919 to gain leadership of the world socialist movement, most European Socialist parties disassociated themselves from the Communists. The term Communism, with a capital C, today still denotes the Marxist-Leninist ideology of the parties founded under the banner of the Comintern and is to be distinguished from lowercase-communism, which denotes any form of society in which property or other important goods are held in common by the community.

Recollected by the rest of her family as the most miserable time of their lives, Tussy never really remembered the pinched Soho years. Twenty-eight Dean Street, without plumbing, gaslight or privacy, was sub-let to the Marxes by a grouchy Irish linguist for £22 per year. The family moved into these lodgings in 1851, shortly after the death of their second son, Little Fawkes. Though Tussy didn't know it, the comprehensive intelligence of a Prussian secret agent sent directly by the Minister of the Interior provides a memorable illustration of Marx family life in the Soho flat where she was born.

2

Introduction

The influence of Marx throughout the late–nineteenth and twentieth centuries was immense, and it is not yet exhausted. But as with any thinker who has changed the course of history, the effects of his work have not always been what he would have predicted or wanted. At the extreme: for over twenty years, world Marxism was dominated by Stalin, whose policies had as little in common with Marx's as the tortures of the Inquisition had with the teachings of Jesus. By stages, the power in Russia passed from the soviets to the party bureaucracy, and 'elections' for the soviets became a one –party matter; and Western social democratic parties back- pedalled on their socialist aims till they became, also by stages; the mildly interventionist liberal parties that they are today. Clearly, neither the Chinese Communist Party nor the British Labour Party nor the SPD has much in common with Marx. But how do these tendencies relate to Marxism? On the subject of different types of democracy, there is some ambiguity in Marx himself. He holds up the Paris Commune of 1871 as a new, higher type of democracy, and Lenin takes this as his starting point in *The State and Revolution*. But Marx also held out the possibility that in the most advanced parliamentary countries socialist revolution might come legally, through the election of a worker's party, to a parliamentary majority. Legally, but not necessarily peacefully, since a capitalist rebellion against the workers' government might occur. Also, it can be argued that, while universal suffrage is now widespread, it has been accompanied by a shift in power from the elected to the unelected parts of the state, which make the prospects for the UK and USA more akin to those of Germany under Bismarck than to those of the UK under Gladstone or the USA under Lincoln.

The Communists in 1917 were close to the Marx of The Civil War in France in their belief that the apparatus of the capitalist state could not be taken over but had to be 'smashed'. And the experience of history has confirmed this belief: where governments committed to socialism have been elected to power, the forces of the old state apparatus have always been strong enough either to deflect them from their socialist purpose or to overthrow them. The typical case is Chile, where Allende's elected socialist coalition was overthrown by the army under General Pinochet, with US support, and replaced by a regime of blood and torture, to the admiration of British Conservatives. On the other hand, practically, the record of communists in power is everywhere one of eventually destroying democracy where it had existed, either in its soviet or its parliamentary guise. While some communist countries have had a better record of economic and social polity than is commonly admitted in the West, none has established popular control either of the state or the economy- hence none can be called socialist in the sense that Marx understood the word. Social democratic governments on the other hand, while also abandoning the goal of popular control of the economy, have presided over the development of what are probably the best societies to live in modern times, if not ever, upon the basis of strong trade unions and co-operative movements, redistributive taxation, a welfare state and a mixed economy. Whether this social democratic option is still on the menu since globalization is a moot point.

Marxist parties do exist that are committed to government of state and economy by elected worker's councils on the model of the soviets during and immediately after the Russian Revolution, while they were still democratic institutions in which communists competed for elections with social democrats, anarchists and even liberals. Marx's 'predictions' are not prophecies, but are the identification of tendencies always inherent in capitalism, which develop as it progresses, and will continue to develop short of either revolution or catastrophic collapse. His mistake regarding these tendencies was usually 'telescoping', that is, exaggerating the speed at which they would develop. As to the tendencies themselves, he was amazingly accurate. This can be seen in several instances.

Globalization

Marx mistakenly thought that the nation state was already on its way out, even within capitalism, in his own time. But, though this was a premature obituary in the mid – nineteenth century, something of the sort is happening today. The coming of supranational institutions to Europe, which Marx thought was imminent, has at last happened. But more importantly, the global market has everywhere undermined the economic sovereignty of nations. National governments no longer protect the interests of their own people against global market forces. There are those who welcome this development and those who resist it. Marx would not belong unambiguously to either camp. His 1847 speech on free trade recognizes the adverse effects that free trade has on the workers, yet concludes by supporting free trade as it will make economic contradictions on a larger scale, leading to the emancipation of the proletariat. Marx was an inveterate optimist, and could not believe that things would go on getting worse. One could argue today that our task for the foreseeable future is not to make the world a better place, but only to slow the pace at which it gets worse, but Marx could not have thought like that.

He clearly thought that globalization is not only inevitable, but potentially beneficial in uniting humankind into one economic community. Yet he could not have welcomed the erosion of even such economic democracy as existed under capitalism, which was itself the achievement of international democratic institutions on a world scale, starting no doubt from some sort of international workers' association such as he tried to build in his own lifetime, and successive generations of Marxists have tried to build since. But eventually the solution would have to be some kind of world federation in a socialist context – a planetary democracy with economic as well as political power, no doubt with many powers decentralized, but with no private institution with the wealth and power to overawe elected ones. It is often assumed, particularly in the wake of the fall of 'state socialism' in Eastern Europe, that the demands for democracy and for the free market go together. Yet the free market means that, within corporations, power is wielded by people unelected by those whom the power affects; and in the relations between corporations, power is at the mercy of impersonal, alienated economic forces, Neither sort of power is compatible with democracy.

What can be learnt from Marx here is that in the modern world the real alignment of forces is 'the market versus democracy', that democracy can only win if it becomes global, and that this cannot be done by rationalizing capitalism, but only by abolishing it.

Proletarianization

In Marx's time the proletariat was a minority everywhere except in Britain, but it was a growing minority, and Marx assumes throughout his work that it was 'the coming class'. Today, this is widely held to be outdated. In the most advanced societies, particularly the English- speaking ones, the proletariat is declining in numbers, and some would say is a minority. But on a world scale, the proletariat is still growing. It is very close to being the majority class of humankind. Its decline in some rich countries is parasitic upon this fact, just as there have always been suburbs of capitalist cities where the proletariat is absent. From Marx's point of view, the growth in the world proletariat is important because the possibility of emancipation for humankind as a whole is bound up with the proletariat. This is not because of any kind of mystical 'proletarian messianism' as is often alleged, but because alone among oppressed classes its conditions of life make it possible for it to unite, to organize democratically, to resist collectively and, under favourable circumstances, to take over the production process. In the 1960s there were controversies between those Marxists who held to the idea of the unique emancipatory potential of the proletariat, and 'Third –Worldists' who turned instead to the peasant classes of the poorer countries. Today, there can be no such controversy. To look to the proletariat for emancipation is for the most part to look to the newly industrialized countries of the 'Third World'.

Concentration of capital

Competition has never had all the virtues that Adam Smith claimed for it, but it did have some virtues. In early capitalism, no single firm was big enough by itself to appreciably alter the state of the market, or to bring pressure to bear on political authorities. Marx always argued that, as capitalism developed, ownership of capital would become more and more concentrated, tending towards monopoly, until not only the interest of the proletariat, but even the 'public interest' within a bourgeois parliamentary state would constrain the government to take over or control great corporations. Yet within Marx's lifetime, there was nothing like the great multinational corporations of today, many of which have turnovers greater than the national income of many medium-sized countries. Marx was something of an optimist about human rationality, and would probably not have believed that elected governments would ever permit such large concentrations of irresponsible power, just as Engels believed that European nations would never again go to war, given the destructive potential of weapons by the end of his life. Be that as it may, concentration of capital has certainly grown apace in the hundred – and – twenty years since Marx's death, and the case for public ownership and democratic control has become giantic need for anyone who values democracy at all.

Increasing inequality

The mature Marx did not believe that workers would always get worse and worse off under capitalism. He defended the value both of labour legislation and of trade unions, as means by which the lot of workers could be improved under capitalism. But he does seem to have held that inequalities of wealth would increase. Yet from the late nineteenth till the late twentieth century, inequalities within developed countries became less marked, precisely because of such trade-union actions and interventions by democratic parliaments as Marx defended – though in Britain, since Thatcher, this trend has been reversed.

However, the global picture is not so rosy. Rich countries get richer and poor countries get, at least relatively often absolutely poorer. Of course, there are those who claim that some inequalities are just, as based on different abilities, but no one in their right mind could claim this of the inequalities that exist between rich and poor countries today.

The question is often posed whether Marx's ideas are 'out of date'. The question about ideas is whether they are true or false, not whether they are fashionable or unfashionable. Indeed, Marxism has gone in and out of fashion several times since Marx's death, and no doubt will continue to do so. But there are two ways in which Marx's ideas could have become dated, rather than merely unfashionable. Firstly, Marx claimed to have inaugurated a science, and while non- scientific ideas do both of these things. If there had been real progress in social science since Marx's time, his theories might have been left behind like Newton's theories were with the discoveries of Einstein. Some think this has happened, but certainly, so far as sociology is concerned, no new theory has won a general consensus, and it is arguable that those social scientists studying societies using Marxist theoretical tools are still producing the best work in this area. In economics the situation is rather different; Marx is widely regarded as 'old hat', but the current theories are not so much refutations of Marxism as they are theories about different things; and once again, none of these theories commands a consensus; the dominance of some over other is probably explained by political rather than scientific considerations. So the claim that Marx is out of date because he has been superseded by superior social scientific the ories is, to say the least, unproven and contentious.

But there is, secondly, another way in which Marx's ideas could have become out of date. Many of them are about a specific period of history, namely capitalism, and more particularly, a capitalism that had outlived its progressive phase. Marx himself would have been very pleased if his ideas had become out of date in one way, namely by the replacement of capitalism with socialism. So it is, legitimate to ask whether changes in the world since Marx's time have rendered his ideas irrelevant.

The main reason why Marx's ideas are treated as out of date in recent times – that is, since about 1990- is that the regimes in Eastern Europe calling themselves Marxist have collapsed. It is odd that this event has been seen in the West as a reason for rejecting Marxism. After all, everyone knew, while those regimes still existed, that they were never good examples of socialism as understood by Marx, and indeed Western Marxists spent a huge proportion of their time and energy analysing exactly what was wrong with them – were they 'state capitalist', or a new form of exploitation called 'bureaucratic collectivism', or degenerated workers' states that needed political revolutions to set them on a socialist course or a kind of socialism that had been deformed by survivals of the autocratic past of most those countries? That they lacked political and industrial democracy, and some of the civil liberties that go with democracy, was well known. Nothing new and bad was discovered about them when the regimes fell; it was all state news. One might have expected a revival of Marxism since it was no longer discredited by association with these regimes, and in the long term, that may yet happen. But at the time, many erstwhile Marxists suddenly came to see Marxism as 'out of date. Later, some turned against it because of the Jacobin terror, some because of the corruption of the Directory, some because of the militarism of Napoleon. All these are honourable reasons for doing so. But anyone who turned against it because Napoleon lost the Battle of Waterloo could only be described as a coward and a turncoat. These who abandoned Marxism in 1990 are in the same category.

Let us start by looking at Marx's own view of the prospects for socialism. We have seen that at some points during the mid-nineteenth century revolution was on the cards. Later, he realized that it had not been, that the world had not yet been ripe for socialism. However, he certainly assumed towards the end of his life that it soon would be. But we have also seen Marx's tendency to 'telescope' future developments, to see as imminent what was indeed coming, but slowly. Almost certainly, a proletarian revolution could not have happened during the nineteenth century. Indeed, when the Russian Revolution did occur in 1917, many Marxists, including Plekhanov, the founder of Russian Marxism and no mean thinker, thought it premature. In a sense, Trotsky and Lenin agreed with them, thinking that a revolution in the industrialized West was necessary if the Russian Revolution was to succeed. But the Western nations were busy exploiting the colonized countries to stop their own revolutions. And during the Cold War period, the Cold War itself precluded revolutions, since all radical opposition was tarred with the brush of the Cold War enemy.

But in the twenty-first century, the global market that Marx predicted has arrived, the old colonized countries have won political independence, and the world proletariat bids fair to become the majority of humankind. Perhaps the conditions for workers' power envisaged by Marx, so far from being dated to the nineteenth century, have only just been realized in the twenty-first century.

Of course, despite their political independence, the 'Third World' countries are still being exploited through investment, debt and unfair trade. That makes workers power in the rich countries an unlikely prospect. But in the newly industrialised countries, it has become a possibility for the first time. Against it, there is the military power of the rich countries which, as the Iraq War has shown, can be used to remove a government that the rich countries do not like. But it is hard to believe that this could be done if the country or countries concerned had a population of over one hundred million and were overwhelmingly behind their socialist government. After all, the USA was beaten in Vietnam, though by a peasant rather than a proletarian movement. And the governments that attacked Iraq no doubt had the bully's instinct for hitting only smaller boys. If we were to see a socialist India, Indonesia or Brazil, the flame might well spread, and the exploiting countries might be unable to stop it.

Firstly, the centre of Marx's view of society is the concept of class. Class exploitation is the invisible form of oppression today. In recent post of UK, a Liberal Democrat member on the TV, saying, truly enough, that parliament was dominated by white middle-class males, and going on to say that we needed more women, ethnic minorities and disabled people in parliament. Despite characterizing the existing parliament as middle class, she did not say that we needed more working-class MPs. Of course, this could have been a slip in a hurried response, but it is fairly typical, not only of liberals but of socialists too. Class is the one form of oppression that they do not notice, despite the fact that the working class is larger and more oppressed than any other oppressed group, and that, whereas something has been achieved by all other oppressed groups in the last fifty years, the working class, in the UK at least, is more oppressed-n and less represented in parliament – than it was fifty years ago. Even if Marx is wrong in holding that class exploitation is the cause of other forms of exploitation, the reminder that such exploitation exists is valuable and timely.

Secondly, for Marx, great inequalities of wealth are the result of exploitation. Everyone today is aware of the division of the world into rich and poor countries. But the terms 'rich' and 'poor' while descriptively accurate, disguise the fact that the rich can only be rich because they exploit the poor, and indeed that, since money is essentially nothing but a token of power over the labour of others, great inequality is not only caused by but essentially consists in the oppression of the poor by the rich. This was not discovered by Marx: several of the Fathers of the Church were quite explicit that you could not be rich except by robbing the poor, so that setting up a flow of wealth the other way was not 'charity' but the repayment of what had been wrongfully appropriated. But Marx was the first to show the mechanism by which this exploitation takes place under market conditions. So the division into rich and poor nations is not a brute fact, but something given by destiny. But most people's only difference from this view today is that they attribute the division to luck rather than to God.

Thirdly, the division into rich and poor countries is one of the two greatest problems confronting humankind today. The environmental crisis is the other. It is often alleged that Marx has nothing to say about this, apart from a few remarks like on the duty of humankind to care for the earth, and the critique of environmentally short-sighted methods in agriculture. However, the distinction between exchange-value driven and use-value driven production may be exactly the distinction needed for an ecological economics. Exchange-value driven production systematically ignores all effects of the production process apart from financial cost and return, hence it ignores all environmental effects, as well as effects on the workers' health and happiness. Use-value driven production takes into account any use-value that the production process either creates or destroys. These will include environmental and human effects as well as 'products'. This means that economic decision-making under socialism would be very different from under capitalism. All foreseeable effects, good and bad, of any decision would have to be taken into account. But this would mean deciding between incommensurable values of various effects. Hence, mathematical calculation would not be the basis of decision- making. You cannot subtract three oranges from five apples.

The fourth question is about the attitude we should take to technology. Here Marx has two lessons to teach – which on the surface may seem to pull in opposite directions, but which are both required for a balanced approach to the place of technology in modern life. On the one hand, Marx sees technology as the foundation of human liberation. He thinks that slavery could not have been abolished without the stream engine and the spinning jenny; in general, human liberation from human oppressors presupposes the liberation of humankind at large from overwork. Only when it is possible for all to have enough leisure and culture to participate in the management of society, is democracy possible in the state or in industry. The reduction of the working day is the foundation of all culture and freedom, and only by technology can the working day be reduced for all. Marx is aware that with technical progress new needs are created, but thinks that, even so, labour can really be lightened by labour –saving technology.

Marx was well aware that the technical progress that was taking place so rapidly in his early lifetime had not lightened labour for the proletarians. It had the potential for doing so, but under capitalist conditions it had been used at first to lengthen the working day. Such paradoxes still happen today, at a more advanced technological level. E-mail enables you to write a letter in two minutes instead of ten, but as a result, where you used to spend the first twenty minutes of the day answering letters, you now spend the first two hours deleting e-mails. But Marx's point is, of course, that the capitalist use of technology militates against its tendency to save labour.

But the capitalist use of technology does more than this, many people have noticed the runaway, out-of-control nature of modern technology. For Marx, this is an example of the out-of-control nature of capitalist markets in general. The laws of the markets make certain outcomes happen even if no one desires them, and there is no procedure available to prevent those unwanted outcomes. This is the 'sorcerer's aspect of capitalism: technology increases human powers, but market forces prevent human being from having power over those powers. If you are careering downhill with faulty brakes, you are a much greater danger to yourself and others than if you are in a lorry. If you are chopping down a rainforest, you cannot do as much harm with an axe as with mechanical means of deforestation. The development of high technology within capitalism means that out-of-control powers have greater and greater effects.

Marx's claim that, just as feudalism could not use steam-mill technology and so had to give way to capitalism, capitalism in turn cannot cope with technology beyond a certain level, and must give way to socialism. As with all parallels between the feudalism – capitalism transition and the capitalism – socialism transition, there are asymmetries. Feudalism just could not produce steam mills; they could not have fitted into its relations of production. Capitalism can produce high technology- very likely there is no ceiling on what it can produce. But it cannot stop that technology from having catastrophic effects on life on Earth. Climate change is a case in point. It is very difficult, if not impossible, for governments of capitalist societies to sufficiently regulate the amount of pollution that causes this, to force powerful rogue states like the USA to conform even to such limits as are agreed.

And finally, the fifth point, in comparison with the issues of world poverty and the environmental crisis, the question of the survival or demise of democracy may seem small fry. Nevertheless there are considerable advantages to living in a democracy. Although it has never been possible in any democracy to elect just any government that the people want, it has been possible to oust a particularly unpopular government without bloodshed. Democracies usually have more personal liberties than undemocratic states, though there are anomalies: for instance, some of the undemocratic communist regimes of Eastern Europe in the 1970s and 1980s had more personal liberties in sexual matters than the highly democratic Irish Republic. But democracies do not usually use torture at home, though those with 'interests' abroad often do there. And democracy was in the twentieth century a mechanism whereby some of the most powerful institutions of society could be brought to defend some of the weakest members of society.

But in recent years, two tendencies can be noted in all parliamentary democracies: political power has shifted from the legislature- usually the only elected part of the state apparatus – to the executive, bureaucratic and military parts of the state, which are unelected; and economic power now eludes the state as a whole, and has shifted to multinational corporations. Marx more than anyone has pointed out both that political power has economic foundations, and that the state is not just the legislature but the coercive and administrative machinery. If the elected part of the state had considerable political and economic power in some countries for a while in the twentieth century, that power itself had a foundation at the point of production in the powerful democratic organizations of the working class, the trade unions. With the decline of trade-union power it is no surprise that democracy has increasingly become a façade, like the survival of the republican institutions of ancient Rome into the age of the emperors. Increasingly, we need to learn from Marx that if we are serious about democracy we must have a democratic army what Machiavelli said of citizens' militia and democratic economic corporations is as well as a democratic legislature. Otherwise we will eventually lose all the advantages that democracy brought. The message of Marx is that if humankind is to be free in the twenty-first century – and perhaps even if it is to survive into the twenty-second – we need common ownership and democratic control of the productive resources of the planet.

The great would religions all formed around some founding figure: a mythical Buddha, a vague Jesus, or a Muhammad just barely emerging from the shadows into the light of empirical detail. In contrast, Marx's life and work was to large extent available to his contemporaries in an era- the 19th century – when historical science was blooming. Today the details of his existence and thoughts have become increasingly avaible to us if we go in search of him. Hegel, Marx's mentor, spoke of "spiritual revolutions" that silently occurred in the "spirit of the age," before bursting like a bud, into actuality. In his so called anti-theological writings, Hegel cites Abraham and Jesus, along with Alexander the Great and Caesar, as world – historical heroes, progenitors of revolutions. Marx was more like a Jesus than a Caesar, conquering with scriptures rather than swords. His role was one of prophecy rather than armed conquest. Yet the end result of his prophecy was a chain of explosive revolutions in Russia, China, Eastern, Europe, Latin America, and elsewhere – of a magnitude unheard of in earlier times.

Karl Marx's influence has been prodigious. Those who call themselves or are labelled Marxists number almost half the planetary inhabitants. The Chinese alone account for one billion, though the 260-80 million Russians claim to be the leading apostles. All in all, between 1.5 and 2 billion people are being led by dedicated Marxists, are being educated in Marxist thought, and thus can be classified as Marxists of one sort or another. Marx's so-called "followers" outnumber those of the largest existing religious bodies: Christianity, Buddhism, and Islam. Their numbers are great – but not as great as the Marxists. Marxism, the "secular religion" of the modern era, extends its sway over a population enormously swollen by the "Demographic Revolution" of the 18th to 20th century. Even allowing for the fact, however, Marxism has come to hold sway over more hearts and minds, or at least to dominate the ideologies of those in power in proportionately more parts of the world than any one of the major historical religions.

There were only eleven mourners at Karl Marx's funeral on 17 March 1883. His name and work will endure through the ages, Friedrich Engels predicted in a graveside oration at Highgate cemetery. It seemed an unlikely boast, but he was right. The history of the twentieth century is Marx's legacy. Stalin, Mao, Che, Castro – the icons and monsters of the modern age have all presented themselves as his heirs. Whether he would recognise them as such is quite another matter. Even in his lifetime the antics of self – styled disciples often drove him to despair. On hearing that a new French party claimed to be Marxist, he replied that in that case 'I, at least, am not a Marxist'. Nevertheless, within one hundred years of his death half thc world's population was ruled by governments that professed Marxism to be their guiding faith. His ideas have transformed the study of economics, history, geography, sociology and literature. Not since Jesus Christ has an obscure pauper inspired such global devotion – been so calamitously misinterpreted.

It is time to strip away the mythology and try to rediscover Karl Marx the man. There have been thousands of books about Marxism, but almost all have been written by academics and zealots for whom it is a near-blasphemy to treat him as a figure of flesh and blood – a Prussian émigré who became a middle-class English gentleman; an angry agitator who spent much of his adult life in the scholarly silence of the British Museum Reading Room; a gregarious and convivial host who fell out with almost all his friends; a devoted family man who impregnated his housemaid; and a deeply earnest philosopher who loved drink, cigars and jokes.

For the West, during the Cold War, he was the demonic begetter of all evil, the founder of an awesomely sinister cult, the man whose baleful influence must be suppressed. In the Soviet Union of the 1950s he assumed the status of a secular God, with Lenin as John the Baptist and, of course, Comrade Stalin himself as the redeeming Messiah. This alone has been quite enough to convict Marx as an accomplice in the massacre and purges: had he lived a few years longer, by now some enterprising journalist would probably have fingered him as a prime suspect in the Jack the Ripper murders too. But why? Marx himself certainly never asked to be included in the Holy Trinity, and would have been appalled by the crimes committed in his name. The bastard creeds espoused by Stalin, Mao or Kim II Sung treated his work rather as modern Christians use the Old Testament: much of it simply ignored or discarded, while a few resonant slogans ('opium of the people', 'dictatorship of the proletariat') are wrenched out of context, turned upside down and then cited as apparently divine justification for the most brutal crimes against humanity.

Only a fool could hold Marx responsible for the Gulag; But there is, alas, a ready supply of fools. In one way or another, the most important facts of our time lead back to one man – Karl Marx. It will hardly be disputed that it is he who is manifested in the very existence of Soviet Russia, and particularly in the Soviet methods. The resemblance between Marx's methods and those of Stalin was apparently so indisputable that they did not bother to adduce any evidence for his preposterous assertion, with the observation that the tree is known by its fruit which like so many proverbs, is rather less axiomatic than it sounds. Should philosophers be blamed for any and every subsequent mutilation of their ideas?

Just as halfwitted or power-hungry followers deified Marx, so his critics have often succumbed to the equal and opposite error of imagining him as agent of Satan. 'There were times when Marx seemed to possessed by demons. He had the devil's view of the world, and the devil's malignity. Sometimes he seemed to know that he was accomplishing works of evil. This school of thought reaches its absurd conclusion in *Was Karl Marx a Satanist*? According to Wurmbdrand, the young Karl Marx was initiated into a 'highly secret Satanist church' which he then served faithfully and wickedly for the rest of his life. No proof can be found, of course, but this merely strengthens the detective's hunch: 'Since the Satanist sect is highly secret, we have only leads about the possibilities of his connections with it. The inversions of the Satanist black mass. Most incriminating; but there's more to come. 'Have you ever wondered, Wurmbrand asks, about Marx's hairstyle? Men usually wore beards in his time, but not beards like this. Marx's manner of bearing himself was characteristic of the disciples of Joanna Southcoott, a Satanic priestess. In fact, the England inhabited by Marx had plenty of bushy-bearded gents, from the cricketer W.G. Grace to the politician Lord Salisbury. Were they, too on speaking terms with the demon?

After the end of the Cold War and the apparent triumph of God over Satan, countless wiseacres declared that we had reached what Francis Fukuyama smugly called the End of History. Communism was as dead as

Marx himself, and the blood-curdling threat with which he concluded the Communist Manifesto, the most influential political pamphlet of all time, now seemed no more than a quaint historical relic: "Let the ruling classes tremble at a communistic revolution. The proletarians have nothing to lose but their chains. They have a world to win Working men of all countries, unite". The only fetters binding the working class today are mock- Rolex watches, but these latter-day proletarians have much else which they'd hate to lose – microwave ovens, holiday timeshares and satellite dishes. They have bought their council houses and their shares in privatised utilities; they made a nice little windfall when their building society turned into a bank. In short, we are all bourgeois now. Even the British Labour Party has gone Thatcherite.

When I started preparing this anthropology, many friends looked at me with pity and incredulity. Why, they wondered, would anyone wish to write about – still less read about – such a discredited outmoded, irrelevant figure? I carried on regardless; and the more I studied Marx, the more astoundingly topical he seemed to be. Today's pundits and politicians who fancy themselves as modern thinkers like to mention the buzz-word globalisation at every opportunity – without realising that Marx was already on the case in 1848. The globe-straddling dominance of McDonald's and MTV would not have surprised him in the least. The shift in financial power from the Atlantic to the Pacific – thanks to the Asian Tiger economies and the silicon boom towns of west- coast America – was predicted by Marx more than a century before Bill Gates was born.

There is, however, one development which Marx had foreseen: that in the late 1990s, long after he had been written off even by fashionable liberals and post-modernist lefties, he would suddenly be hailed as a genius by the wicked old bourgeois capitalists themselves. The first sign of this bizarre reassessment appeared in October 1997, when a special issues of the New Yorker billed Karl Marx as the next big thinker, "a man with much to teach us about political corruption, monopolisation, alienation, inequality and global markets. The longer I spend on Wall Street, the more convinced I am that Marx was right", a wealthy investment banker told the magazine. We are absolutely convinced that Marx's approach is the best way to look at capitalism. Since then right-wing economists and journalists have been queuing up to pay similar homage. Ignore all that communist nonsense, they say: Marx was really 'a student of capitalism'.

Even this intended compliment serves only to diminish him. Karl Marx was a philosopher, a historian, an economist, a linguist, a literary critic and a revolutionist. Although he may not have had a job as such, he was a prodigious worker: his collected writings, few of which were published in his lifetime, fill fifty volumes. What neither his enemies nor his disciples are willing to accept is the most obvious that this mythical ogre and saint was a human being. The McCarthyite witch-hunt of the 1950, the wars in Vietnam and Korea, the Cuban Missile Crisis, the invasions of Czechoslovakia and Hungary, the massacre of students in Tiananmen Square – all these bloody blemishes on the history of the twentieth century were justified in the name of Marxism or anti-Marxism. No mean feat for a man who spent much of his adult life in poverty, plagued by carbuncles and liver pains, and was once pursued through the streets of London by the Metropolitan Police after a rather over exuberant pub crawl.

3

A Self-potrait

We have not yet mentioned Marx's youthful literary ventures, or the three volumes of poetry he dedicated, as a student, to his future wife Jenny von Westphalen. These may perhaps be passed over, without too much contention, as amongst his least enduring creations. But they do, at least, have the virtue of revealing the man behind the myths. This anthology begins in this vein with Marx's co-called 'Confessions', his answers to questions put to him as part of a parlour game by his daughters Jenny and Laura, sometime in the 1860s. Here we learn, among other things, that Marx's 'favourite heroes' were Spartacus and Kepler, his 'favourite poets' Shakespeare, Goethe, and Aeschylus and his 'idea of misery' submission. It is salutory to find that his 'favourite motto' doubt everything. His 'favourite virtue in man' was strength. In women, however, it was 'weakness' his 'favourite heroine' was not a Boadicea or a Joan of Arc, but Goethe's fictional Gretchen. Marx may, of course, simply have been teasing his female children; hut he was, amongst many other things, a very Victorian, if Bohemian, paterfamilias. Such ephemera serve to remind us that this, was not the only respect in which Marx was a man of his time and place.

Like most other Victorians, Marx thought both 'race' and family natural categories and had little trouble in distinguishing between 'civilisation' (which for him was white, western, and modern) and 'barbarism'.

–Editor

- Your favourite virtue - Simplicity.
- Your favourite virtue in man - Strength.
- Your favourite virtue in woman - Weakness.

- Your chief characteristic - Singleness of purpose.
- Your idea of happiness - To fight.
- Your idea of misery - Submission,
- The vice you excuse most - Gullibility.
- The vice you detest most - Servility.
- Your pet aversion - Martin Tupper.
- Favourite occupation - Bookworming.
- Poet - Shakespeare, Aeschylus, Goethe.
- Prose writer - Diderot.
- Hero - Spartacus, Kepler.
- Heroine - Gretchen.
- Flower - Daphne.
- Colour - Red.
- Name - Laura, Jenny.
- Dish - Fish.
- Favourite maxim - I regard nothing human as alien to me.
- Favourite motto - Doubt Everything.

– (*Confessions*, 1860s; Riazanov, Karl Marx, p. 269)

4

Marx The Poet

The philosopher-king was Plato's ideal; poets were to be banished from his realm. In political developments since his time, few if any philosopher-kings have ruled. Poets, however, even if ineffectively have mixed with politics. One thinks of Byron in the Greek War of Independence or Alfred de Vigny celebrating the instruction in Paris in July 1830. In general, however, poetry and politics are not seen as particularly compatible professions.

It may come as something of a surprise, therefore, to note that Marx was a poet before he became a philosopher and then a revolutionary. The fact is that Marx's first published works were two poems in the in 1841. Written in 1837, they were included in the book of verse dedicated to his father. One called "The Fiddler," speaks in Faust- like terms: With Satan I have struck my deal. He chalks the signs, beats time for me, I play the death march fast and free. The other, 'Nocturnal Love', also sounds the death note: You have drunk poison, Love with me you must away. The sky is dark above, No more I see the day.

The sentiments are typical of the romantic genre. Marx was about eighteen years old when he gave expression to them. He had already written "three volumes" of poems, which he had sent to his fiancée, Jenny, and which have not survived. We are more fortunate with another collection, which the author entitled 'Book of Love', followed by another, 'Book of Songs', which were dedicated to his beloved, Jenny, and later rededicated in part to his father as his father approached death. Some of the poems in this collection, while still typically romantic in their sentiments, strike a personal note as well, sounding themes that persist into later life and work.

Never can I do in peace
That with which my Soul's obsessed,
Never task things at my ease;
I must press on without rest.

Others only know elation
When things go their peaceful way,
Free with self-congratulation,
Giving thanks each time they pray.

I am caught in endless strife,
Endless ferment, endless dream;
I cannot conform to Life,
Will not travel with the stream.

Heaven I would comprehend,
I would draw the world to me;
Loving, hating, I intend
That my star shine brilliantly....

.... Worlds I would destroy for ever,
Since I can create no world,
Since my call they notice never,
Coursing dumb in magic whirl.

Therefore let us risk our all,
Never resting never ting;
Not in silence dismal, dull
Without action or desiring;
Not in brooding introspection
Bowed beneath a yoke of pain.

The first note struck is that of "endless strife": the writer is in turmoil and pain. The next note informs us that the writer feels out of step, "alienated," we might say, from the world around him. He cannot conform; he wishes to be free to go his own way. Then comes the note of ambition: "I intend that my star shine brilliantly"- at whatever cost. And then the call to action: if the world will not notice him, i. e., respond to his ambition, then he will destroy it. The youthful poet's dreams will be fulfilled, but exactly with what content and how is left vague. The poem is filled with adolescent yearnings. With so many of his generation – the early 19th century- he is on the edge of "brooding introspection." The threat of depression hangs over the poem and its author. He turns, violently, to action to avoid his melancholy. Or at least he indicates that action is, or will be, his desired course.

What sort of action? He does not know as yet. Another of the poems, "To Jenny," gives us some hints. It is not the expected outpouring of Jenny," which concludes, Love is Jenny, Jenny, is Love's Name".

Words – lies, hollow shadows, nothing more,
    Crowding Life from all sides round!
In you, dead and tired, must I outpour
    Spirits that in me abound?
Yet Earth's envious Gods have scanned before
    Human fire with gaze profound;
And forever must the Earthing poor
    Mate his bosom's glow with sound.
For, if passion leaped up, vibrant, bold,
    In the Soul's sweet radiance,
Daringly it would your would bring you down low,
    Would oursoar the Zephyr –Dance.
Ripe a world above you then would grow.

The allusion to the "envious Gods" and "human lire" recalls to us the story of Prometheus. Who defied the Gods and brought fire to mankind. The poet appears to be telling us that his words will be like fire and as a result will "dethrone' the Gods; and then create a world "above" them. Here we have the same theme of destroying the existing world, only now the means are indicated-words-and the action's result indicated-the creation of another world more to the poet's heart's desire.

The youthful poet struggles in another of his poems, “My World,” to discern its lineaments. Even if he encompassed all the existing universe- “Drank l all the stars’ bright radiance. All the light by suns over”, spilled,” his pains would not be assuaged, and his dreams would remain unfulfilled. Above all existing worlds is “my own will,” he declares. It drives him as “endless battle... Demon-wise into the far mists driving towards a goal I cannot near.” Overcome by a feeling of hopelessness, he turns suddenly in the remainder of the poem to his Jenny and in her eyes finds an answer: she and the All are one.

Love, and Jenny, are the solid moorings for the author as he moves out into the confusing and disturbing world around him, but his will is clearly driving him forward, to both destruction and creation. Demon, or God. It is not clear on which side he is arraigning himself. The demons, of course, are also gods, as a mention of Satan reminds us. Will the poet be a Satan a Prometheus in the Greek version, defying the gods? And what would this mean?

We have other fragmentary works from our aspiring author. At about ‘the sometime as his poems, he was also writing a play Oulanem and a “humoristic or satirical, novel,. Scorpion and Felix. As literary works, they are dreadful. Unlike the poems, they are obscure, crabbed, “clever,” ‘and utterly uninspired. They were wisely left unfinished, and unpublished

Marx wrote his poety in the late 1830s at it time when the romantic inspiration ran high and the “Young Germans” wee prominent.

At the time he was writing his own poetry, Marx was not particularly concerned with the miserable lot of the workers but rather with the Romantic anguish over the growing quantification and objectification of life as a result of capitalism and science. Marx’s sentiments, therefore, were initially pre-capitalist in their coloring, hardly differing in this regard from conservative critics. As Edmund Burke, an unlikely ally at first glance, had remarked, “The age....was one of sophisters, economists, and calculators.”

It was not just Romantic poets but idealist philosophers, such as Kant, Schiller, Fichte and Hegel, who were reacting against the atomistic, mechanistic, and calculating features of the Enlightenment. They stressed, instead, the autonomous, moral, and self-creating aspects of humans- Marx later noted that Hegel conceives of the self-creation of man as a process”

– and claimed the external world to be a field on which man might battle for, as well as express, his inner spiritual and even aesthetic nature.

Coleridge wrote of how "the philosophy of mechanism, which, in everything that is most worthy of the human intellect, strikes Death," and Keats exclaimed how "in these cold and enfeebling times. Romance lives but in the same vein asked rhetorically.

"Is the view of nature and of social relations which shaped Greek imagination and thus Greek mythology possible in the age of automatic machinery and railways and locomotives and electric telegraphs? Where does Vulcan come in as against Roberts and Co., Jupiter as against the lightening rod, and Hermes as against the credit mobilier? All mythology masters and dominates and shapes the forces of nature in and through imagination; hence it disappears as soon man gains mastery over the forces of nature. What becomes of the Goddess Frame side by side with Printing House Square? Or is the Iliad at all possible in a time of the hand –operated or the later steam press? Are not singing and reacting and the muse necessary put out of existence by printer's bar; and do not necessary prerequisites of epic poetry according vanish"?

Epic poetry, such as the lliad, was no longer possible, at least in its old form. But Marx wrote another kind of epic poem in Capital-where his allusion to Dante's Divine Comedy suggests what he had in mind—and created a new mythology of enormous potency. In embracing the Romantic attitude, young Marx was joining his gen eration's questioning of the Enlightenment, its values, and its commercial underpinnings. Engels missed this point when he spoke of the strands that went into Marx's protean synthesis. Romantic anti-capitalist feelings entered into Marx's philosophic and revolutionary critique as much, for example, as English classical economic theory.

Marx, in embracing Romantic anti-capitalism, and rejecting Enlightenment values (except for the core belief in progress), was also challenging his father, a typical follower of the philosophes, and the older man, in response to his son's letters, did not hesitate to make his own views known. For him, the spate of high -flown romantic rhetoric represented the utterances of "new monsters." As he wrote his son, "You are following in the footsteps of the new monsters that mumble their words until they can no longer hear themselves speak; they have only confused ideas or none at all, and so a flood of words is described as the birth of a genius".

Reading Marx's texts, one is struck by the "flood of words," by the way effusive language is often substituted for careful analysis. Even his sympathetic headmaster at the gymnasium, remarked of Marx's school essay that he "constantly seeks for elaborate picturesque expressions .... Therefore many passage lack the necessary clarity." The "old" Marx did not give up his youthful tricks He seems intoxicated by the sound of certain words and turns of phrase. He is utterly enamoured of chiastic phrases, where the order of syntactical elements is inverted; "The social emancipation of the Jew: is the emancipation of society from Judaism"; or, "Man makes religion; religion does not make man" or, playing on the title of Proudhon's book, The Philosophy of Poverty, Marx entitles his critique, The Poverty of Philosophy.

5

Hegel and Marx

During the long years of exile in London, Marx's only forays into English culture were occasional outing to watch the leading Shakespearean actors Salvini and Irving. It is no coincidence that one of the Marx children, Eleanor, went on the stage and another, little Jenny, yearned to do likewise. Marx's household was obliged to live in a perpetual flurry of allusions to English literature. There was a question for every occasion – to flatten a political enemy, to enliven a dry economic text, to heighten a family joke, or to authenticate an intense emotion. Why, then, were Karl and Jenny so reluctant to tell her parents of the betrothal? Perhaps Karl thought that the difference in their ages would count against him: marriages to older women were still rare enough to seem a crime against the laws of nature. Or perhaps they feared that, for all his generosity of spirit, the old man would try to dissuade his adored daughter from throwing in her lot with a brilliant but volatile nonconformist. Life with Karl Marx would never be dull, but it held little promise of stability or prosperity.

Apart from Jenny, the most important passion of Marx's youth was a dead philosopher, Hegel. It followed much the same course as many love affairs: shy wariness, followed by the intoxicating trill of a first embrace, followed by rejection of the beloved as the *amour fou* wanes. But he remained grateful for this initiation into the secrets of adulthood. Long after repudiating Hegelianism and declaring his intellectual independence, Marx spoke affectionately of the man who led him out of innocence. He had earned the right to chide Hegel with the robust honesty of an intimate friend; strangers were permitted no such licence.

'The mystificatory side of Hegelian dialectic I criticised nearly thirty years ago, at a time when it was still the fashion,' he wrote in 1873. 'But just as I was working at the first volume of Capital, it was the good pleasure of the peevish arrogant, mediocre epigones, who now talk big in cultured Germany, to treat Hegel in the same way as the brave Moses Mendelssohn in Lessing's time treated Spinoza, i.e. as a "dead dog". I therefore openly avowed myself the pupil of that might thinker, and even here and there, in the chapter on the theory of value, coquetted with the modes of expression peculiar to him. The mystification which dialectic suffers in Hegel's hands by no means prevents him from being the first to present its general form of working in a conscious and comprehensive manner'. It was very rare indeed for Marx to pay such a compliment to someone with whom he had disagreed.

Marx's thought shows the influence of Hegel's dialectical philosophy in many ways. He first became acquainted with it during his student days in Berlin, adopting in the first place a republican interpretation of Hegel's philosophy of history such as was represented by, for example, Eduard Cans. Like Hegel, Marx interprets world history as a dialectical progression, but following Fcuetbach's materialist reinterpretation of Hegel, Marx comprehends 'material labour as the essence, as the self-validating essence, of humanity' (Economic and Philosophical Manuscripts). Marx's critical reformulation of Hegel's philosophy of history consists in the elimination of the nutritious subject of world history, the so-called 'world spirit' and in the prolongation of the dialectical process of historical development into the future That realm of freedom which Hegel asserted to be fully realized here and now, lies for Marx in the future as a real possibility of the present. The dialectic of productive forces and productive relations which effects historical progress offers in contrast to Hegel's dialectic of world spirit no guarantee that the realm of freedom (see Emancipation) will be realized; it presents only the objective possibility of such a development. Should the historically possible revolutionizing of society not come about, then a relapse into barbarism (Luxemburg) or the 'common ruin of the contending classes' (Marx) is also possible.

In place of the constitutional bourgeois state, which for Hegel constituted the end point of historical development, Marx puts forward the concept of 'the free association of producers'. This is a social order which dispenses with any kind of coercive force standing over and above it, and whose members manage their own affairs through consensus. For Hegel, the process through which an individual liberates himself from his natural existence, from external coercion, is a process of 'spiritualization'; through philosophical insight into his objective situation, the individual comes to see that what appeared to be external constraints upon his will are in fact necessary conditions of his existence as a thinking being with a will of its own, and with this insight comes reconciliation with the objective reality. Hegel and conservative Hegelians held that such insight, reconciliation and liberation could only be perfectly attained by philosophically educated state officials, while the young Hegelians, generalizing this idea, identified the process of 'spiritualization' with that of the individual's maturation to citizenship. Nonetheless, in both interpretations the individual is left with a certain 'double identity': on the one hand, he is a natural individual feeling himself to be subject to external and coercive forces; on the other hand, he is a 'spiritual being' possessed of the knowledge that that which apparently denies him his freedom is in fact his freedom and reality itself. Liberation is reconciliation. For Marx, however, liberation is only possible when this duplication of human identity into human being and citizen, into natural individual and spiritualized being, is no longer necessary, has been overcome; when human beings no longer have to objectify their own social constraints in an 'alien essence standing over and above them' - the state later also capital. Despite all his criticisms of Hegel Marx nevertheless retains the Hegelian conviction that humanity makes progress in the course of history. He also adopts – indeed as a matter of course - Hegel's Eurocentrism; and his own Eurocentrism is at its most obvious in his writings on India and China.

In Marx's work on the critique of political economy, a second influence of Hegel makes itself felt. The comprehension of this influence is particularly essential for an adequate understanding of Marx's main work, Capital, for it concerns the method which underlies his analysis of the capitalist mode of production. Here Marx makes use of Hegel's dialectical method, which he claims to have put back on its feet, in order to present the internal dynamic and systematic structure of capitalist production. The capitalist system of production relations constitutes a totality, an all-inclusive unity which for this very reason must be examined and presented as an interconnected whole. However, empirical research and the processing of specific empirical data must precede the presentation of the totality. The dialectical self-movement of the at once subjective and objective categories, value, money and capital, must be a feature of the object under investigation, not the result of an externally imposed methodological-scheme. Marx stresses the difference between his way of handling empirical relationships and facts and that of Hegel who, as Marx maintained in his early *Critique of Hegel's Philosophy of the State*, develops a scheme of categories first – in his Logic – and then presents social institutions such as the family, civil society, the state and their internal structures in abstract conformity with his scheme. According to Marx the only adequate dialectical exposition of an object of investigation is one which is sensitive to the dynamic and structural individuality of the object. The self-moving 'subject' of the capitalist mode of production, that for the sake of which capitalist production takes place at all, is capital itself, which is, however, not something independently real, but rather something which arises out of the unconscious interaction and collaboration of individuals and classes, and which will therefore disappear once capitalist society has been transcended. It is not a real subject of production but a 'pseudo-subject'. For this reason it is at best misleading to assert that Marx's category of 'capital' plays the same role in his thought as does the category of 'spirit' in Hegel's thought and system. Whereas the World spirit according to Hegel's idealist philosophy actually produces history, capital is only the seemingly real subject of the capitalist mode of production.

The actual 'subjectlessness' of this mode of production (Althusser) is by no means only a methodological achievement of Marx; the idea that capital on the one hand objectively appears as the independently real subject of production yet on the other is not 'really real', is not really an independent subject at all, contains an implicit criticism of the mode of production which constitutes it. The free association of producers, according to Marx, is destined to take the place of capitalism, a social order which ruthlessly and short-sightedly exploits nature, in which individuals and classes are determined by the structural laws of the mode of production to serve the 'pseudo-subject', capital. The free association of producers, so Marx maintains, will regulate the metabolic interchange between society and nature rationally and, in contrast to capitalist society — where production is subservient and responsive only to the interests of capital - its production will be directed towards satisfying the producers' material requirements and their needs for social activity, social life and individual development. It will, as the real subject of production, take the place of the 'pseudo-subject', capital, the mere objectively existing 'appearance' of a subject of production. Only in this not yet realized subject will the Hegelian World Spirit find its empirical embodiment.

Marx only used Hegel's dialectic methodologically and tacitly to ground his belief in historical progress. Engels, however, in *Anti-Dubring*, attempted to go beyond this, to draft and of materialist dialectical ontology and theory: development. Marx owed indeed more to Darwin arid nineteenth-century natural science and scientific world-views than to Hegel. The so-called 'dialectical materialism' arose, to whose further development and elaboration Plekhanov, Lenin, Stalin and a series of Soviet thinkers contributed.

This chapter draws mainly on Marx's writings of the 1840s, and illustrates major themes in his critique of the philosophical historiographies current in Germany at the time. In retrospect this can be seen as a ground-clearing exercise, a 'settling of accounts', as Marx put it later, with his 'former philosophical conscience'. He charges Hegelian and post-Hegelian idealist philosophy with the creation of imaginary historical subjects, through the abstraction of ideas from the material conditions and social relations that they, in his view, express. But Marx is as critical of classical materialism. It too, he argues, remains 'abstract'; it does not set out from 'real, active men', but philosophical 'phrases' like 'matter', 'substance', or 'the world of things'. It is, as Marx makes explicit in a comment on Proudhon, the dualism of material and ideal, 'life and ideas', that he rejects. Marx's alternative is made clearest in his criticisms of Feuerbach: his materialism starts out from 'human activity itself as objective activity'. Such a materialism, focused on 'the changing of circumstances and of human activity or self-change', is necessarily historical.

– Editor

'The mystificatory side of Hegelian dialectic I criticised nearly thirty years ago, at a time when it was still the fashion,' he wrote in 1873. 'But just as I was working at the first volume of *Capital*, it was the good pleasure of the peevish arrogant, mediocre epigones, who now talk big in cultured Germany, to treat Hegel in the same way as the brave Moses Mendelssohn in Lessing's time treated Spinoza, as a "dead dog". I therefore openly avowed myself the pupil of that might thinker, and even here and there, in the chapter on the theory of value, coquetted with the modes of expression peculiar to him. The mystification which dialectic suffers in Hegel's hands by no means prevents him from being the first to present its general form of working in a conscious and comprehensive manner'.

Dear Father,

There are moments in one's life which are like frontier posts marking the completion of a period but at the same time clearly indicating a new direction.

In accordance with my state of mind at the time, lyrical poetry was bound to be my first subject. But owing to my attitude and whole previous development it was purely idealistic. All the poems of the first three volumes I sent to Jenny (von Westphalen, then Marx's fiancee) are marked by attacks on our times, diffuse and inchoate expressions of feeling, nothing natural, everything built out of moonshine, complete opposition between what is and what ought to be.

Poetry, however, could be and had to be only an accompaniment; I had to study law and above all felt the urge to wrestle with philosophy.

First of all came what I was pleased to call the metaphysics of law, i.e. basic principles, reflections, definitions of concepts, divorced from all actual law and every actual form of law, as occurs in Fichte, only in my case it was more modern and shallower. From the outset an obstacle to grasping the truth here was the unscientific form of mathematical dogmatism, in which the author argues hither and thither, going round and round the subject dealt wilh, without the latter taking shape as something living and developing in a many-sided way. A triangle gives the mathematician scope for construction and proof, it remains a mere abstract conception in space and does not develop into anything further. It has to be put alongside something else, then it assumes other positions, and this diversity added to it gives it different relationships and truths. On the other hand, in the concrete expression of a living world of ideas, as exemplified by law, the state, nature, and philosophy as a whole, the object itself must be studied in its development; arbitrary divisions must not be introduced, the rational character of the object itself must develop as something imbued with contradictions in itself and find its unity in itself.

From the idealism which, by the way, I had compared and nourished with the idealism of Kant and Fichte, I arrived at the point of seeking the idea in reality itself. If previously the gods had dwelt above the earth, now they became its centre.

I had read fragments of Hegel's philosophy, the grotesque craggy melody of which did not appeal to me. Once more I wanted to dive into the sea, but with the definite intention of establishing that the nature of the mind is just as necessary, concrete and firmly based as the nature of the body. My aim was no longer to practice tricks of swordsmanship, but to bring genuine pearls into the light of day (Letter to his father, Nov. 1837).

Philosophers do not spring up like mushrooms out of the ground; they are products of their time, of their nation, whose most subtle, valuable and invisible juices flow in the ideas of philosophy. The same spirit that constructs railways with the hands of workers, constructs philosophical systems in the brains of philosophers. Philosophy does not exist outside the world, any more than the brain exists outside man because it is not situated in the stomach. Every true philosophy is the intellectual quintessence of its time. (The leading article in no. 179 of the K & lnische Zeitung, 1842).

Consciousness can never be anything else than conscious being, and the being of men is their actual life-process. If in all ideology men and their relations appear upside-down as in a camera obscura, this phenomenon arises just as much from their historical life-process as the inversion of objects on the retina does from their physical life-process.

In direct contrast to German philosophy which descends from heaven to earth, here it is a matter of ascending from earth to heaven. That is to say, not of setting out from what men say, imagine, conceive, nor from men as narrated, thought of, imagined, conceived, in order to arrive at men in the flesh; but setting out from real, active men, and on the basis of their real life-process demonstrating the development of the ideological reflexes and echoes of this life-process. The phantoms formed in the brains of men are also, necessarily, sublimates of their material life-process, which is empirically verifiable and bound to material premises. Morality, religion, metaphysics, and all the rest of ideology as well as the forms of consciousness corresponding to these, thus no longer retain the semblance of independence. They have no history, no development; but men, developing their material production and their material intercourse, alter, along with this their actual world, also their thinking and the products of their thinking. It is not consciousness that determines life, but life that determines consciousness. For the first manner of approach the starting point is consciousness taken as the living individual; for the second manner of approach, which conforms to real life, it is the real living individuals themselves, and consciousness is considered solely as their consciousness.

This manner of approach is not devoid of premises. It starts out from the real premises and does not abandon them for a moment. Its premises are men, not in any fantastic isolation and fixity, but in their actual, empirically perceptible process of development under definite conditions. As soon as this active life-process is described, history ceases to be a collection of dead facts, as it is with the empiricists (themselves still abstract), or an imagined activity of imagined subjects, as with the idealists.

Where speculation ends, where real life starts, there consequently begins real, positive science, the expounding of the practical activity, of the practical process of development of men. Empty phrases about consciousness end, and real knowledge has to take its place. When the reality is depicted, a self-sufficient philosophy loses its medium of existence. At the best its place can only be taken by a summing-up of the most general results, abstractions which are derived from the observation of the historical development of men. These abstractions in themselves, divorced from real history, have no value whatsoever. They can only serve to facilitate the arrangement of historical material, to indicate the sequence of its separate strata. But they by no means afford a recipe or schema, as does philosophy, for neatly trimming the epochs of history. On the contrary, the difficulties begin only when one sets about the examination and arrangement of the material whether of a past epoch or of the present - and its actual presentation. (The German Ideology)

The ideas of the ruling class are in every epoch the ruling ideas: i.e., the class which is the ruling material force of society is at the same time its ruling intellectual force. The class which has the means of material production at its disposal, consequently also controls the means of mental production, so that the ideas of those who lack the means of mental production are on the whole subject to it. The ruling ideas are nothing more than the ideal expression of the dominant material relations, the dominant material relations grasped as ideas; hence of the relations which make the one class the ruling one, therefore, the ideas of its dominance.

If now in considering the course of history we detach the ideas of the ruling class from the ruling class itself and attribute to them an independent existence, if we confine ourselves to saying that these or those ideas were dominant at a given time, without bothering ourselves about the conditions of production and the producers of these ideas, if we thus ignore the individuals and world conditions which are the source of the ideas, then we can say, for instance, that during the time the aristocracy was dominant, the concepts honour, loyalty, etc., were dominant, during the dominance of the bourgeoisie the concepts freedom, equality, etc. The ruling class itself on the whole imagines this to be so.

Once the ruling ideas have been separated from the ruling individuals and, above all, from the relations which result from a given stage of the mode of production, and in this way the conclusion has been reached that history is always under the sway of ideas, it is very easy to abstract from these various ideas 'the Idea', the thought, etc., as the dominant force in history, and thus to consider all these separate ideas and concepts as 'forms of self-determination' of the Concept developing in history. It follows then naturally, too, that all the relations of men can be derived from the concept of man, man as conceived, the essence of man, Man. This has been done by speculative philosophy.

The whole trick of proving the hegemony of the spirit in history is thus confined to the following three attempts.

No. 1. One must separate the ideas of those ruling for empirical reasons, under empirical conditions and as corporeal individuals, from these rulers, and thus recognise the rule of ideas or illusions in history.

No. 2. One must bring an order into this rule of ideas, prove a mystical connection among the successive ruling ideas, which is managed by regarding them as 'forms of self-determination of the concept (this is possible because by virtue of their empirical basis these ideas really are connected with one another and because, conceived as mere ideas, they become self-distinctions, distinctions made by thought).

No. 3. To remove the mystical appearance of this 'self-determining concept' it is changed into a person - 'self-consciousness - or, to appear thoroughly materialistic, into a series of persons, who represent the 'concept' in history, into the 'thinkers', the 'philosophers', the ideologists, who again are understood as the manufacturers of history. Thus the whole body of materialistic elements has been eliminated from history and now full rein can be given to the speculative steed.

We shall now demonstrate in detail the one-sidedness and the limitations of Hegel, as observed in the closing chapter of the *Phenomenology*. This chapter ('Absolute Knowledge') contains the concentrated essence of the Phenomenology, its relation to the dialectic, and Hegel's consciousness of both and their interrelations.

For the present, let us observe that Hegel adopts the standpoint of modern political economy. He sees labour as the essence, the self-confirming essence, of man; he sees only the positive and not the negative side of labour. Labour is man's coming to be for himself within alienation or as an alienated man. The only labour Hegel knows and recognizes is abstract mental labour. So that which above all constitutes the essence of philosophy - the alienation of man who knows himself or alienated science that thinks itself - Hegel grasps as its essence, and is therefore able to bring together the separate elements of previous philosophies and resent his philosophy as the philosophy. What other philosophers did-that they conceived separate moments of nature and of man's life as moments of self-consciousness, indeed, of abstract self-consciousness - this Hegel knows by doing philosophy. Therefore his science is absolute.

Let us now proceed to our subject.

'Absolute Knowledge'. The last chapter of the Phenomenology.

The main point is that the object of consciousness is nothing else but self-consciousness, or that the object is only objectified self-consciousness, self-consciousness as object. (The positing of man — self-consciousness.)

It is therefore a question of surmounting the object of consciousness. Objectivity as such is seen as an estranged human relationship which does not correspond to human nature, to self-consciousness. The reappropriation of the objective essence of man, produced in the form of estrangement as something alien, therefore means transcending not only estrangement but also objectivity. That is to say, man is regarded as a non-objective, spiritual being.

Hegel describes the process of surmounting the object of consciousness in the following way:

The object does not only show itself as returning into the self, (according to Hegel that is a one-sided conception of the movement, a conception which grasps only one side). Man is equated with self. But the self is only abstractly conceived man, man produced by abstraction, Man is self. His eyes, his ears, etc., have the quality of self; each one of his essential powers has this quality of self. But therefore it is quite wrong to say that self-consciousness has eyes, ears, essential powers. Self-consciousness is rather a quality of human nature, of the human eye, etc.; human nature is not a quality of self-consciousness.

The self abstracted and fixed for itself is man as abstract egoist, egoism raised to its pure abstraction in thought.

For Hegel human nature, man, is equivalent to self-consciousness. All estrangement of human nature is therefore nothing but estrangement of self-consciousness. Hegel regards the estrangement of self-consciousness not as the expression, reflected in knowledge and in thought, of the real estrangement of human nature. On the contrary, actual estrangement, estrangement which appears real, is in its innermost hidden nature - which philosophy first brings to light - nothing more than the appearance of the estrangement of real human nature, of self-consciousness. The science which comprehends this is therefore called phenomenology. All reappropriation of estranged objective being therefore appears an incorporation into self-consciousness; the man who takes hold of his being is only the self-consciousness which takes hold objective being. The return of the object into the self is therefore the reappropriation of the object.

Expressed comprehensively, the surmounting of the object of consciousness means:

(1) That the object as such presents itself to consciousness as something disappearing.

(2) That it is the alienation of self-consciousness which establishes thingness.

(3) That this alienation has not only a negative but also a positive significance.

(4) That this significance is not only for us or in itself, but for self-consciousness itself,

(5) For self-consciousness the negative of the object, its own supersession of itself, has a positive significance - or self-consciousness knows the nullity of the object - in that self-consciousness alienates itself, for in this alienation it establishes itself as object or establishes the object as itself, for the sake of the indivisible unity of being-for-itself.

(6) On the other hand, this other moment is also present in the process, namely, that self-consciousness has superseded and taken back into itself this alienation and objectivity, and is therefore at home in its other-being as such.

(7) This is the movement of consciousness, and consciousness is therefore the totality of its moments.

(8) Similarly, consciousness must have related itself to the object in terms of the totality of its determinations, and have grasped it in terms of each of them. This totality of determinations makes the object intrinsically a spiritual being, and it becomes that in reality for consciousness through the apprehending of each one of these determinations as determinations of self or through what we earlier called the spiritual attitude towards them.

(1) That the object as such presents itself to consciousness as something disappearing is the above-mentioned return of the object into the self.

(2) The alienation of self-consciousness establishes thingness. Because man is equivalent to self-consciousness, his alienated objective being or thingness (that which is an object for him, and the only true object for him is that which is an essential object, i.e. his objective essence; since it is not real man, and therefore not nature, for man is human nature, who becomes as such the subject but only the abstraction of man, self-consciousness, thingness can only be alienated self-consciousness) is the equivalent of alienated self-consciousness, and thingness is established by this alienation. It is entirely to be expected that a living, natural being equipped and endowed with objective, i.e. material essential powers should have real natural objects for the objects of its being, and that its self-alienation should take the form of the establishment of a real, objective world, but as something external to it, a world which does not belong to its

> being and which overpowers it. There is nothing incomprehensible or mysterious about that. It would only be mysterious if the contrary were true. But it is equally clear that a self-consciousness; through its alienation, can only establish thingness, i.e. an abstract thing, a thing of abstraction and not a real thing. It is also clear that thingness is therefore in no way something independent or substantial vis-a-vis self-consciousness; it is a mere creature, a postulate of self-consciousness. And what is postulated, instead of confirming itself, is only a confirmation of the act of postulating; an act which, for a single moment, concentrates its energy as product and apparently confers upon that product - but only for a moment - the role of an independent, real being.

When real, corporeal man, his feet firmly planted on the solid earth and breathing all the powers of nature, establishes his real, objective essential powers as alien objects by externalization, it is not the establishing which is subject; it is the subjectivity of objective essential powers whose action must therefore be an objective one. An objective being acts objectively, and it would not act objectively if objectivity were not an inherent part of its essential nature. It creates and establishes only objects because it is established by objects, because it is fundamentally nature. In the act of establishing it therefore does not descend from its 'pure activity' to the creation of objects; o. the contrary, its objective product simply confirms its objective activity, its activity as the activity of an objective, natural being.

Here we see how consistent naturalism or humanism differ both from idealism and materialism and is at the same time their unifying truth. We also see that only naturalism is capable of comprehending the process of world history.

Man is directly a natural being. As a natural being and as a living natural being he is on the one hand equipped with natural' powers, with vital powers, he is an active natural being; these powers exist in him as dispositions and capacities, as drives. On the other hand, as a natural, corporeal, sensuous, objective being he is a suffering, conditioned and limited being, like animals and plants. That is to say, the objects of his drives exist outside him as objects independent of him; but these objects are objects of his need, essential objects, indispensable to the exercise and confirmation of his essential powers. To say that man is a corporeal, living, real, sensuous, objective being with natural powers means that he has real, sensuous objects as the object of his being and of his vital expression, or that he can only express his life in real, sensuous objects. To be objective, natural and sensuous and to have object, nature and sense outside oneself, or to be oneself object, nature and sense for a third person is one and the same thing. Hunger is a natural need; it therefore requires a nature and an object outside itself in order to satisfy and still itself. Hunger is the acknowledged need of my body for an object which exists outside itself and which is indispensable to its integration and to the expression of its essential nature. The sun is an object for the plant, an indispensable object which confirms its life, just as the plant is an object for the sun, an expression of its life-awakening power and its objective essential power.

A being which does not have its nature outside itself is not a natural being and plays no part in the system of nature. A being which has no object outside itself is not an objective being. A being which is not itself an object for a third being has no being for its object, i.e. it has no objective relationships and its existence is not objective.

A non-objective being is a non-being.

Imagine a being which is neither an object itself nor has an object. In the first place, such a being would be the only being; no other being would exist outside it, it would exist in a condition of solitude. For as soon as there are objects outside me, as soon as I am not alone, I am another, a reality other than the object outside me. For this third object I am therefore a reality other than it, i.e. its object. A being which is not the object of another being therefore presupposes that no objective being exists. As soon as I have an object, this object has me for its object. But a non-objective being is an unreal, non-sensuous, merely thought, i.e. merely conceived being, a being of abstraction. To be sensuous, i.e. to be real, is to be an object of sense, a sensuous object, and thus to have sensuous objects outside oneself, objects of one's sense perception. To be sensuous is to suffer (to be subjected to the actions of another).

Man as an objective sensuous being is therefore a suffering being, and because he feels his suffering, he is a passionate being. Passion is man's essential power vigorously striving to attain its object.

But man is not only a natural being; he is a human natural being; i.e. he is a being for himself and hence a species-being, as which he must confirm and realize himself both in his being and in his knowing. Consequently, human objects are not natural objects as they immediately present themselves, nor is human sense, in its immediate and objective existence, human sensibility and human objectivity. Neither objective nor subjective nature is immediately present in a form adequate to the human being. And as everything natural must come into being, so man also has his process of origin in history. But for him history is a conscious process, and hence one which consciously supersedes itself. History is the true natural history of man.

Critique of Hegel's Philosophy of Right

The foundation of religious criticism is: Man makes religion, religion does not make man. Religion is indeed the self-consciousness and self-esteem of man who has either not yet won through to himself or has already lost himself again. But man is no abstract being squatting outside the world. Man is the world of man, state, society. This state and this society produce religion, which is an inverted consciousness of the world, because they are an inverted world. Religion is the general theory of this world, its encyclopedic compendium, its logic in popular form, its spiritual point d'honneur, its enthusiasm, its moral sanction, its solemn complement and its universal basis of consolation and justification. It is the fantastic realization of the human essence since the human essence has not acquired any true reality. The struggle against religion is therefore indirectly the struggle against that world whose spiritual aroma is religion.

Religious suffering is at one and the same time the expression of real suffering and a protest against real suffering. Religion is the sigh of the oppressed creature, the heart of a heartless world and the soul of soulless conditions. It is the opium of the people. The abolition of religion as the illusory happiness of the people is the demand for their real happiness. To call on them to give up their illusions about their condition is to call on them to give up a condition that requires illusions. The criticism of religion is therefore in embryo the criticism of that vale of tears of which religion is the halo.

Criticism has plucked the imaginary flowers on the chain not in order that man shall continue to bear that chain without fantasy or consolation but so that he shall throw off the chain and pluck the living flower. The criticism of religion disillusions man, so that he will think, act and fashion his reality like a man who has discarded his illusions and regained his senses, so that he will move land around himself as his own true sun. Religion is only the illusory sun which revolves around man as long as he does not revolve around himself.

It is therefore the task of history, once the other-world of truth has vanished, to establish the truth of this world. It is the immediate task of philosophy, which is in the service of history, to unmask self-estrangement in its unholy forms once the holy form of human self-estrangement has been unmasked. Thus the criticism of heaven turns into the criticism of earth, the criticism of religion into the criticism of law and the criticism of theology into the criticism of politics.

The following exposition – a contribution to this undertaking - concerns itself not directly with the original but with a copy, with the German philosophy of the state and of law. The only reason for this is that it is concerned with Germany.

If we were to begin with the German status quo itself, the result - even if we were to do it in the only appropriate way, i.e. negatively - would still be an anachronism. Even the negation of our present political situation is a dusty fact in the historical junk room of modern nations. If I negate powdered wigs, I am still left with unpowered wigs. If I negate the situation in Germany in 1843, then according to the French calendar I have barely reached 1789, much less the vital centre of our present age.

Indeed, German history prides itself on having travelled a road which no other nation in the whole of history has ever travelled before, or ever will again. We have shared the restorations of modern nations without ever having shared their revolutions. We have been restored firstly because other nations dared to make revolutions and secondly because other nations suffered counterrevolutions: on the one hand, because our masters were afraid, and on the other, because they were not afraid. With our shepherds to the fore, we only once kept company with freedom, on the day of its interment.

One school of thought that legitimizes the infamy of today with the infamy of yesterday, a school that stigmatizes every cry of the serf against the knout as mere rebelliousness once the knout has aged a little and acquired a hereditary significance and a history, a school to which history shows nothing but its a posteriori, as did the God of Israel to his servant Moses, the historical school of law - this school would have invented German history were it not itself an invention of that history. A Shylock, but a cringing Shylock, that swears by its bond, its historical bond, its Christian-Germanic bond, for every pound of flesh cut from the heart of the people.

Now only flourished inside its cranium. In a word; You cannot transcend philosophy without realizing it.

The same mistake, but with the factors reversed, was committed by the theoretical political party, which has its origins in philosophy.

This party saw in the present struggle only the critical struggle of philosophy with the German world and failed to realize that previous philosophy itself belongs to this world and is its complement, even though an ideal complement. It was critical towards its counterpart, but not towards itself, for it took the presuppositions of philosophy as its point of departure and either took for granted the conclusions of that philosophy or passed off demands and conclusions drawn from other quarters as direct philosophical demands and conclusions. But this is to ignore the fact that such demands and conclusions - assuming that they are legitimate - can be achieved only through the negation of previous philosophy, i.e. of philosophy as philosophy. We shall save for later a more detailed account of this party. Its basic defect can be summed up as follows: It believed that it could realize philosophy without transcending it.

The criticism of the German philosophy of the state and of law, which received its most consistent, thorough and complete formulation from Hegel, is both these things: it is at once a critical analysis of the modern state and of the reality connected with it and a decisive negation of all previous forms of political and juridical consciousness in Germany, whose most refined and universal expression, elevated to the level of a science, is precisely the speculative philosophy of law. Only Germany could develop the speculative philosophy of law, this abstract and high-flown thought of the modern state, the reality of which remains part of another world (even if this other world is only the other side of the Rhine). Conversely, the German conception of the modern state, which abstracts from real man, was only possible because and in so far as the modern state itself abstracts from real man or satisfies the whole man in a purely imaginary way. The Germans have thought in politics what other nations have done. Germany has been their theoretical conscience. The abstraction and arrogance of Germany's thought always kept pace with the one sided and stunted character of their reality. So if the status quo of the German political system is an expression of the consummation of the ancient regime, the completion of the thorn in the flesh of the modern state, then the status quo of German political thought is an expression of the imperfection of the modern state, the damaged condition of the flesh itself.

As the determined opponent of the previous form of German political consciousness, the criticism of the speculative philosophy of law finds its progression not within itself but in tasks which can only be solved in one way - through practice [Praxis].

We must then ask ourselves: can Germany attain a practice, that is to say, a revolution that raises it not only to the official level of modern nations but to the human level that will be their immediate future?

Clearly the weapon of criticism cannot replace the criticism of weapons, and material force must be overthrown by material force. But theory also becomes a material force once it has gripped the masses. Theory is capable of gripping the masses when it demonstrates ad hominem, and it demonstrates ad hominem as soon as it becomes radical. To be radical is to grasp things by the root. But for man the root is man himself. Clear proof of the radicalism of German theory and its practical energy is the fact that it takes as its point of departure a decisive and positive transcendence of, religion. The criticism of religion ends with the doctrine that for man the supreme being is man, and thus with the categorical imperative to overthrow all conditions in which man is a debased, enslaved, neglected and contemptible being - conditions that are best described in the exclamation of a Frenchman on the occasion of a proposed tax on dogs: Poor dogs! They want to treat you like human beings!

For Germany, theoretical emancipation has a specific practical significance even from a historical point of view. For Germany's revolutionary past, in the form of the Reformation, is also theoretical. Just as it was then the monk, so it is now the philosopher in whose brain the revolution begins.

Luther certainly conquered servitude based on devotion, but only by replacing it with servitude based on conviction. He destroyed faith in authority, but only by restoring the authority of faith. He transformed the priests into laymen, but only by transforming the laymen into priests. He freed mankind from external religiosity, but only by making religiosity the inner man. He freed the body from its chains, but only by putting the heart in chains.

But even if Protestantism was not the true solution, it did pose the problem correctly. It was now no longer a question of the struggle of the layman with the priest outside himself, but rather of his struggle with his own inner priest, with his priestly nature. And if the Protestant transformation of the German laymen into priests emancipated the lay priests - the princes together with their clergy, the privileged and the philistines - the philosophical transformation of the priestly Germans into men will emancipate the people. But just as emancipation did not stop with the princes, so will secularization of property not stop with the dispossession of the churches, which was set going above all by hypocritical Prussia. At that time the Peasants War, the most radical episode in German history, suffered defeat because of theology. Today, when theology itself has failed, the most unfree episode in German history, our status quo, will founder on philosophy. On the eve of the Reformation official Germany was Rome's most unquestioning vassal. On the eve of its revolution Germany is the unquestioning vassal of lesser powers than Rome - of Prussia and Austria, of clod-hopping squires and philistines.

But a major difficulty appears to stand in the way of a radical German revolution.

The point is that revolutions need a passive element, a material basis. Theory is realized in a people only in so far as it is a realization of the people's needs. But will the enormous gap that exists between the demands of German thought and the responses of German reality now correspond to the same gap both between civil society and the state and civil society and itself? Will the theoretical needs be directly practical needs? It is not enough that thought should strive to realize itself; reality must itself strive towards thought.

But Germany did not pass through the intermediate stages of political emancipation at the same time as modern nations. Even the stages that it has left behind in theory it has not yet reached in practice. How is Germany to override not only its own limitations but also those of the modern nations, to override limitations which in point of fact it ought to experience and strive for as liberation from its real limitations? A radical revolution can only be the revolution of radical needs, but the preconditions and seedbeds for such needs appear to be lacking.

Yet, even if Germany has only kept company with the development of the modern nations through the abstract activity of thought, without taking an active part in the real struggles of this development, it has nevertheless shared in the sufferings of this development without sharing in its pleasures and its partial satisfaction. Abstract activity on the one hand corresponds to abstract suffering on the other. Germany will therefore one day find itself at the level of European decadence before it has ever reached the level of European emancipation. It will be like a fetish-worshipper suffering from the diseases of Christianity.

If we examine the German governments, we find that as a result of the circumstances of the time, the situation in Germany, the standpoint of German education and finally their own happy instincts they are driven to combine the civilized defects of the modern political world, whose advantages we lack, with the barbaric defects of the ancient regime, of which we have our full measure. In this way Germany must participate more and more, if not in the reason then at least in the unreason even of those state forms which have progressed beyond its own status quo. For example, is there any country in the world which shares as naively as so-called constitutional Germany all the illusions of the constitutional state without sharing any of the realities? Or was it just an accident that the idea of combining the torments of censorship with the torments of the French September laws, which presuppose freedom of the press, was the invention of a German government ? Just as the gods of all nations could be found in the Roman Pantheon, so the sins of all state forms will be found in the Holy Roman German Empire. That this eclecticism will take on unheard-of proportions is assured in particular by the politico-aesthetic gourmandise of a German king, who proposes to play all the roles of royalty - feudal and bureaucratic, absolute and constitutional, autocratic and democratic - if not in the person of the people then at least in his own person, and if not for the people, then at least for himself. Germany, as a world of its own embodying all the deficiencies of the present political age, will not be able to overcome the specifically German limitations without overcoming the universal limitation of the present political age.

It is not radical revolution or universal human emancipation which is a Utopian dream for Germany; it is the partial, merely political revolution, the revolution which leaves the pillars of the building standing. What is the basis of a partial and merely political revolution? Its basis is the fact that one part of civil society emancipates itself and attains universal domination, that one particular class undertakes from its particular situation the universal emancipation of society. This class liberates the whole of society, but only on condition that the whole of society finds itself in the same situation as this class, e.g. possesses or can easily acquire money and education.

No class of civil society can play this role without awakening a moment of enthusiasm in itself and in the masses; a moment in which this class fraternizes and fuses with society in general, becomes identified with it and is experienced and acknowledged as its universal representative', a moment in which its claims and rights are truly the rights and claims of society itself and in which it is in reality the heart and head of society. Only in the name of the universal rights of society can a particular class lay claim to universal domination. Revolutionary energy and spiritual self-confidence are not enough to storm this position of liberator and to ensure thereby the political exploitation of all the other spheres of society in the interests of one's own sphere. If the revolution of a people and the emancipation of a particular class of civil society are to coincide, if one class is to stand for the whole of society, then all the deficiences of society must be concentrated in another class, one particular class must be the class which gives universal offence, the embodiment of a general limitation; one particular sphere of society must appear as the notorious crime of the whole of society, so that the liberation of this sphere appears as universal self-liberation. If one class is to be the class of liberation par excellence, then another class must be the class of overt oppression. The negative general significance of the French nobility and the French clergy determined the positive general significance of the class which stood nearest to and opposed to them - the bourgeoisie.

But in Germany every particular class lacks not only the consistency, acuteness, courage and ruthlessness which would stamp it as the negative representative of society; equally, all classes lack that breadth of spirit which identifies itself, if only for a moment, with the spirit of the people, that genius which can raise material force to the level of political power, that revolutionary boldness which flings into the face of its adversary the defiant words: I am nothing and I should be everything. The main feature of German morality and honour, not only in individuals but in classes, is that modest egoism which asserts its narrowness and allows that narrowness to be used against it. The relationship of the different spheres of German society is therefore epic rather than dramatic. Each begins to experience itself and to set up camp alongside the others with its own particular claims, not as soon as it is oppressed but as soon as circumstances, without any contribution from the sphere concerned, create an inferior social stratum which it in its turn can oppress. Even the moral self-confidence of the German middle class is based simply on an awareness of being the general representative of the philistine mediocrity of all the other classes. It is therefore not only the German kings who mount the throne mal~a-propos, but every sphere of civil society which experiences defeat before it celebrates victory, develops its own limitations before it overcomes the limitations confronting it, and asserts its narrow-mindedness before it has had a chance to assert its generosity. As a result, even the opportunity of playing a great role has always passed by before it was ever really available and every class, as soon as it takes up the struggle against the class above it, is involved in a struggle with the class beneath it. Thus princes struggle against kings, bureaucrats against aristocrats, and the bourgeoisie against all of these, while the proletariat is already beginning to struggle against the bourgeoisie. The middle class scarcely dares to conceive of the idea of emancipation from its own point of view, and already the development of social conditions and the progress of political theory have demonstrated this point of view to be antiquated or at least problematical.

In France it is enough to be something for one to want to be everything. In Germany no one may be anything unless he renounces everything. In France partial emancipation is the basis of universal emancipation. In Germany universal emancipation is the conditio sine qua non of any partial emancipation. In France it is the reality, in Germany the impossibility, of emancipation in stages that must give birth to complete freedom. In France each class of the people is a political idealist and experiences itself first and foremost not as a particular class but as the representative of social needs in general. The role of emancipator therefore passes in a dramatic movement from one class of the French people to the next, until it finally reaches that class which no longer realizes social freedom by assuming certain conditions external to man and yet created by human society, but rather by organizing all the conditions of human existence on the basis of social freedom. In Germany, however, where practical life is as devoid of intellect as intellectual life is of practical activity, no class of civil society has the need and the capacity for universal emancipation unless under the compulsion of its immediate situation, of material necessity and of its chains themselves.

So where is the positive possibility of German emancipation? This is our answer. In the formation of a class with radical chains, a class of civil society which is not a class of civil society, a class which is the dissolution of all classes, a sphere which has a universal character because of its universal suffering and which lays claim to no particular right because the wrong it suffers is not a particular wrong but wrong in general', a sphere of society which can no longer lay claim to a historical title, but merely to a human one, which does not stand in one-sided opposition to the consequences but in all-sided opposition to the premises of the German political system; and finally a sphere which cannot emancipate itself without emancipating itself from - and thereby emancipating - all the other spheres of society, which is, in a word, the total loss of humanity and which can therefore redeem itself only through the total redemption of humanity. This dissolution of society as a particular class is the proletariat.

The proletariat is only beginning to appear in Germany as a result of the emergent industrial movement. For the proletariat is not formed by natural poverty but by artificially produced poverty; it is formed not from the mass of people mechanically oppressed by the weight of society but from the mass of people issuing from society's acute disintegration and in particular from the dissolution of the middle class. (Clearly, however, the ranks of the proletariat are also gradually swelled by natural poverty and Christian-Germanic serfdom.)

When the proletariat proclaims the dissolution of the existing world order, it is only declaring the secret of its own existence, for it is the actual dissolution of that order. When the proletariat demands the negation of private property, it is only elevating to a principle for society what society has already made a principle or the proletariat, what is embodied in the proletariat, without its consent, as the negative result of society. The proletarian then finds that he has the same right, in relation to the world which is coming into being, as the German King in relation to the world as it is at present when he calls the people his people just as he calls his horse his horse. By calling the people his private property, the king is merely declaring that the owner of private property is king.

Just as philosophy finds its material weapons in the proletariat, so the proletariat finds its intellectual weapons in philosophy; and once the lightning of thought has struck deeply into this virgin soil of the people, emancipation will transform the Germans into men.

Let us sum up the result:

The only liberation of Germany which is practically possible is liberation from the point of view of that theory which declares man to be the supreme being for man. Germany can emancipate itself from the Middle Ages only if it emancipates itself at the same, time from the partial victories over the Middle Ages. In Germany no form of bondage can be broken without breaking all forms of bondage. Germany, which is renowned for its thoroughness, cannot make a revolution unless it is a thorough one. The emancipation of the German is the emancipation of man. The head of this emancipation is philosophy, its heart the proletariat. Philosophy cannot realize itself without the transcendence of the proletariat, and the proletariat cannot transcend itself without the realization of philosophy.

When all the inner conditions are met, the day of the German resurrection will be heralded by the crowing of the Gallic cock.

(From *Critique of Hegel's Philosophy of Life: Introduction*)

6

Feuerbach

Ludwig Feuerbach was born on 28 July 1804, Bavaria; died on 13 September 1872, Nuremberg. Noted materialist philosopher whose *Essence of Christianity* (1841), with its doctrine that religion is the projection of human wishes and a form of alienation, attracted world attention, and whose critique of Hegel and of religion had an important influence on the young Marx and Engels.

The son of a noted, progressive jurist and criminologist Paul Johann Feuerbach, Feuerbach came to philosophy by way of theology, beginning his studies at Heidelberg in 1823. In 1824 he moved to Berlin and attended Hegel's lectures; in 1825 he lost his religious faith, became a philosophical Hegelian and transferred to the Faculty of Philosophy, completing his degree at Erlangen in 1828. His *Thoughts on Death and Immortality* (1830) caused a scandal by denying the immortality of the soul. In 1829 he had become a Dozent in philosophy at Erlangen and he continued lecturing until 1832, when he stopped in protest against the university's failure to appoint him professor because of his anti-religious views. He lived the rest of his life as a private scholar, publishing in the 1830s a number of pioneering studies in the history of modern philosophy, followed by articles increasingly critical, from a 'materialist' standpoint, of Hegel's idealism. *The Essence of Christianity* (1841) and *Basic Propositions of the Philosophy of the Future* and *Preliminary Theses for the Reform of Philosophy* (both 1843) created a generation of Feuerbachians, following him in rejecting monarchist, the claims of Absolute Reason and of religion as illegitimate attempts to abstract human powers from man, to substitute thought for man thinking, and to set these up to dominate man. Further studies of religion followed and on the outbreak of the revolution of 1848 Feuerbach was hailed, at least by his students at Heidelberg, as its intellectual father and hero - though he himself took a passive and sceptical attitude to it, believing that Germany was not yet sufficiently emancipated from theological illusions to become a republic. In 1850 Feuerbach was converted to the medical materialism of Moleschott, and summed up his view that man is determined by the nature and quality of his food rather than by homilies against sin, in the German pun 'Man is what he eats'. He wrote little of consequence after that except some fragments on ethics, and no longer attracted public attention. In 1868 he read Marx's Capital and praised it for its exposure of horrible, inhuman conditions; in 1870 he joined the Social Democratic Party.

Feuerbach was neither a systematic nor a carefully consistent philosopher; he threw off aphorisms and ideas and has not left behind him a coherently worked out and carefully analysed position on any of the major problems of philosophy that are central to his work. Both his 'materialism' and his theory of knowledge are matters for interpretation and possible dispute. Marx's treatment of him in the *Theses on Feuerbach* as a contemplative materialist who neglected the active side of mind is simply wrong; so is the charge that he saw praxis only in its 'dirty Jewish' vulgarly practical aspects. Greatly influential in Germany in the 1840s, and in Russia and France still in the 1850s and 1860s, Feuerbach has had later receptions and revivals, and from becoming the leading anti-theological figure of the nineteenth century, he has become a central figure in twentieth-century theology with elevation of man as the content of religion. Feurbach's elevation of love as the principle of union between human beings, his doctrine of the I-Thou as the minimum content of all truly human activities (thinking, speech and love) have appealed to modern theologians and to some other philosophers standing on the margins of technical developments, but they have not much interested Marxists. Feuerbach's critique of religion, his conception of alienation, his materialism and his critique of Hegel have in recent years attracted renewed study and become part of the new philosophical treatment of Marxist thought. Marx himself saw Feuerbach's critique of religion as ending in the proposition that man is the highest being for man, and thus providing the starting-point for a truly revolutionary philosophy. Feuerbach's claim that Hegel reverses the role of subject and predicate, creating man as an attribute of thought instead of thought as an attribute of man, is certainly one source of Marx's decision to 'turn Hegel on his head', and Feuerbach's genetic critical method of inquiry, seeking the origin and function of such social institutions as religion, is applied by Marx to the state in 1843 and may be said to be one of the ingredients of his materialist conception of history. It is only with the discovery and rediscovery of Marx's early philosophical writings, however, that the relationship between Marx and Feuerbach has come to be thoroughly studied and well understood. Marx himself saw Feuerbach as an important but passing phase in his own intellectual development and maintained no lasting interest in him, though he did order from London, in the 1860s, the seven volumes of Feuerbarchs collected works. Engels's Ludwig Feuerbach, though an important text in the development of official Soviet dialectical materialism, is neither a valuable study of Feuerbach's own philosophy nor a major contribution to a sophisticated Marxist philosophical position. Among classical Marxists, and philosophers working in the Soviet Union until recently, there has been much lip-service to Feuerbach as an important but inadequate forerunner of Marxism, but only one serious study, by Deborin (1923). Deborin's claim that Feuerbach was an important philosopher and that Marxism is a variety of Feuerbachianism, on which the first edition of the book ended, was removed from subsequent editions, and his incorrect estimation of the relationship between Feuerbach and Marx was one of the charges made against him when he was denounced and removed from his philosophical post at Stalin's behest. Kamenka treats Feuerbach as important historically and as basically sound in his non-atomistic empiricism, his active theory of mind and his critique of religion, but does not regard him as a systematic or great philosopher.' Wartofsky (1977) treats Feuerbach as raising much more profound issues and attempts to show that Feuerbach's philosophical development is of the deepest significance for a dialectical understanding of the progress of thought.

Feuerbach's conception of the sensuous world is confined on the one hand to mere contemplation of it, and on the other to mere feeling; he posits 'Man' instead of 'real historical man'. 'Man' is really 'the German'. In the first case, the contemplation of the sensuous world, he necessarily lights on things which contradict his consciousness and feeling, which disturb the harmony he presupposes, the harmony of all parts of the sensuous world and especially of man and nature. To remove this disturbance, he must take refuge in a double perception, a profane one which perceives 'only the flatly obvious', and a higher, philosophical, one which perceives the 'true essence' of things. He does not see that the sensuous world around him is not a thing given direct from all eternity, remaining ever the same, but the product of industry and of the state of society; and, indeed a product in the sense that it is an historical product, the result of the activity of a whole succession of generations, each standing on the shoulders of the preceding one, developing its industry and its intercourse, and modifying its social system according to the changed needs. Even the objects of the simplest 'sensuous certainty' are only given him through social development, industry and commercial intercourse. The cherry-tree, like almost all fruit trees, was, as is well known, only a few centuries ago transplanted by commerce into our zone, and therefore only by this action of a definite society in a definite age has it become 'sensuous certainty' for Feuerbach.

Incidentally, when things are seen in this way, as they really are and happened, every profound philosophical problem is resolved quite simply into an empirical fact. For instance, the important question of the relation of man to nature goes so far as to speak of 'the antitheses in nature and history', as though these were two separate 'things' and man did not always have before him an historical nature and a natural history which gave rise to all the 'unfathomably lofty works' on 'substance' and 'self-consciousness', crumbles of itself when we understand that the celebrated 'unity of man with nature' has always existed in industry and lias existed in various forms in each epoch according jo the lesser or greater development of industry, and so has the 'struggle' of man with nature, right up to the development of his productive forces on a corresponding basis.

Certainly Feuerbach has a great advantage over the 'pure' materialists since he realises that man too is an 'object of the senses'. But apart from the fact that he only conceives man as an 'object of the senses', not as 'sensuous activity', because he still remains in the realm of theory and conceives of men not in their given social connection, not under their existing conditions of life, which have made them what they are, he never arrives at the actually existing, active men, but stops at the abstraction 'man', and gets no further than recognising 'the actual, individual, corporeal man' emotionally he knows no other 'human relations' 'of man to man' than love and friendship, and even these idealised. He gives no criticism of the present conditions of life. Thus he never manages to conceive the sensuous world as the total living sensuous activity of the individuals composing it.

Marx contends that as far as Feucrbach is a materialist he does not deal with history, and as far as he considers history he is not a materialist. With him materialism and history diverge completely.

Marx's polemical piece, The German Ideology, didn't find a publisher until 1932. The only public demand for it came from Marx himself, who was now being caricatured by the Young Hegelians as an unthinking disciple of Ludwig Feuerbach. This infuriated him: Feuerbach's demystification of Hegel had indeed been a glorious moment of revelation, but Marx had long since concluded that the critique merely substituted one myth for another. Feuerbach, the man who had turned Hegel upside down, was now due for the same treatment – as Marx put it, a 'settlement of accounts'.

His exercise in philosophical book keeping began in the spring of 1845 when he scribbled down the brief notes now known as the Theses on Feuerbach. 'The chief defect of all previous materialism is that things, reality, sensuousness, are conceived only in the form of the object, or of contemplation, but not as sensuous human activity, practice.' Feuerbach had exposed the secular basis of religion, but then allowed the secular realm itself to float off into clouds of abstraction. 'The question whether objective truth can be attributed to human thinking,' Marx argued, 'is not a question of theory but is a practical question…All social life is essentially practical. The philosophers have only interpreted the world in various ways; the point is to change it.' The theory without practice was a form of scholastic masturbation-pleasurable. Marx and Hegels proceeded to spend the winter of 1845-46 composing their German Ideology.

The book begins with one of Marx's attention – grabbing generalisation: Hitherto men have always formed wrong ideas about themselves, about what they are and what they ought to be. This is followed by another favourite trick, the provocative parable:

Once upon a time a valiant fellow had the idea men were drowned in water only because they were possessed with the idea of gravity. If they were to get this notion out of their heads, say by avowing it to be a superstitious, a religious concept, they would be sublimely proof against any danger from water. In his whole life he fought against the illusion of gravity, of whose harmful consequences all statistics brought him new and manifold evidence. This valiant fellow was the type of the new revolutionary philosophers in Germany. These thinkers were sheep labouring under the delusion that they were wolves, whose vapid bleating 'merely imitates in a philosophic form the conceptions of the German middle class'.

One sheep was Ludwig Feuerbach himself, whose conception of the world was 'confined on the one hand to mere contemplation of it, and on the other to mere feeling'. He thus failed to notice that even the simplest natural objects are in fact products of historical circumstance. The cherry – tree, like almost all fruit – trees, was as is well known, only a few centuries ago transplanted by commerce into our zone, and therefore only by this action of a definite society in a definite age has it become a "sensuous certainty". But Feuerbach thinks the cherry-tree was simply there, one of nature's altruistic gifts.

The German Ideology is a most revealing account of what the twenty-seven-year old Marx had learned from his philosophical and political adventures,. Having rejected God, Hegel and Feuerbach in quick succession, he and Engels were now ready to unveil their own scheme of practical theory or theoretical practice– otherwise known as historical materialism. 'The premises from which we began, they announced, are not arbitrary ones, not dogmas, but real premises from which abstraction can only be made in the imagination. They are the real individuals, their activity and the material conditions of their life. These premises can thus be verified in a purely empirical way.' Whereas Feuerbach had argued that you are what you eat, Marx and Engels insisted that you are what you produce and how you produce it. 'The division of labour inside a nation leads at first to the separation of industrial and commercial from agricultural labour, and hence to the separation of town and country and to the conflict of their interests. Its further development leads to the separation of commercial from industrial labour.' And so on, these various refinements in the division of labour reflected the development of property – from primitive tribal property to ancient communal and state property, thence to feudal or estate property and onwards to bourgeois property. 'The social structure and the state are continually evolving out of the life – process of definite individuals.

Though the new materialism of Marx and Engels was presented as the negation of idealism, their own vision of paradise turned out to be a pastoral idyll bizarrely ironic in view of Marx's contempt for country life, which he usually described as 'rural idiocy'. Under the present division of labour, they noted, each man was trapped in an exclusive sphere of activity.

He is a hunter, a fisherman, a shephered, or a critical critic, and must remain so if he does not want to lose his means of livelihood; whereas in communist society where nobody has one exclusive sphere of activity but each can become accomplished in any branch he wishes, society regulates the general production and thus makes it possible for me to do one thing today and another tomorrow, to hunt in the morning, fish in the afternoon, rear cattle in the evening, criticise, just as I have a mind, without ever becoming hunter, fisherman, shepherd or critic.

Engels certainly enjoyed hunting and criticising, but did his heart really thrill at the promise of postprandial cattle –rearing?

The Marxist paradise was evoked rather more enticingly in the interminable diatribe against Stirner, who had suggested that the division of labour applied only to those tasks which any reasonably trained person could perform – baking or ploughing, for instance. No one, he maintained, could have done Raphael's works for him. This was an unfortunate example: Raphael had teams of assistants and pupils to complete his frescoes, as Marx and Engels were quick to point out. Besides, the communists didn't believe that everyone should or could produce the work of a Raphael, but only that a potential Raphael must be allowed to develop without hindrance.

Stirner imagines that Raphael produced his pictures independently of the division of labour that existed in Rome at the time. If he were to compare Raphael with Leonardo da Vinci and Titian, he would see how greatly Raphael's works of art depended on the flourishing of Rome at that time, which occurred under Florentine influence, while the works of Leonardo depended on the state of things in Florence, and the works of Titian, at a later period, depended on the totally different development of Venice. Raphael as much as any other artist was determined by the technical advances in art made before him by the organisation of society and the division of labour. In a communist society there are no painters but only people who engage in painting among other activities.

The question of who would clean the lavatories or hew the coal was neither asked nor answered. When someone tried to catch him out by wondering aloud who would polish the shoes under communism, Marx replied crossly 'You should'.

Since its belated publication this century, extravagant claims have been made for The German Ideology as a 'comprehensive exposition' of the

Marxist conception of history. Marx himself was more realistic about its limitations. We abandoned the manuscript to the gnawing criticism of the mice,' he wrote, 'all the more willingly as we had achieved our main purpose – self – clarification.' The tattered pages of the surviving manuscript do indeed appear to have been nibbled at the margin by small rodents.

Why, though, should versions of most of these ideas become a feature of 19th century German philosophy, from the attacks on Hegel's philosophy of the 1830s onwards? Part of the answer is that philosophy now becomes very explicitly connected to politics. Kant, the Idealists, and the early Romantics were not apolitical: they all supported at least some aspects of the French Revolution and wrote on political philosophy: However, perhaps because of the repression to which radical political views were subjected by German states, they do not convey an explicit sense that political activity necessarily goes to the core of philosophy. One reason why a new kind of connection to politics becomes central is the awareness, initiated by Herder, Schlegel, and Hegel, that philosophy is subject to history in ways that had previously not been appreciated. The disruptive changes brought about by the scientific revolution, industrialization, and urbanization mean that the idea of a stable world order falls prey to the pressures of the historical world. Given the brutality that accompanies nascent capitalism, it is not surprising that suspicion of metaphysics becomes connected to the idea that philosophy may conspire with social injustice.

The 'Young Hegelians', a group of predominantly left-wing thinkers that included Ludwig Feuerbach and the early Marx, criticize Hegel but do not completely reject his ideas. Their initial focus is religion, though their main objective is social transformation. One of the decisive changes in 19th century theology is the incursion of new approaches to history into theology. This gives rise to questions about the historical basis of the Gospels, which is revealed to be very shaky. The wider truth of religion therefore becomes more questionable, and one response to this is the idea that the value of religion may not lie in the literal truth of the scriptures. The value of religion can be construed in both a destructive and a constructive manner. As a means of control that sustains traditional hierarchies, the value of religion for the ruling classes is as a form of 'ideology'. As a means of making life more tolerable when change seems impossible, religion keeps hope alive among the oppressed. Marx's remark about religion is the 'opium of the people' does not mean religion is something that just makes them sleep: it makes their pain tolerable. Without religion, though, many forms of authority lose their foundation, leaving the way open for radical social change. Such change needs, however, to offer in reality the kind of hope previously offered only to the imagination.

In Marx's period, there is a more and more explicit tension between an Enlightenment faith in reason's city for solving problems, .and the tragic sense that human life is necessarily transient painful. If there is no hope of individual redemption without religion, the hope has to be that the individual can contribute to the life of the species, by making a better future for humankind. However, whether the idea of such a future is a real consolation to the individual in distressing circumstances is by no means certain. Moreover, in the 19th century and since, the individual self-transcendence too often ends up taking the form of self-sacrifice to the political ends of the nation.

Feuerbach's strategy is to salvage the content of religion that is left when 'dogmatic' beliefs become untenable. He maintains, in a way later to be echoed by Freud, that the content of the notion of God is a 'projection'. Awareness of this will reveal how humankind has alienated' its own best attributes by projecting them onto an external source: 'the Christian God is himself just an abstraction from human love', and the secret of theology is anthropology, of the divine being it is the human being'. Criticism of religion is destruction of an illusion which has a thoroughly destructive effect on humankind'. Feuerbach employs an inversion suggested in aspects of early Romantic philosophy; which also occurs in Schelling's critique of Hegel. Idealism, in this view, makes mind the 'subject' and reality the 'predicate'. In idealism, philosophical abstractions are supposed to be the primary reality. The importance of this idea becomes clear when putatively Hegelian ideas, such as that of 'the State' as the real subject, of which individuals are the predicates, are used to legitimate an unjust, feudal status quo. However, Feuerbach's insistence on sensuous human existence as the prior reality; out of which abstractions are generated, runs the risk of falling prey to Hegel's criticisms of immediacy: as we saw, individual rights cannot exist without mediation through the collective form of the state. This is, though, another case in which considering the issue in purely philosophical terms may obscure the real significance of a philosophical conception. It is Marx who is one of the first to bring this sort of danger to light.

–Editor

Theses on Feuerbach

Thesis 1

Hence, in opposition to materialism, the active side was developed in abstract fashion by idealism which naturally does not know of real, sensible activity as such. Feuerbach appeals to sensible objects-ones really distinct from thought objects: but he does not conceive human activity itself as activity which belongs the objective world. Hence in the 'Essence of Christianity' he considers only the theoretical stance as the genuinely human one, whilst practice is conceived and set off only in its grubby Jewish form. Hence he does not grasp the meaning of 'revolutionary', of 'practical-critical' activity."

Thesis 2

The question whether truth about the objective world is attained by human thinking is not a question of theory, but a practical question. In practice must man prove the truth, that is reality and power, this- worldliness of his thinking. The dispute over the reality on non- reality of thinking - that is isolated from practice- is a purely scholastic question.

Thesis 3

The materialist doctrine about change of circumstances and education forgets that circumstances are hanged by men and the educator himself must be educated. Hence it must sunder society into two parts of which one is superior to society. The coincidence of the changing of circumstances and of human activity or self-change can be conceived and rationally understood only as icvolittionaiy practice?

Thesis 4

Feuerbach starts from the fact of religious elf-estrangement, of the duplication of the world into a religious and a secular one. His work consists in resolving the religious would into its secular basis. But that the secular basis takes off from itself and establishes itself as realm m the doubts can only be explained in terms of the inwardly even and inwardly contradictory character of this secular basis. Therefore this itself must both be understood in its contradiction and revolutionized in practice. Thus once for example the earthly family is revealed as the secret of the holy family, the former must itself be destroyed in theory and in practice.

Thesis 5

Feuerbach, not satisfied with abstract thinking, appeals to observation; but he does not conceive the sensible world as practical human activity involving the senses."

What is said here is substantially only a reprise of part of what has already been said in Thesis and one may therefore pass on immediately to the next thesis, which resumes the critique of Feuerbach on religion initiated in Thesis 4.

Thesis 6

Feuerbach resolves the essence of religion into the essence of man. Hut the essence of man is no abstraction indwelling in each separate individual. In its reality it is the ensemble of social relations.

Feuerhach, who does not enter into the critique of this real essence, is hence obliged:

(1) to abstract from the course of history and to set off the religious I attitude as something self-contained, and to assume an abstract-isolated- human individual.

(2) Hence the essence can be conceived only as 'genus', as an inner, mute, universal character uniting the many individuals in a natural way.

Thesis 7

Hence Feuerbach does not sec that the 'religious attitude' itself is a social product and that the abstract individual which he analyzes belongs to a definite form of society.'

The first clause of this thesis only sums up what has just gone before. The second clause makes explicit an implication of the doctrines just outlined and in effect poses a question (precisely what form of society?) which is in fact answered in Theses 9 and 10. Hut before this answer is presented Marx generalizes the insight illustrated in the preceding criticism of Feuerbach's traditional materialist view of religion.

Thesis 8

All social life is essentially practical. All mysteries that turn theory towards mysticism find their rational solution in human practice and in the comprehension of this practice.

Thesis 9

The highest point attained by materialism based on observation, that is materialism which docs not comprehend the sensible world as practical activity, is the observation of separate individuals and of civil society."

Thesis 10

The standpoint of the old materialism is civil society, the standpoint of the new, human society or social humanity.

Thesis 11

The philosophers have only interpreted the world in different ways, the point is to change it.

(*From Marx*: *Early Writings* translated by Rodny Livingstone, Penguin Books, England, 1975).

7

Alienation

The concept of alienation, regarded today as one of the central concepts of Marxism, and widely used by both Marxists and non-Marxists, entered the dictionaries of philosophy only in the second half of the twentieth century. However, before it was recognized as an important philosophical term it was widely used outside philosophy: in everyday life, in the sense of turning or keeping away from friends or associates; in economy and law, as a term for the transfer of property from one person to another (buying and selling, stealing, making a gift); in medicine and psychiatry, as a name for deviation from normality, insanity. And before it was developed as a metaphilosophical revolutionary concept in Marx, it was developed as a philosophical concept by Hegel and Feuerbach. In his elaboration of alienation Hegel in turn had a number of precursors. Some of them used the term without coming close to its Hegelian or Marxian meaning, some anticipated the idea without using the term, and in some cases there was even a kind of meeting between the idea and the term.

The Christian doctrine of original sin and redemption has been regarded by many as one of the first versions of the story of man's alienation and de-alienation. Some have insisted that the concept of alienation found its first expression in Western thought in the Old Testament concept of idolatry. The relationship of human beings to logos in Heraclitus can also be analysed in terms of alienation. And some have maintained that the source of Hegel's view of nature as a self-alienated form of the Absolute Spirit can be found in Plato's view of the natural world as an imperfect picture of the noble world of Ideas. In modern times the terminology and problematic of alienation can be found especially in the social theorists. Thus Hugo Grotius used alienation as a name for transfer of sovereign authority over oneself to another person.

But regardless of whether they use the term like Grotius or not like Hobbes and Locke, the very idea of the social contract can be interpreted as an attempt at making progress in de-alienation achieving more freedom, or at least security through a deliberate partial alienation. This list of precursors could easily be enlarged. But probably no thinker before Hegel could be read and understood in terms of alienation and de-alienation better than Rousseau. To mention just two among the many relevant points, the contrast Rousseau draws between the natural man and the social man could be compared with the contrast between the non-alienated and the self-alienated man; and his project of overcoming the contradiction between the general and the particular could be regarded as a programme for abolishing self-alienation. However, despite all precursors, including Rousseau, the true philosophical history of alienation begins with Hegel.

Although the idea of alienation appears in the earty writings of Hegel, its explicit elaboration as a philosophical term begins with his *Phenomenology of Mind*. And although the discussion of alienation is most direct and concentrated in the section entitled 'Mind alienated from itself; Culture', it is really the central concept and the leading idea of the whole book. In the same way, although there is no concentrated, explicit discussion of alienation in his later works, the whole philosophical system of Hegel, as it is briefly presented in his Encyclopaedia of the Philosophical Sciences and more extensively in all of his later works and lectures, was constructed with the help of ideas of alienation and de-alienation.

In one basic sense the concept of self-alienation is applied in Hegel to the Absolute. The Absolute Idea (Absolute Mind), which is the only reality for Hegel, is a dynamic Self engaged in a circular process of alienation and de-alienation. It becomes alienated from itself in nature and returns from its self-alienation in the Finite Mind, man who is the Absolute in the process of de-alienation. Self-alienation and de-alienation are in this way the form of Being of the Absolute.

In another basic sense self-alienation can be applied to the Finite Mind, or man. In so far as he is a natural being, man is a self-alienated spirit. But in so far as he is a historical being, able to achieve an adequate knowledge of the Absolute, he is able to become a de-alienated being, the Finite Mind fulfilling its vocation to accomplish the construction of the Absolute. Thus the basic structure of man can also be described as self-alienation and de-alienation.

There is a further sense in which alienation can be attributed to man. It is an essential characteristic of finite mind to produce things. To express itself in objects, to objectify itself in physical things, social institutions and cultural products; and every objectification is of necessity an instance of alienation: the produced objects become alien to the producer. Alienation in this sense can be overcome only in the sense of being adequately known.

A number of further senses of alienation have been discovered in Hegel, for example by Schacht who has concluded that Hegel uses the term in two quite different senses: 'alienation,' which means 'a separation or discordant relation, such as might obtain between the individual and the social substance, or between one's actual condition and essential nature', and 'alienation' which means a surrender or sacrifice of particularity and wilfulness, in connection with the overcoming of alienation, and the reattainment of unity.

Feuerbach criticized Hegel's view that nature is a self-alienated form of Absolute Mind and that man is Absolute Mind in the process of de-alienation. For Feuerbach man is not a self-alienated God, but God is self-alienated man, he is merely man's essence abstracted, absolutized and estranged from man. Thus man, is alienated from himself when he creates, and puts above himself, an imagined alien higher being and bows before him as a slave. The de-alienation of man consists in the abolition of that estranged picture of man which is God. Feuerbach's concept of alienation was first criticized and extended by Moses Hess, but a criticism along the same lines was carried out more fully and deeply by Hess's younger friend, Marx. Marx praised Hegel for having grasped 'the self-creation of man as a process, objectification as loss of the object, as alienation and transcendence of this alienation. But he criticized Hegel for having identified objecnfication with alienation, and for having regarded man as self-consciousness, and the alienation of man as the alienation of his consciousness: 'For Hegel, human life, man is equivalent to self-consciousness. All alienation of human life is therefore nothing but alienation of self-consciousness. All re-appropriation of alienated objective life appears therefore as an incorporation in self-consciousness.

Marx agreed with Feuerbach's criticism of religious alienation, but he stressed that religious alienation is only one among the many forms of human self-alienation. Man not only alienates a part of himself in the form of God; he also alienates other products of his spiritual activity in the form of philosophy, common sense, art, morals; he alienates products of his economic activity in the form of the commodity, money, capital; he alienates products of his social activity in the form of the stale, law, social institutions. There are many forms in which man alienates the products of his activity from himself and makes of them a separate, independent and powerful world of objects to which he is related as a slave, powerless and dependent. However, he not only alienates his own products from himself, he also alienates himself from the very activity through which these products are produced, from the nature in which he lives and from other men. All these kinds of alienation are in the last analysis one; they are different aspects or forms of man's self-alienation, different forms of the alienation of man from his human 'essence' or 'nature', from his humanity.

Alienation tells Marx an action through which a person, a group, an institution, or a society becomes alien (1) to the results or products of its own activity and or (2) to the nature in which it lives, andor (3) to other human beings, and in addition and through any or all of (1) to (3) - also (4) to itself to its own historically created human possibilities.

Thus conceived, alienation is always self-alienation, i.e. the alienation of man of his self from himself from his human possibilities. And self-alienation is not just one among the forms of alienation, but the very essence and basic structure of alienation. On the other hand 'self-alienation' is not merely a descriptive concept; it is also prescriptive term – an appeal, or a call for a revolutionary change of the world de-alienation.

The criticism of alienation was not an end in itself for Marx. His aim was to pave the way for a radical revolution and for the realization of communism understood as 'the re-integration of man, his return to himself, the supersession of man's self-alienation', as the positive abolition of private property, of human self-alienation, and thus the real appropriation of human nature through and for man. Although the terms alienation and de-alienation are not very much used in Marx's later writings, all of them, including Capital, present a criticism of the existing alienated man and society and a call for de-alienation. And there is at least one great work of the later Marx, the Grundrisse, in which the terminology of alienation is widely used.

The Economic and Philosophical Manuscripts were first published in 1932, and the Grundrisse first published in 1939 became accessible in practice only after their re-publication in 1953. These may have been among the main 'theoretical' reasons, practical reasons too and for the neglect of the concepts of alienation and de-alienation in all interpretations of Marx in the 19th century and in the first decades of the twentieth. Some important aspects of alienation were discussed for the first time in Lukacs's History and Class Consciousness under the term Reification, but there is no general and explicit discussion of alienation in the book. Thus the discussion only began after the publication of the Economic and Philosophical Manuscripts in 1932. Herbert Marcuse was among the first to stress the importance of the Manuscripts and to draw attention to the concept of alienation in them, Cornu was one of the first to study the 'young Marx' more carefully, and Lefebvre was perhaps the first who tried to introduce the concept of alienation into the then established interpretation of Marxism.

A more widespread and intense discussion of alienation began after the second world war. Those who have taken part in it include not only Marxists but also existentialists and personalists, and not only philosophers but also psychologists, sociologists, literary critics, writers. Among non-Marxists it was especially Heidegger who gave an important impulse to the discussion of alienation. In *Being and Time* (1967) he used it to describe one of the basic traits of the inauthentic mode of man's Being. Others too have found an analogy between Marx's self-alienation and Heidegger's inauthenticity and also between revolution and Heidegger's Kehre. Further important impulses came from Sanre, who used 'alienation' in both his existentialist and his Marxist phase; Paul Tillich, in whose combination of Protestant theology, existential philosophy and Marxism the concept of alienation plays a prominent role; Kojeve, who interpreted Hegel with the help of insights from the young Marx; Hyppolite discussed alienation especially the relationship between alienation and objectificarion.

Among the Marxists, Lukacs studied alienation in Hegel and Marx, and tried to specify his own concept of alienation and its relationship to reification; Bloch, who used the concept without a special insistence on it, tried to draw a clear distinction between alienation and objectifical and Fromm not only carefully studied the concept of alienation in Marx, but made it a key tool of analysis in his sociological, psychological and philosophical studies.

The Stalinist and structuralist Marxists like Althusser who tried to revive and develop Marx's theory of alienation in the 1950s and 1960s for idealism and Hegelianism. Such opponents of the theory of alienation have insisted that what was called alienation in the early Marx was much more adequately described in later works by scientific terms such as private property, class domination, exploitation, division of labour, etc. But it has been argued in reply that the concepts of alienation and de-alienation cannot be fully reduced to any of the concepts which have been offered as replacements, and that for a truly revolutionary interpretation of Marx the concept of alienation is indispensable. As a result of these debates the number of Marxists who still oppose any use of alienation has considerably declined.

Many who were ready to accept Marx's concept of alienation did not accept that of self-alienation, which seemed to them unhistorical, because it implied that there is a fixed and unchangeable human essence or nature. Against such a view it has been argued that alienation from oneself should be understood not as alienation from a factual or ideal human nature, but as alienation from historically created human possibilities, especially from the human capacity for freedom and creativity. Thus instead of supporting a static or unhistorical view of man the idea of self-alienation is a call for a constant renewal and development of man. To be self-alienated means 'to be self-alienated from oneself as one's own deed, self-activity, self-production, self-creation; to be alienated from history as human praxis and a human product'. Thus 'a man is alienated or self-alienated, when he is not becoming man', and this occurs when 'that which is and was, is taken as the authentic and only truth, or when one operates inside a ready-made world, and is not active practically-critically in a revolutionary way.

A further controversial point is whether alienation applies in the first place to individuals, or to society as a whole. According to some of those who see it as applying in the first place to individuals, the non-adjustment of the individual to the society in which he lives is a sign of his alienation. Others in fact dispute the importance of any external change in circumstances and suggest that the individual's moral effort, 'a revolution within the self, is the only cure. And those who regard self-alienation as a neurotic phenomenon are quite consistent in offering a psychoanalytical treatment for it. At the other pole stand those philosophers and sociologists who, basing themselves on a degenerate variant of Marxism called 'economic determinism', regard individuals as passive products of social and economic organization. For such Marxists the problem of de-alienation is reduced to the problem of social transformation, and the problem of social transformation to the problem of the abolition of private property.

As against both the above-mentioned views a third conception has been proposed according to which de-alienation of society and of individuals are closely connected, so that neither can be carried out without the other, nor can one be reduced to the other. It is possible to create a social system that would be favourable to the development of de-alienated individuals, but it is not possible to organize a society which would automatically produce such individuals. An individual can become a non-alienated, free and creative being only through his own activity. But not only can de-alienation not be reduced to de-alienation of society; the de-alienation of society in its turn cannot be conceived simply as a change in the organization of the economy that will be followed automatically by a change in all other spheres or aspects of human life. Far from being an eternal fact of social life, the division of society into mutually independent and conflicting spheres (economy,, politics, law, arts, morals, religion, etc.), and the predominance of the economic sphere, are according to Marx characteristics of a self-alienated society. The de-alienation of society is therefore impossible without the abolition of the alienation of the different human activities from each other.

Equally, the problem of de-alienation of economic life cannot be solved by the mere abolition of private property. The transformation of private property into state property does not introduce an essential change in the situation of the worker, or the producer. The de-alienation of economic life also requires the abolition of state property, its transformation into real social property, and this cannot be achieved without organizing the whole of social life on the basis of the self-management of the immediate producers. But if the self-management of producers is a necessary condition of the de-alienation of the economic life, it is not of itself a sufficient condition. It does not solve automatically the problem of de-alienation in distribution and consumption, and is not by itself sufficient even, for the de-alienation of production. Some forms of alienation in production have their roots in the nature of present-day means of production, so that they cannot be eliminated by a mere change in the form of managing production.

The act of transforming human properties, relations and actions into properties, relations and actions of man-produced things which have become independent of man and govern his life. Also transformation of human beings into thing-like beings which do not behave in a human way but according to the laws of the thing-world. Reificarion is a 'special' case of alienation, its most radical and widespread form characteristic of modem capitalist society.

There is no term and no explicit concept of reification in Hegel, but some of his analyses seem to come close to it his analysis of die observing reason in the *Phenomenology of Mind*, or his analysis of property in his *Philosophy of Right*. The real history of the concept of reification begins with Marx and with Lukacs's interpretation of Marx, Although the idea of reification is implicitxs already in the early works of Marx, an explicit analysis and use of reification begins in his later writings and reaches its peak in the Gnndrisse, and Capital. The two most concentrated discussions of reification arc to be found in Capital 1, ch, I sect. 4, and in Capital III, ch. 48. In the first of these, on commodity fetishism, there is no definition of reification but basic elements for a theory of reification are nevertheless given in a number of pregnant statements:

The mystery of the commodity form, therefore, consists in the fact that in it the social character of men's labour appears to them as an objective characteristic, a social natural quality of the labour product itself. . . The commodity form, and the value relation between the products of labour which stamps them as commodities, have absolutely no connexion with their physical properties and with the material relations arising therefrom. It is simply a definite social relation between men, that assumes, in their eyes, the fantastic form of a relation between things. This Marx calls the fetishism which attaches itself to the products of labour, so soon as they are produced as commodities, and which is therefore inseparable from the production of commodities. To the producers the social relations connecting the labours of one individual with that of the rest appear, not as direct social relations between individuals at work, but as what they really are, thinglike relations between persons and social relations between things. To them their own social action takes the form of the action of things, which rule the producers instead of being ruled by them.

In the second discussion, Marx summarizes briefly the whole previous analysis which has shown that reification is characteristic not only of the commodity, but of all basic categories of capitalist production (money, capital, profit, etc.). He insists that reification exists to a certain extent in 'all social forms insofar as they reach the level of commodity production and money circulation', but that 'in the capitalist mode of production and in capital which is its dominating category this enchanted and perverted world develops still further'. Thus in the developed form of capitalism reification reaches its peak:

Despite the fact that the problem of reification was discussed by Marx in *Capital*, published partly during his lifetime, and partly soon after his death, which was generally recognized as his master work, his analysis was very much neglected for a long time. A greater interest in the problem developed only after Lukacs drew attention to it and discussed it in a creative way, combining influences coming from Marx with those from Max Weber who elucidated important aspects of the problem in his analyses of bureaucracy and rationalization and from Simmel who discussed the problem in *The Philosophy of Money*. In the central and longest chapter of *History and Class Consciousness* on 'Reification and the Consciousness of the Proletariat, Lukacs starts from the viewpoint that 'commodity fetishism is a specific problem of our age, the age of modern capitalism', and also that it is not a marginal problem but 'the central structural problem of capitalist society'. The 'essence of commodity-structure', according to Lukacs, has already been clarified, in the following way: 'Its basis is that a relation between people takes on the character of a thing and thus acquires a "phantom objectivity", an autonomy that seems so strictly rational and all-embracing as to conceal every trace of its fundamental nature: the relation between people'. Leaving aside 'the importance of this problem for economics itself Lukacs undertook to discuss the broader question: 'how far is commodity exchange together with its structural consequences able to influence the total outer and inner life of society?' He points out that two sides of the phenomenon of reification or commodity fetishism have been distinguished (which he calls the 'objective and the 'subjective'): 'Objectively a world of objects and relations between things springs into being (the world of commodities and their movements on the market). Subjectively– where the market economy has been fully developed - a man's activity becomes estranged from himself, it turns into a commodity which, subject to the non-human objectivity of the natural laws of society, must go its own way independently of man just like any consumer article. Both sides undergo

> the same basic process and are subordinated to the same laws. Thus the basic principle of capitalist commodity production, 'the principle of rationalization based on what is and can be calculated" extends to all fields, including the worker's 'soul', and more broadly, human consciousness. 'Just as the capitalist system continuously produces and reproduces itself economically on higher levels, the structure of reification progressively sinks more deeply, more fatefully and more definitively into the consciousness of man'.
>
> The publication of Marx's *Paris Manuscripts* was a great support for the kind of interpretation of Marx begun by Lukacs, but this was fully recognized only after the second world war. Although the discussion of rcification never became as extensive and intense as that about alienation, a number of outstanding Marxists such as Goldmann, Gabel and Kosik have made valuable contributions to it. Not only have the works of Marx and Lukacs been discussed afresh, but also Heidegger's *Being and Time*, which concludes with the following remarks and questions: 'That the ancient ontology works with "thing-concepts" and that there is a danger "of reifying consciousness" has been well known for a long time. But what does reification mean? Where does it originate from?... Why does this reification come again and again to domination? How is the Being of consciousness positively structured so that reification remains inadequate to it?' Goldmann maintained that these questions are directed against Lukacs and that the influence of Lukacs can be seen in some of Heidegger's positive ideas. **–Editor**

This fact simply means that the object that labour produces, its product, stands opposed to it as something alien, as a power independent of the producer. The product of labour is labour embodied and made material in an object, it is the objectification of labour. The realization of labour is its objectification. In the sphere of political economy this realization of labour appears as a loss of reality for the worker, objectification as loss of and bondage to the object, and appropriation as estrangement, as alienation.

So much does the realization of labour appear as loss of reality that the worker loses his reality to the point of dying of starvation. So much does objectification appear as loss of the object that the worker is robbed of the objects he needs most not only for life but also for work. Work itself becomes an object which he can only obtain through an enormous effort and with spasmodic interruptions. So much does the appropriation of the object appear as estrangement that the more objects the worker produces the fewer can he possess and the more he falls under the domination of his product, of capital.

All these consequences are contained in this characteristic, that the worker is related to the product of his labour as to an alien object. For it is clear that, according to this premise, the more the worker exerts himself in his work, the more powerful the alien, objective world becomes which he brings into being over against himself, the poorer he and his inner world become, and the less they belong to him. It is the same in religion. The more man puts into God, the less he retains within himself. The worker places his life in the object; but now it no longer belongs to him, bur to the object. The greater his activity, therefore, the fewer objects the worker possesses. What the product of his labour is, he is not Therefore, the greater this product, the less is he himself. The externalization [Entausserwg] of the worker in his product means not only that his labour becomes an object, an external existence, but that it exists outside him, independently of him and alien to him, and begins to confront him as an autonomous power; that the life which he has bestowed on the object confronts him as hostile and alien.

Let us now take a closer look at objectification, at the production of the worker, and the estrangement, the toss of the object, of his product, that this entails.

The worker can create nothing without nature, without the sensuous external world. It is the material in which his labour realizes itself, in which it is active and from which and by means of which it produces.

But just as nature provides labour with the means of fife in the sense that labour cannot live without objects on which to exercise itself, so also it provides the means of life in the narrower sense, namely the means of physical subsistence of the worker.

The more the worker appropriates the external world, sensuous nature, through his labour, the more he deprives himself of the means of life in two respects: firstly, the sensuous external world becomes less and less an object belonging to his labour, a means of life of his labour; and secondly, it becomes less and less a means of life in the immediate sense, a means for the physical subsistence of the worker.

In these two respects, then, the worker becomes a slave of his object; firstly in that he receives an object of labour, i.e. he receives work, and secondly in that he receives means of subsistence. Firstly, then, so that he can exist as a worker, and secondly as a physical subject. The culmination of this slavery is that it is only as a worker that he can maintain himself as a physical subject and; only as a physical subject that he is a worker.

The estrangement of the worker in his object is expressed according to the laws of political economy in the following way: the more the worker produces, the less he has to consume; the more values he creates, the more worthless he becomes; the more his product is shaped, the more misshapen the worker; the more civilized his object, the more barbarous the worker; the more powerful the work, the more powerless the worker; the more intelligent the work, the duller the worker and the more he becomes a slave of nature.

Political economy conceals the estrangement in the nature of labour by ignoring the direct relationship between the worker and production. It is true that labour produces marvels for the rich, but it produces privation for the worker. It produces palaces, but hovels for the worker. It produces beauty, but deformity for the worker. It replaces labour by machines, but it casts some of the workers back into barbarous forms of labour and turns others into machines. It produces intelligence, but it produces idiocy and cretinism for the worker.

The direct relationship of labour to its products is the relationship of the worker to the objects of his production. The relationship of the rich man to the objects of production and to production itself is only a consequence of this first relationship, and confirms it. Later we shall consider this second aspect. Therefore when we ask what is the essential relationship of labour, we are asking about the relationship of the worker to production.

Up to now we have considered the estrangement, the alienation of the worker only from one aspect, i.e. his relationship to the products of his labour. But estrangement manifests itself not only in the result, but also in the act of production, within the activity of production itself. How could the product of the worker's activity confront him as something alien if it were not for the fact that in the act of production he was estranging himself from himself? After all, the product is simply the resume of the activity, of the production. So if the product of labour is alienation, production itself must be active alienation, the alienation of activity, the activity of alienation. The estrangement of the object of labour merely summarizes the estrangement, the alienation in the activity of labour itself.

What constitutes the alienation of labour? Firstly, the fact that labour is external to the worker, i.e. does not belong to his essential being; that he therefore does not confirm himself in his work, but denies himself, feels miserable and not happy, does not develop free mental and physical energy, but mortifies his flesh and ruins his mind. Hence the worker feels himself only when he is not working; when he is working he does not feel himself. He is at home when he is not working, and not at home when he is working. His labour is therefore not voluntary but forced, it is forced labour. It is therefore not the satisfaction of a need but a mere means to satisfy needs outside itself. Its alien character is clearly demonstrated by the fact that as soon as no physical or other compulsion exists it is shunned like the plague. External labour, labour in which man alienates himself, is a labour of self-sacrifice, of mortification.

Finally, the external character of labour for the worker is demonstrated by the fact that it belongs not to him but to another, and that in it he belongs not to himself but to another. Just as in religion the spontaneous activity of the human imagination, the human brain and the human heart detaches itself from the individual and reappears as the alien activity of a god or of a devil, so the activity of the worker is not his own spontaneous activity. It belongs to another, it is a loss of his self.

The result is that man (the worker) feels that he is acting freely only in his animal functions - eating, drinking and procreating, or at most in his dwelling and adornment - while in his human functions he is nothing more than an animal.

It is true that eating, drinking and procreating, etc., are also genuine human functions. However, when abstracted from other aspects of human activity and turned into final and exclusive ends, they are animal.

We have considered the act of estrangement of practical human activity, of labour, from two aspects:

(1) the relationship of the worker to the product of labour as an alien object that has power over him. This relationship is at the same time the relationship to the sensuous external world, to natural objects, as an alien world confronting him in hostile opposition.

(2) The relationship of labour to the act of production within labour. This relationship is the relationship of the worker to his own activity as something which is alien and does not belong to him, activity as passivity, power as impotence, procreation as emasculation, the worker's own physical and mental energy, his personal life – for what is life but activity? - as an activity directed against himself, which is independent of him and does not belong to him. Self-estrangement, as compared with the estrangement of the object mentioned above.

We now have to derive a third feature of estranged labour from the two we have already looked at. Man is a species-being, not only because he practically and theoretically makes the species - both his own and those of other things - his object, but also - and this is simply another way of saying the same thing - because he looks upon himself as the present, living species, because he looks upon himself as a universal and therefore free being.

Species-life, both for man and for animals, consists physically in the fact that man, like animals, lives from inorganic nature; and because man is more universal than animals, so too is the area of inorganic nature from which he lives more universal. Just as plants, animals, stones, air, light, etc., theoretically form a part of human consciousness, partly as objects of science and partly as objects of art - his spiritual inorganic nature, his spiritual means of life, which he must first prepare before he can enjoy and digest them - so too in practice they form a part of human life and human activity. In a physical sense man lives only from these natural products, whether in the form of nourishment, heating, clothing, shelter, etc. The universality of man manifests itself in practice in that universality which makes the whole of nature his inorganic body, (1) as a direct means of life and (2) as the matter, the object and the tool of his life activity. Nature is man's inorganic body, that is to say nature in so far as it is not the human body. Man lives from nature, i.e. nature is his body, and he must maintain a continuing dialogue with it if he is not to die. To say that man's physical and mental life is linked to nature simply means that nature is linked to itself, for man is a part of nature. Estranged labour not only (1) estranges nature from man and; (2) estranges man from himself, from his own active function, from his vital activity; because of this it also estranges man from his species. It turns his species-life into a means for his individual life. Firstly it estranges species-life and individual life, and secondly it turns the latter, in its abstract form, into the purpose of the former, also in its abstract and estranged form.

For in the first place labour, life activity, productive life itself appears to man only as a means for the satisfaction of a need, the need to preserve physical existence. But productive life is species-life. It is life-producing life. The whole character of a species, its species-character, resides in the nature of its life activity, and free conscious activity constitutes the species-character of man. Life itself appears only as a means of life.

The animal is immediately one with its life activity. It is not distinct from that activity; it is that activity. Man makes his life activity itself an object of his will and consciousness. He has conscious life activity. It is not a determination with which he directly merges. Conscious life activity directly distinguishes man from animal life activity. Only because of that is he a species-being. Or rather, he is a conscious being, i.e. his own life is an object for him, only because he is a species-being. Only because of that is his activity free activity. Estranged labour reverses the relationship so that man, just because he is a conscious being, makes his life activity his being, a mere means for his existence.

The practical creation of an objective world, the fashioning of inorganic nature, is proof that man is a conscious species-being, i.e. a being which treats the species as its own essential being or itself as a species-being. It is true that animals also produce. They build nests and dwellings, like the bee, the beaver, the ant, etc. But they produce only their own immediate needs or those of their young; they produce one-sidedly, while man produces universally; they produce only when immediate physical need compels them to do so, while man produces even when he is free from physical need and truly produces only in freedom from such need; they produce only themselves, while man reproduces the whole of nature; their products belong immediately to their physical bodies, while man freely confronts his own product Animals produce only according to the standards and needs of the species to which they belong, while man is capable of producing according to the standards of every species and of applying to each object its inherent standard; hence man also produces in accordance with the laws of beauty.

It is therefore in his fashioning of the objective that man really proves himself to be a species-being. Such production is his active species-life. Through it nature appears as his work and his reality. The object of labour is therefore the objectification of the species-life of man: for man reproduces himself not only intellectually, in his consciousness, but actively and actually, and he can therefore contemplate himself in a world he himself has created. In tearing away the object of his production from man, estranged labour therefore tears away from him his species-life, his true species-objectivity, and transforms his advantage over animals into the disadvantage that his inorganic body, nature, is taken from him.

In the same way as estranged labour reduces spontaneous and free activity to a means, it makes man's species-life a means of his physical existence.

Consciousness, which man has from his species, is transformed through estrangement so that species-life becomes a means for him.

Estranged labour therefore turns man's species-being - both nature and his intellectual species-powers - into a being alien to him and a means of his individual existence. It estranges man from his own body, from nature as it exists outside him, from his spiritual essence [Wesen], his human essence.

An immediate consequence of man's estrangement from the of man's self-estrangement; but since it has not yet comprehended the positive essence of private property or understood the human nature of need, it is still held captive and contaminated by private property. True, it has understood its concept, but not yet its essence.

Communism is the positive supersession of private property as human self-estrangement, and hence the true appropriation of the human essence through and for man; it is the complete restoration of man to himself as a social, i.e. human, being, a restoration which has become conscious and which takes place within the entire wealth of previous periods of development. This communism, as fully developed naturalism, equals humanism, and as fully developed humanism equals naturalism; it is the genuine resolution of the conflict between man and nature, and between man and man, the true resolution of the conflict between existence and being, between objectification and self-affirmation, between freedom and necessity, between individual and species. It is the solution of the riddle of history and knows itself to be the solution.

The entire movement of history is therefore both the actual act of creation of communism - the birth of its empirical existence -and, for its thinking consciousness, the comprehended and known movement of its becoming:, whereas the other communism, which is not yet fully developed, seeks in isolated historical forms opposed to private property a historical proof for itself, a proof drawn from what already exists, by wrenching isolated moments from their proper places in the process of development and advancing them as proofs of its historical pedigree. But all it succeeds in showing is that by far the greater part of this development contradicts its assertions and that if it did once exist, then the very fact that it existed in the past refutes its claim to essential being.

It is easy to see how necessary it is for the whole revolutionary movement to find both its empirical and its theoretical basis in the movement of private property or, to be more exact, of the economy.

This material, immediately sensuous private property is the material, sensuous expression of estranged human life. Its movement - production and consumption - is the sensuous revelation f of the movement of all previous production, i.e. the realization or reality of man. Religion, the family, the state, law, morality, science, art, etc., are only particular modes of production and therefore come under its general law. The positive supersession of private property, as the appropriation of human life, is therefore the positive supersession of all estrangement, and the return of man from religion, the family, the state, etc., to his human, i.e. social existence. Religious estrangement as such takes place only in the sphere of consciousness, of man's inner life, but economic estrangement is that of real life - its supersession therefore embraces both aspects. Clearly the nature of the movement in different countries initially depends on whether the actual and acknowledged life of the people has its being more in consciousness or in the external world, in ideal or in real life. Communism begins with atheism, but atheism is initially far from being communism, and is for the most part an abstraction. The philanthropy of atheism is therefore at first nothing more than an abstract philosophical philanthropy, while that of communism is at once real and directly bent towards action.

(From *Marx: Early Writings*, translated by Rodny Livingstone, Penguin Books, England, 1975)

8

Money, The Universal Whore

Money, in as much as it possesses the property of being able to buy everything and appropriate all objects, is the object most worth possessing. The universality of this property is the basis of money's omnipotence; hence it is regarded as an omnipotent being. Money is the pimp between need and object, between life and man's means of life. But that which mediates my life also mediate the existence of other men for me. It is for me the other person.

What, man confound it, hands and feet and head and backside, all are yours! And what we take while life is sweet, Is that to be declared nut ours? Six stallions, say, I can afford, Is not their strength my property? I tear along, a sporting lord As if their legs belonged to me. (Goethe, Fazssi—Mephistopheles) Shakespeare–in Timon of Athens'.

Gold? Yellow, glittering, precious gold? No. gods, I am no idle votanst: roots, you clear heavens! Thus much of this will make black while; foul, fair; Wrong, right; base, noble; old, young coward, valiant.

Why, this will lug your priests and servants from your sides, Pluck stout men's pillows from below their heads; This yellow slave will knit and break religions; bless the accurse; Make the hoar leprosy adored; place thieves. And give them title, knee, and approbation, With senators on the bench: this is it That makes the wrapper's widow wed again; She whom the spinal-house and ulcerous sores Would cast the gorge at, this embalms and spices To the April day again. Come, damned earth, Thou common whore of mankind, that putty's odds Among the rout of nations, I will make thee, Do they right nature.

And later on; O thou sweet king-killer, and dear divorce Twit natural son and sire! Thou bright defiler of Hymen's purest bed Thou valiant Mars

Thou ever young fresh, loved whose blush doth thaw the consecrated snow That lies on Dian's lap! Thou viable gin, that solder's close And mark's them kiss! That sneak's with every tongue. To every purpose! O thou touch of hearts Think, thy slave man rebels; and by thy virtue Set them into confounding odds, that beasts may have the world in empire Shakespeare paints a brilliant picture of the nature of money. To understand him let us begin by expounding the passage from Goethe.

That which exists for me through the medium of money, that which I can pay for, i.e. which money can buy, that am I, the possessor of the money. The stronger the power of my money, the stronger am I, The properties of money are my, the possessor's, properties and essential powers. Therefore what I am and what I can do is by no means determined by my individuality. I am ugly, but I can buy the most beautiful woman. Which means to say that I am not ugly, for the effect of ugliness, its repelling power, is destroyed by money. As an individual, I am lame, but money procures me twenty-four legs. Consequently. I am not lame. I am a wicked, dishonest, unscrupulous and stupid individual, but money is respected, and also is its owner. Money is the highest good, and consequently its owner is also good. Moreover, money spares me the trouble of being dishonest, and I am therefore presumed to be honest. I am mindless, but if money is the trite mind of all things, how can its owner he mindless? What is more, he can buy clever people for himself, and is not he who has power over clever people cleverer than them? Through money I can have anything the human heart desires. Do I not therefore possess all human abilities? Does not money therefore transform all my incapacities into their opposite?

If money is the bond which ties me to human life and society to me, which links me to nature and to man, is money not the bond of all bonds'! Can it not bind and loose all bonds? Is it therefore not the universal means of separation? It is the true agent of separation and the true cementing agent, it is the chemical power of society. Shakespeare brings out two properties of money in particular:

(1) It is the visible divinity, the transformation of all human and natural qualities into their opposites, the universal confusion and inversion of things; it brings together impossibilities.

(2) It is the universal whore, the universal pimp of men and peoples.

The inversion and confusion of all human and natural qualities, the bringing together of impossibilities, the divine power of money lies in its mealier as the estranged and alienating species-essence of man which alienates itself by selling itself. It is the alienated capacity of mankind.

What I as a man cannot do, i.e. what all my individual powers cannot do, can do with the help of money. Money therefore transforms each of these essential powers into something which it is not, into its opposite. If I desire a meal or want to take the mail coach because I am not strong enough to make the journey on foot, money can procure me both the meal and the mail coach, i.e. it transfers my wishes from the realm of imagination, it translates them from their existence as thought, imagination and desires into their sensuous, real existence, from imagination into life, and from imagined being into real being. In this mediating role money is the truly creative power.

Demand also exists for those who have no money, but their demand is simply a figment of the imagination. For me or for any other third party it has no effect, no existence. For me it therefore remains unreal and without an object. The difference between effective demand based on money and ineffective demand based on my need, my passion, my desire, etc., is the difference between being and thinking, between a representation which merely exists within me and one which exists outside me as a real object.

(From *Marx: Early Writings* translated by Rodny Livingstone, Penguin Books, England, 1975)

9

Civil Society

Although the term 'civil society' was used by writers such as Locke and Rousseau to describe civil government as differentiated from natural society or the state of nature, the Marxist concept derives from Hegel. In Hegel, civil or bourgeois society, as the realm of individuals who have left the unity of the family to enter into economic competition, is contrasted with the state, or political society. It is an arena of particular needs, self-interest, and divisiveness, with a potential for self-destruction. For Hegel it is only through the state that the universal interest can prevail, since he disagrees with Locke, Rousseau or Adam Smith that there is any innate rationality in civil society which will lead to the general good.

Marx uses the concept of civil society in his critique of Hegel and German idealism, in such writings as '*On the Jewish Question*', 'Contribution to the Critique of Hegel's Philosophy of Right: Introduction' and Economic and Philosophical Manuscripts. His discussion is in the Hegelian language of that period of his work. The term practically disappears in later works although it can be argued that some of the implications which his earlier discussion has for his view of politics remain. Civil society is also used in his early writings as a yardstick of the change from feudal to bourgeois society. Defined by Marx as the site of crass materialism, of modern property relations, of the struggle of each against all, of egotism, civil society arose, he insists, from the destruction of medieval society. Previously individuals were part of many different societies, such as guilds or estates each of which had a political role, so that there was no separate civil realm. As these partial societies broke down, civil society arose in which the individual became all important. The old bonds of privilege were replaced by the selfish needs of atomistic individuals separated from each other and from the community. The only links between them are provided by the law, which is not the product of their will and does not conform to their nature but dominates human relationships because of the threat of punishment. The fragmented, conflictual nature of civil society with its property relations necessitates a type of politics which does not reflect this conflict but is abstracted and removed from it. The modern state is made necessary by the characteristics of civil society. The fragmentation and misery of civil society escape the control of the state which is limited to formal, negative activities and is rendered impotent by the conflict which is the essence of economic life. The political identity of individuals as citizens in modern society is severed from their civil identity and from their function in the productive sphere as tradesman, day-labourer, or landowner.

In Marx's analysis two divisions grow up simultaneously, between individuals enclosed in their privacy, and state between the public and private domains, or between state and society. Marx contrasts the idealism of universal interests as represented by the modern state and the abstractness of the concept of a citizen who is moral because he goes beyond his narrow interest, with the materialism of real, sensuous man in civil society. The irony according to Marx is that in modern society the most universal, moral, social purposes as embodied in the ideal of the state are at the service of human beings in a partial, depraved state of individual egotistical desires, of economic necessity, it is in this sense that the essence of the modern state is to be found in the characteristics of civil society, in economic relations. For the conflict of civil society to be truly superseded and for the full potential of human beings to be realized, both civil society and its product, political society, must be abolished, necessitating a social as well as a political revolution to liberate mankind.

Although Gramsci continues to use the term to refer to the private or non-state sphere, including the economy, his picture of civil society is very different from that of Marx, It is not simply a sphere of individual needs but of organizations, and has the potential of rational self-regulation and freedom. Gramsci insists on its complex organization, as the 'ensemble of organisms commonly called "private" where hegemony and 'spontaneous consent' are organized. He argues that any distinction between civil society and the state is only methodological, since even a policy of nonintervention like laissez-faire is established by the state itself. In his notes, the metaphors he uses to describe the precise relationship between the state and civil society vary. A fully developed civil society is presented as a trench system able to resist the 'incursions' of economic crises and to protect the state, while elsewhere in a note contrasting Russia in 1917, with its "primordial and undeveloped civil society, with countries in the West, the state is described as an outer ditch behind which stands a sturdy and powerful system of defence in civil society. Whereas Marx insists on the separation between the state and civil society, Gramsci emphasizes the interrelationship between the two, arguing that whereas the everyday, narrow use of the word state may refer to government, the concept of state in fact includes elements of civil society. The state narrowly conceived as government is protected by hegemony organized in civil society while the hegemony of the dominant class is fortified by the coercive state apparatus. Yet the state also has an 'ethical function' as it tries to educate public opinion and to influence the economic sphere. In turn, the very concept of law must be extended, Gramsci suggests, since elements of custom and habit can exert a collective pressure to conform in civil society without coercion or sanctions,

In any actual society the lines of demarcation between civil society and the state may be blurred, but Gramsci argues against any attempt to equate or identify the two, be it in the works of various Italian fascist thinkers or by the French Jacobins. And while he accepts a role for the state in developing civil society, he warns against perpetuating statolatry or state worship. In fact, the withering away of the state is redefined by Gramsci in terms of a full development of the self-regulating attributes of civil society.

Where in Marx's writings civil society is portrayed as the terrain of individual egotism, Gramsci refers to Hegel's discussion of the estates and corporations as organizing elements which represent corporate interests in a collective way in civil society, and the role of the bureaucracy and the legal system in regulating civil society and connecting it to the state. He points out, however, that Hegel did not have the experience of modern mass organizations, which Marx also lacked despite his greater feeling for the masses. These differences may relate to Gramsci's emphasis on the need to analyse the actual organization of civil society and the interconnections between the state and society including the economy. It should be pointed out that in both Marx and Gramsci the term 'civil society' contains elements from both the economic base and the non-political aspects of the superstructure and therefore does not fit neatly into this metaphor.

A reading of the concept of civil society in both Marxist and non-Marxist thinkers leads to an examination of the concept of politics itself. It involves the relationship between individuals, and between individuals and the community, a view of society as organized or not, the delineation of public and private. Although the term disappears in Marx's later works, the theme of the withering away of politics as a separate sphere uncontrolled by society, and its substitution by a new type of democracy reappears in The Civil War in France, is found in Lenin's State and Revolution, and is further developed by Gramsci.

Most recently civil society has occupied a prominent place in debates in Eastern Europe as a result of the challenge to the socialist regimes there, and has entered discussions in the West about changes in the role of the state, the concept of citizenship, and the need to protect civil liberties. Civil society embraces the whole material intercourse of individuals within a definite stage of the development of productive forces. It embraces the whole commercial and industrial life of a given stage, and insofar, transcends the state and the nation though, on the other hand again, it must assert itself in its external relations as nationality and internally must organize itself as state. The term 'civil society' emerged in the eighteenth century, when property relations had already extricated themselves from the ancient and medieval community. Civil society as such only develops with the bourgeoisie; the social organisation evolving directly out of production and intercourse, which in all ages forms the basis of the state and the rest of the idealistic superstructure, has, however, always been designated by the same name. **–Editor**

Civil society and state are separated. Hence the citizen of the state is also separated from the citizen as a member of civil society. He must therefore effect a fundamental division with himself. As an actual citizen he finds himself in a two-fold organization: the bureaucratic organization, which is an external, formal feature of the distant state, the executive, which docs not touch him or his independent reality, and the social organization, the organization of civil society. But in the latter he stands as a private person outside the state; this social organization does not touch the political state as such. The former is a state organization for which he always provides the material. The second is a civil organization the material of which is not the state. In the former the state stands as formal antithesis to him, in the second he stands as material antithesis to the state. Hence, in order to behave as an actual citizen of the state, and to attain political significance and effectiveness, he must step out of his civil reality, disregard it, and withdraw from this whole organization into his individuality; for the sole existence which he finds for his citizenship of the state is his sheer, blank individuality, since the existence of the state as executive is complete without him, and his existence in civil society is complete without the slate. He can be a citizen of the state only in contradiction to these sole available communities, only as an individual. His existence us a citizen of the state is an existence outside his communal existences and is therefore purely individual. The separation of civil society and political state necessarily appears as a separation of the political citizen, the citizen of the state, from civil society, from his own, actual, empirical reality, for as an idealist of the state he is quite another being, a different, distinct, opposed being. Civil society here effects within itself the relationship of state and civil society which already exists on the other side as bureaucracy.

The 'bureaucracy' is the state formalism of civil society. It is the 'state consciousness', the 'state will', the 'state power', as one corporation - and thus a particular, closed society within the state. 'The 'state formalism' which bureaucracy is, is the 'state as formalism'; and it is as a formalism of this kind that Hegel has described bureaucracy. Since this 'state formalism' constitutes itself as actual power and itself becomes its own material content, it goes without saying that the 'bureaucracy' is a web of practical illusions, or the 'illusion of the state'. The bureaucratic spirit is a Jesuitical, theological spirit through and through. The bureaucrats are the Jesuits and theologians of the state. The bureaucracy is the religious republic.

Since by its very nature the bureaucracy is the 'state as formalism', it is also this as regards its purpose. The actual purpose of the state therefore appears to the bureaucracy as an objective hostile to the state. The spirit of the bureaucracy is the 'formal state spirit'. The bureaucracy therefore turns the 'formal state spirit' or the actual spiritlessness of the state into a categorical imperative. The bureaucracy takes itself to be the ultimate purpose of the state. Because the bureauracy turns its 'formal' objectives into its content, it comes into conflict everywhere with 'real' objectives. It is therefore obliged to pass off the form for the content and the content for the form. State objectives are transformed into objectives of the department, and department objectives into objectives of the state. The bureaucracy is a circle from which no one can escape. Its hierarchy is a hierarchy of knowledge. The top entrusts the understanding of detail to the lower levels, whilst the lower levels credit the top with understanding of the general, and so all are mutually deceived.

The bureaucracy is the imaginary state alongside the real state - the spiritualism of the state. Each thing has therefore a double meaning, a real and a bureaucratic meaning, just as knowledge (and also the will) is both real and bureaucratic. The really existing, however, is treated in the light of its bureaucratic nature, its other-worldly, spiritual essence. The bureaucracy has the state, the spiritual essence of society, in its possession, as its private property. The general spirit of the bureauracy is the secret, the mystery, preserved within itself by the hierarchy and against the outside world by being a closed corporation. Avowed political spirit, as also political-minded ness, therefore appear to the bureaucracy as treason against its mystery. Hence, authority is the basis of its knowledge, and the deification of authority is its conviction. Within the bureaucracy itself, however, spiritualism becomes crass materialism the materialism of passive obedience, of faith in authority, of the mechanism of fixed and formalistic behaviour, and of fixed principles, views and traditions. In the case of the individual bureaucrat, the state objective turns into his private objective, into a chasing after higher posts, the making of a career. In the first place, he looks on actual life as something material, for the spirit of this life has its distinctly separate, existence in the bureaucracy. The bureaucracy must therefore proceed to make life as material as possible. Secondly, actual life is material for the bureaucrat himself, i.e., so far as it becomes an object of bureaucratic manipulation; for his spirit is prescribed for him, his aim lies beyond him, and his existence is the existence of the department. The state only continues to exist as various fixed bureaucratic minds, bound together in subordination and passive obedience. Actual knowledge seems devoid of content, just as actual, life seems dead; for this imaginary knowledge and this imaginary life are taken for the real thing. The bureaucrat must therefore deal with the actual state jesuitically, whether this Jesuitry is conscious or, unconscious. However, once its antithesis is knowledge, this Jesuitry is likewise bound to achieve self-consciousness and then become deliberate Jesuitry.

Whilst the bureaucracy is on the one hand this crass materialism, it manifests its crass spiritualism in the fact that it wants to do everything, i.e., by making the will the causa prima. For it is purely an active form, of existence and receive its content from without and can prove its existence, therefore, only by shaping and restricting this content For; the bureaucrat the world is a mere object to be manipulated by him.

When Hegel calls the executive the objective aspect of the sovereignty dwelling in the monarch, that is right in the same sense in which the Catholic Church was the real presence of the sovereignty, substance and spirit of the Holy Trinity. In the bureaucracy the identity of state interest and particular private aim is established in such a way that the state interest becomes a particular private aim over against other private aims.

The abolition of the bureaucracy is only possible by the general interest actually – and not, as with Hegel, merely in thought, in abstraction - becoming the particular interest, which in turn is only possible as a result of the particular interest actually becoming the general interest.

In the genuine state it is not a question of the opportunity of every citizen to devote himself to the general estate as one particular estate, but the capacity of the general estate to be really general that is, to be the estate of every citizen. But Hegel proceeds from the premise of the pseudo-general, illusory-general estate - the premise of generality as a particular estate (the bureaucracy).

The identity which he has constructed between civil society and the state is the identity of two hostile armies, where every soldier has the opportunity to become, by 'desertion', a member of the 'hostile' army; and indeed Hegel herewith correctly describes the present empirical position.

It is the same with his construction of the 'examinations'. In a rational state, to sit an examination should be demanded of a shoemaker rather than an executive civil servant. For shoemaking is a skill without which one can be a good citizen of the state and a social human being; whereas the necessary 'political knowledge' is a requirement without which a person in the state lives outside the state, cut of from himself, from the air. The 'examination' is nothing but a Masonic rite, the legal recognition of a knowledge of citizenship as a privilege.

The examination - this 'link' between the 'office of state' and the 'individual', this objective bond between the knowledge of civil society and the knowledge of the state - is nothing but the bureaucratic baptism of knowledge, the official recognition of the transubstantiation of profane into sacred knowledge (in every examination, it goes without saying the examiner knows all). One does not hear that the Greek or Roman statesmen passed examinations. But of course, what is a Roman statesman against a Prussian government official!

The transformation of state activities into official posts presupposes the separation of the state from society.

It is an historical advance which has transformed the political estates of medieval society into social estates, so that, just as the Christians are equal in heaven, but unequal on earth, so the individual members of the nation are equal in the heaven of their political world, but unequal in the earthly existence of society. The real transformation of the political estates into civil estates took place in the absolute monarchy. The bureaucracy maintained the notion of unity against the various estates within the state. Nevertheless, the social difference of the estates, even alongside the bureaucracy of the absolute executive power, remained a political difference, political within and alongside the bureaucracy of the absolute executive power. Only the French Revolution completed the transformation of the political into social estates, or changed the differences of estate of civil society into mere social differences, into differences of civil life which are without significance in political life. With that the separation of political life from civil society was completed.

The estates of civil society were likewise transformed in the process: civil society was changed by its separation from political society. Estate in the medieval sense continued only within the bureaucracy itself, where civil and political position are directly identical. As against this stands civil society as civil estate. Difference of estate here is no longer a difference of needs and of work as independent bodies. The only general, superficial and formal difference still remaining here is that of town and country. Within society itself, however, the difference was developed in mobile and not fixed circles, of which free choice is the principle. Money and education are the main criteria. The estate of civil society has for its principle neither need, that is, a natural element, nor politics. It consists of separate masses which form fleetingly and whose very formation is fortuitous and does not amount to an organisation.

Only one thing is characteristic, namely, that lack of property and the estate of direct labour, of concrete labour, form not so much an estate of civil society as the ground upon which its circles rest and move. The estate proper is confined to the members of the executive authority. The present-day estate of society already shows its difference from the earlier estate of civil society in that it does not hold the individual as it formerly did as something communal, as a community, but that it is partly accident, partly the work and so on of the individual which docs, or does not, keep him in his estate, an estate which is itself only an external quality of the individual, being neither inherent in his labour nor standing to him in fixed relationships as an objective community organised according to rigid laws. It stands, rather, in no sort of real relation to his material actions, to his real standing. The physician does not form a special estate within civil society. One merchant belongs to a different estate from another, to a different social position. For just as civil society is separated from political society, so civil society has within itself become divided into estate and social position, however many relations may occur between them. The principle of the civil state or of civil society is enjoyment and the capacity to enjoy. In his political significance the member of civil society frees himself from his estate, his true civil position; it is only here that he acquires importance as a human being, or that his quality as member of the state, as social being, appears as his human quality. For all his other qualities in civil society appear inessential to the human being, the individual, as external qualities which indeed are necessary for his existence in the whole, i.e., as a link with the whole, but a link that he can just as well throw away again. (Present-day civil society is the realized principle of individualism; the individual existence is the final goal; activity, work, content, etc., are mere means.) The real human being is the private individual of the present-day state constitution.

In general, the estate has the significance that difference and separation constitute the very existence of the individual. His way of life, activity, etc., instead of turning him into a member, a function of society, make of him an exception to society, are his privilege. That this difference is not merely individual but is established as a community, estate or corporation, not only docs not cancel its exclusive nature but is rather an expression of it. Instead of the individual function being a function of society, it turns, on the contrary, the individual function into a society for itself.

Not only is the estate based on the separation of society as the prevailing law; it separates the human being from his general essence, it turns him into an animal that is directly identical with its function. The Middle Ages are the animal history of human society, its zoology.

The modern era civilisation, makes the opposite mistake. It separates the objective essence of the human being from him as merely something external, material. It does not accept the content of the human being as hi true reality.

The state abolishes, in its own way, distinctions of birth, social rank, education, occupation, when it declares that birth, social rank, education, occupation, are non-political distinctions, when it proclaims, without regard to these distinctions, that every member of the nation is an equal participant in national sovereignty, when it treats all elements of the real life of the nation from the standpoint of the state. Nevertheless, the state allows private property, education, occupation, to act in their way, i.e., as private property, as education as occupation, and to exert the influence of their special nature. Far from abolishing these feat distinctions, the state only exists on the presupposition of their existence; it feels itself to be apolitical state and asserts its universality only in opposition to these elements of its being.

The political state is, by its nature, man's species-life, as opposed to his material life. All the preconditions of this egoistic life continue to exist in civil society outside the sphere of the state, but as qualities of civil society. Where the political state has attained its true development, man - not only in thought, in consciousness, but in reality, in life leads a twofold life, a heavenly and an earthly life: life in the political community, in which he considers himself a communal being, and life in civil society, in which he acts as a private individual, regards other men as a means; degrades himself into a means, and becomes the plaything of alien powers. The relation of the political state to civil society is just as spiritual as the relation of heaven to earth. The political suite stands in the same opposition to civil society, and it prevails over the latter in the same way as religion prevails over me narrowness of the secular world, i.e., by likewise always having to acknowledge it, to restore it, and allow itself to be dominated by it. In his most immediate reality, in civil society, man is a secular being. Here, where he regards himself as a real individual, and is so regarded by others, he is a fictitious phenomenon. In the state, on the other hand, where man is regarded as a species-being, he is the imaginary member of an illusory sovereignty, is deprived of his real individual life and endowed with an unreal universality.

Political emancipation is at the same lime the dissolution of the old society on winch the state alienated from the people, the sovereign power, is based. Political revolution is a revolution of civil society. What was the character of the old society? It can be described in one word feudalism. The character of the old civil society was directly political, that is to say, the elements of civil life, for example, property, or the family, or the mode of labour, were raised to the level of elements of political life in the form of seignority, estates, and corporations. In this form they determined the relation of the individual to the state as a whole, i.e., his political relation, that is, his relation of separation and exclusion from the other components of society.

(From Marx: *Early Writings*, translated by Rodny Livingstone, Penguin Books, England, 1975)

10

Historical Materialism

Historical materialism is one of the most important component parts or discoveries of Marx's thought. In contemporary Marxism, especially since the end of the seventies, historical materialism has become topical again. Marx's materialist conception of history, or the so-called "historical materialism," is actually a set of methodological principles of historical approach. Thus, in *The German Ideology* he terms it the "materialist method" or "method of approach" and illustrates its premises, conditions, and basic concepts. This set of tentative principles is abstracted from his serious study of the history of Europe and, in turn, serves as a guiding thread for his studies.

According to Marx, the first premise of all human history is the existence of, living human individuals and their needs. Thus, the first fact to be established is the physical organization of these individuals and their consequent relation to the rest of nature. Among other premises Marx mentions, the natural conditions in which humans find themselves–geological, climatical, and so on—are of basic importance. Accordingly, both the internal and the external nature of human existence constitute the premises of history. Furthermore, Marx points out that before everything else human existence involves eating and drinking, shelter, clothing, among other things. The first historical act is thus the production of the means to satisfy these needs, the production of material life itself.

In addition, Marx frequently mentions population, which is basically the biological aspect of society. He argues that the increase of population may lead, to a more intensive division of labour, increased productivity, and, the multiplication of needs. In sum, the existence of human individuals and their needs, the natural, conditions in which humans find themselves, population, and so on, constitute the natural bases of history.

As early as 1844, Marx was already concerned about the relationship between humans and nature as well as among humans. In the *Economic and Philosophic Manuscripts* of 1844, Marx declares that "communism as completed naturalism is humanism and as completed humanism is naturalism. It is the genuine solution of the antagonism between man and man". In his view, the relationship between humans and nature is more basic than that between humans. In order to survive, the human species must exploit nature and, consequently, be conditioned by it. According to Marx, material production is rooted in nature, and social relations and consciousness are rooted in material production. There is no gulf or opposition between nature and society or between natural history and human history. Marx even regards the human species as part of nature and "the social movement as a process of natural history".

Moreover, on a methodological or epistemological level, Marx claims the unity of the natural and the human sciences and a natural science of humans. Natural science will, in time, incorporate into itself the science of man, just as the science of man will incorporate into itself natural science. It is obvious that Marx tries to combine naturalism and humanism in his materialist conception of history in order to solve the traditional opposition between humanism and naturalism as well as the antagonism between human beings and nature and between human beings themselves.

However, in Marx's thought, nature is not "nature in itself" but rather "man-made nature"or humanized nature. Thus, productive labour, technology, natural sciences, and industry all represent the historical relationship of humans and nature and the various forms of the unity of humans with nature. From these social practices one is able to grasp "the human essence of nature or the natural essence of man". Accordingly, the histories of the natural sciences, technology, and industry are of fundamental importance in human history.

The sum of productive forces, capital funds and social forms of intercourse according to Marx, is the real basis of history. Civil society is regarded by Marx as the true source and theatre of all history.

By contrast, the idealistic conception of history neglects the real basis of history. It considers it a minor matter quite irrelevant to the course of history. Accordingly, history is always written according to an extraneous standard; the material production of life seems to be primeval history, while material history appears to be separated from ordinary life. In this way, Marx argues, the relation of humans to nature is excluded from history and, hence, the antithesis of nature and history is created. He asserts that the exponents of the idealistic conception of history have only been able to see in story the political actions of princes and states, religious and other types of theoretical struggles, and, in particular, each historical epoch has had to share the illusions of that epoch.

The "idea", the "conception" of the people in question about their real practice, is transformed into the sole determining, active force, which controls and ' determines their practice. In this connection Marx offers an example: when the crude form in which the division of labour appears with the Indians and the Egyptians calls forth the caste-system in their state and religion, the idealistic historian thus mistakenly believes that the caste-system is the power which has produced this crude social form.

Thus, Marx concludes that while the French and the English at least hold by political illusions, which is moderately close to reality, the Germans move in the realm of the "pure spirit" and make religious illusion the driving force of history. The Hegelian philosophy of history is the endpoint of this German historiography, which it is not concerned with real interests, but with pure thought. Furthermore, as far as the relationship between ideas and classes is concerned, Marx declares that "the ideas of the ruling class are in every epoch the ruling ideas, i.e. the class which is the ruling material force of society, is at the same time its ruling intellectual force".

By contrast, in Marx's view, the idealistic historian separates the ruling ideas from the ruling class and from the social relationships which result from a given stage of a mode of production. In this way, the conclusion has been reached that history is always under the sway of ideas; it is very easy to abstract from these various ideas "the idea," "the notion," and so on, as the dominant force in history, and thus to understand all these separate ideas and concepts as "forms of self-determination" on the part of the concept developing in history. It follows that all human relationships can be derived from the concept of the human being. Marx criticizes idealistic historians for they take every epoch at its word and believe that everything it says and imagines about itself is true. In the end of his criticism of the idealistic view of history, Marx points out the social origin of the view.

Although Marx is profoundly influenced by Feuerbach, he criticizes Feuerbach severely and tries to transcend him. Marx's general criticism of Feuerbach in particular, or old materialism in general, is that the doctrines are purely "contemplative"; they only concern themselves with interpretation and thus give no guide for action. Marx says that the chief defect of all previous materialism including that of Feuerbach is that things, reality, the sensible world are conceived only in the form of objects of observation, but not as human sensuous activity, not as practical, not subjectivity. Feuerbach wants sensible objects distinguished from the objects of thought, but he does not understand human activity itself as objective activity. Consequently, he regards the theoretical attitude as the only genuine human activity, while practical activity is apprehended only in its Jewish manifestation. He therefore does not recognize the significance of revolutionary, 'practical-critical' activity.

In contrast to the contemplative character of old materialism, Marx's doctrine can be called practical or historical materialism. Thus, in his second thesis on Feuerbach Marx insists that the question whether human thinking can pretend to objective truth is not a theoretical 'but practical question. Man must prove the truth, i.e. the reality and power, the 'this-sidedness' of his thinking in practice. The dispute over the reality or non-reality of thinking that is isolated from practice is a purely scholastic question.

The unity of theory and practice is the paramount principle of Marxism. Both the attainment and the test of truth involve practice. Even the simple act of understanding and the test of its validity should be related to practice.

Although the primacy of practice is exaggerated in Maoism to the extent the autonomy of theory is denied, the theoretical tendency can be traced back to Marx's own emphasis on practice. Marx argues that all social life is essentially practical. All the mysteries which lead theory towards mysticism find rational resolution in human practice and in the comprehension of this practice.

Furthermore, Marx criticizes Feuerbach for his separation of materialism from history. He points out that insofar as Feuerbach is a materialist he does not deal with history, and insofar as he considers history he is not a materialist, and Feuerbach says "man" instead of "real historical man". Moreover, Marx maintains that "liberation" is a historical not, a mental act, and is brought about by historical conditions, the development of industry, commerce, agriculture, and the conditions of intercourse.

The old materialism asserts the primacy of circumstances over humans. However, Marx argues, humans make circumstances as much as circumstances shape humans. Thus, he criticizes the old materialism for forgetting that circumstances are changed by humans and that the educator must himself be educated. Materialism therefore has to divide society into two parts, one of which is superior to society. By contrast, Marx claims that the coincidence of the changing of circumstances and of human activity or self-changing can only be grasped as revolutionary practice. The dialectical unity of the changing of humans and circumstances is achieved through revolution in Marx's thought, whereas in old materialism there remains a one-sided determinism of circumstances or education.

In contrast to historical idealism, Marx claims that the production of material life is fundamentally important in human society. Material production is the defining characteristic of the human species as well as the determining factor of social life. Thus, Marx, writes in the German Ideology that men can be distinguished from animals by consciousness, by religion or anything else you like. They themselves begin to distinguish themselves from animals as soon as they begin to produce their means of subsistence, a step which is conditioned by physical organization. By producing their means of subsistence, men are indirectly producing their actual material life. The way in which men produce their means of subsistence depends in the first place on the nature of the actual means of subsistence which they find in existence and have to reproduce. This mode of production should not be regarded simply as the reproduction of the physical existence of individuals. It is already a definite form of activity of these individuals, a definite way of expressing their life, a definite mode of life on their part. As individuals express their lives, so they are. What they are, therefore, coincides with their production, both with what they produce and with how they produce.

Furthermore, material production involves, among other things, definite relations of production, the development of the latter corresponds to that of the former. In Marx's own words: "in the social production of their life, men enter into definite relations that are indispensable and independent of their will, relations of production which correspond to a definite stage of development of their material productive forces". The sum total of the relations of production constitute the economic structure of a society, the real foundation, upon which rises a legal and political structure and to which definite forms of social consciousness correspond.

This architectonic analogy is good because it illustrates the relative position and some relation or some aspects of the relation between the productive forces and the relations of production, legal and political structure and social consciousness; however it hides other relation or aspects of the relation among these elements, for instance, in the case of architecture, the influence of superstructure on substructure is almost negligible. Unfortunately, this limitation of the architectonic analogy has created profound theoretical and practical problems. Marx goes on to assert that: "The mode of production of material life conditions the social, political and intellectual life process in general. It is not the consciousness of men that determines their being, but, on the contrary, their social being that determines their consciousness". Here Marx seems to suggest a sort of ontological determination either between material production and superstructure or between social being and consciousness.

Moreover, what concerns Marx is the transformation of societies, especially the capitalist societies in which he lived. Thus, from a dynamic point of view, he observes that a certain stage of their development, the material productive forces come in conflict with the existing relations of production. From forms of development of productive forces these relations turn into their fetters. Then begins an epoch of social revolution. As for social revolution, Marx criticizes utopians and conspirators for disregarding the .material conditions of revolution. Marx chides them vividly: "For them, the one and only condition for a revolution is that their plot be sufficiently organized. They are all chemists of revolution and share the mental disarray, the narrowness of mind and the prejudices of the alchemists of former times".

In short, they wish to bring about revolutionary miracles. In contrast to Utopians and conspirators, Marx tends to stress the development of productive forces, the contradiction between the productive forces and the relations of production, the formation of revolutionary classes, and so on. According to Marx, a revolution can not take place without the material conditions for it. Even revolutionary, theory or science is regarded by Marx as the product of historical movement. Marx's materialist theory of revolution is much more conservative or realistic than the revolutionary messianism of many neo-Marxists.

Furthermore, the communist revolution, according to Marx, is a novelty in history. It is a social, and not merely political, revolution, since it is directed at the abolition of private property and at the division of labour, it is a type of mass movement, in contrast to the movement of minorities, carried out by the majority, in order to serve the interests of the majority, it makes the alteration of humans on a mass scale. Marx, assets that "the communist revolution is necessary because the ruling class can not be overthrown in any other way; the class overthrowing it can. only in a revolution succeed in ridding itself of all the muck of ages and become fitted to found society anew". In other words, the communist revolution' is, among other things, a means of their own education.

As a result of social revolution, the old relations of production in which the productive forces have developed since then are abolished, and new relations arise. Marx wrote a large number of letters, manuscripts, articles, pamphlets, and books throughout his life. Consequently, there are some ambiguities and inconsistencies in this massive quantity of writings over which later Marxists dispute endlessly. Moreover, there are some potential tensions or disjunctions in Marx's thought which are usually kept in delicate balance by virtue of his intellectual skill. However, most of the later Marxists lack this skill. They usually hold one pole of the antinomies against the other. Therefore, at least some issues or differences among later Marxists may be traced back to the potential tensions or ambiguities in Marx's thought.

In some texts, for example, the 1859 "Preface" and The Communist Manifesto, Marx seems to see his doctrine as a general theory of history or society and disregards the discontinuity or qualitative difference between capitalist societies and non-capitalist societies. Moreover, in these texts, unlike in *Capital*, Marx does not emphasize the historical nature of laws or regularities.

By contrast, in *Capital* and the *Grundrisse*, Marx emphasizes the qualitative differences or discontinuities between capitalist societies and pre-or non-capitalist societies. In his view, the most crucial difference between capitalist societies and pre-capitalist societies is the complete separation of the direct producers and the means of production. It follows that there is a gap between historical materialism as a general theory of history and as a special theory of capitalist society. In his letter to Mikhailovsky, Marx regards *Capital* as an "historical sketch of the genesis of capitalism in Western Europe" and objects to understanding it as a general historic-philosophic.

In some of his formulations, Marx seems to regard the productive forces as the driving force of history. The most well-known instance of this is provide in the 1959 "Preface". On the other hand, *The Communist Manifesto* Marx declares that the history of all hitherto existing societies is the history of class struggle. Karl Korsch notes this ambiguity in Marx when he designates the former as the objective formula, and the latter, the subjective formula. Korsch observes that the two formulae are two independent forms of Marxian thought equally original and one is not derived from the other.

Many of Marx's formulations stress the determining role of productive forces. Sometimes this stress even implies a sort of technological determinism. For instance, in an oft-quoted passage Marx observes that social relations are clearly bound up with the productive forces. In acquiring new productive forces men change their mode of production; and in changing their mode of production, in their way of earning a living, they change social relations. The hand-mill gives you society with the feudal lord; the steammill society with the industrial capitalist.

The social relations into which the producers enter with one another, the conditions under which they exchange their activities and participate in the whole act of production, which naturally vary according to the character of the means of production. With the invention of a new instrument of warfare, firearms, the whole internal organization of the army necessarily changed; the relationship within which individuals can constitute an army and act as an army were transformed and the relations of different armies to one another also changed.

From these observations Marx draws a conclusion about the determination of production relations by productive forces: "Thus the social relations within which individuals produce, the social relations of production, change, are transformed, with the change and development of the means of production, the productive forces."

On the other hand, in some places Marx seems to regard the relations of production as the condition or social framework of production, and thus assigns a rather active role to production relations. He says that in production, men not only act on nature but also on one another. They produce only by cooperating in a certain way and mutually exchanging their activities. In order to produce, they enter into definite connections and relations with one another and only within these social connections and relations does their action on nature, does production, take place.

Moreover, in *Capital* and the *Grundrisse* the emphasis is laid on the relations of production. Marx holds that the relationship between the owners of the means of production and the direct producers reveals the innermost secret, the hidden basis of the entire social structure." Similarly, in The Communist Manifesto the class struggle is regarded as the driving force of history. The emphasis on the relations of reduction here is obvious and overwhelming. Thus it is no accident that the history of Marxist thought is full of disputes or debates between "right wing" and "left wing," or between "opportunists" and "adventurists."

It seems that there are ambiguities or inconsistencies in Marx's view of the development of productive forces. Analytically, we want to ask: in Marx, is the development of productive forces continuous or discontinuous, automatic or contingent? In some passages the productive forces appear to develop continually. For instance, in *The Poverty of Philosophy,* we read: "There is a continuous movement of growth of the productive forces, of destruction of social relations, of formation of ideas; nothing is immutable but the abstract movement."

Furthermore, according to Marx, the continuous development of productive forces renders human history coherent. Thus Marx in a letter to Annenkov says that every succeeding generation finds itself in possession of the productive forces acquired by the previous generations, which serve it as the raw material for new production, a coherence arises in human history, a history of humanity which takes shape is all the more a history of humanity as the productive forces of man and therefore his social relations have been more developed.

On the other hand, capitalist society is distinguished from pre-capitalist societies by its rapid technical progress. Thus, in *Capital* Marx writes: "The technical basis of modern industry is therefore revolutionary, while all earlier modes of production were essentially conservative". Or again, in The Communist Manifesto Marx observes that the bourgeoisie can not exist without constantly revolutionalizing the instruments of production, and thereby the relations of production, ad with them the whole relations of society. Conservation of the old modes of production in an unaltered form was, on the contrary, the first condition of existence for all earlier industrial Classes. Constant revolutionizing, uninterrupted disturbance of all social conditions, everlasting uncertainty and agitation distinguish the bourgeois epoch from all earlier ones.

In other words, the development of productive forces in pre-capitalist societies, in contrast to capitalist societies, are relatively static. This also can be seen from Marx's comments on the Asiatic modes of production. For instance he writes in Capital I: "the oriental empires always show an unchanging social infrastructure coupled with unceasing change in the persons and tribes who managed to ascribe to themselves the political superstructure".

Engels credited Marx with being the originator of historical materialism, which he saw as one of Marx's two great scientific discoveries (the other being the theory of surplus value), while Marx wrote that Engels had arrived at the materialist conception of history independently. In accord with the theory itself they stressed the historical and material preconditions of its formulation.

Although scholars disagree about the degree of continuity of various themes between Marx's early and later writings, few would deny that the materialist view of history which Marx and Engels began to hammer out at the time of German Ideology (1845-46) - though not without its intellectual antecedents - constitutes that which is, and was believed by them to be, distinctive of their world view. Earlier adumbrations of this conception in their writings may or may not demonstrate that one or the other of them had already reached a recognizably Marxist perspective prior to 1844-45. At this time, however, they began quite self-consciously to utilize historical materialism as, in Marx's words, the 'guiding thread' of all their subsequent studies.

Historical materialism is not, strictly speaking, a philosophy; rather, it is best interpreted as an empirical theory. Thus Marx and Engels frequently underscore the scientific character of their enterprise, and German Ideology claims that its approach rests not on philosophically derived abstractions or dogmas, but rather on observation and an accurate depiction of real conditions; in short, on premises that 'can thus be verified in a purely empirical way'. Occasionally, Marx and Engels offer simple a priori arguments in favour of historical materialism, but these are not very compelling. A theory which makes such bold claims about the nature of history and society can be vindicated, if at all, only by its ability to provide a viable research programme for social and historical investigations.

These claims receive their most memorable statement in a very compact passage from Marx's 'Preface' to *A Contribution to the Critique of Political Economy*. Although the reliability of the 'Preface' has not gone unchallenged, its authority is bolstered by the fact that Marx refers to it at least twice in *Capital* as a guide to his materialist perspective. The themes of the 'Preface' reverberate throughout the Marxian corpus and must be interpreted in the light of the elaboration they receive elsewhere. In the 'Preface' Marx contends that the economic structure of society, constituted by its relations of production, is the real foundation of society. It is the basis 'on which rises a legal and political superstructure and to which correspond definite forms of social consciousness'. On the other hand society's relations of production themselves 'correspond to a definite stage of development of society's material productive forces'. In this manner, 'the mode of production of material life conditions the social, political and intellectual life process in general'.

As the society's productive forces develop, they clash with existing production relations, which now fetter their growth. Then begins an epoch of social revolution' as this contradiction divides society and as people become, in a more or less ideological form, 'conscious of this conflict and fight it out.' The conflict is resolved in favour of the productive forces and new, higher relations of production, whose material preconditions have 'matured in the womb of the old society', emerge which better accommodate the continued growth of society's productive capacity. The bourgeois mode of production represents the most recent of several progressive epochs in the economic formation of society, but it is the last antagonistic form of production. With its demise the prehistory of humanity will come to a close.

The growth of the productive forces thus explains the general course of human history. The productive forces, however include not just the means of production (tools, machines, factories and so on), but labour power – the skills, knowledge, experience, and other human faculties used in work. The productive forces represent the powers society has at its command in material production.

The relations of production, which are said to correspond to society's productive level, link productive forces and human beings in the process of production. These relations are of two broad types: on the one hand those technical relations that are necessary for the actual production process to proceed; on the other the relations of economic control which are legally manifested as property ownership that govern access to the forces and products of production.

The related concept Mode of Production is similarly equivocal.

Sometimes Marx uses it in the restricted sense of the technical nature or manner of producing, as when capitalism is said to introduce 'constant daily revolutions in the mode of production'. More frequently, Marx employs the concept in a second sense, namely that of the social system of producing, which is carried on within, and as a result of, a certain set of ownership relations. Thus, capitalist relations of production define a specific connection between people and productive forces, while the capitalist mode of production involves the production of commodities, a certain manner of obtaining surplus, labour time determination of value, and so on. In addition, Marx sometimes uses 'mode of production' to encompass both the technical and social properties of the way production proceeds. More than one mode of production may subsist within any actual social formation, but the Introduction to the Grund-rise maintains that 'in all forms of society there is one determinate kind of production which assigns ranks and influence to all the others'.

The expansion of the productive forces determines the relations and mode of production which obtain because, as Marx wrote to Annenkov, 'men never relinquish what they have won'. In order to retain 'the fruits of civilization' they will change their way of producing - either their material or social relations of production or both – to accommodate the acquired productive forces and facilitate their continued advance. The resulting economic structure in turn shapes the legal and political superstructure. Thus the productive forces do not fashion the social world directly. Only the broad contours of history, the main forms of society's socio-economic evolution, are set by the development of society's productive capacity.

The relations of production can influence the momentum and qualitative direction of the development of the productive forces. Capitalism in particular is distinguished by its tendency to raise society to a productive level undreamt of before. This is in line with historical materialism, however, since Marx's thesis is that the relations of production which emerge do so precisely because they have the ability to promote the development of society's productive capacity. Relatedly, it is often noted that the productive forces which marked the birth of capitalism are not those forces - for example, the factories and machinery typical of large-scale mechanized production - that are distinctive of capitalism. Historical materialism, though, envisages the emergence of capitalism as a response to the then existing level of productive forces.

Some present-day Marxists deny the dominant role of the productive forces in favour of the idea that relations and forces are mutually determining. But while Marx certainly allows for their interaction and indeed describes specific instances of the relations of production influencing the productive forces, in all his general theoretical pronouncements the basic determination runs the other way. Because historical materialism sees the productive forces as enjoying explanatory primacy, it is able to give an answer to the question of why in general different socio-economic formations arise when they do.

The legal and political institutions of society are clearly super-structural for Marx: their fundamental character is determined by the nature of the existing economic structure. Which other social institutions are properly part of the superstructure is a matter of debate. Certainly Marx thought that the various spheres and realms of society reflect the dominant mode-of-production and that the general consciousness of an epoch is shaped by the nature of its production. The Marxist theory of ideology contends, in part, that certain ideas originate or are widespread because they sanction existing social relations or promote particular class interests. The economy's determination of legal and political structures, though, will tend to be relatively direct, while its influence over other social realms, culture, and consciousness generally is more attenuated and nuanced. Historical materialism perceives a general hierarchy among the realms of social life, but these relations must be elaborated, not just for society in general, but also for each specific type of socio-economic organization. It is a law for Marx that the superstructure is derived from the base, but this is a law about laws; in each social formation, more specific laws govern the precise nature of this general derivation, In line with this, an important footnote in Capital 1 (ch. 1, sect. 4) suggests that the mode of production of an era determines the relative importance of the various spheres of the social world of that period. The nature and strength of the mechanisms hypothesized by the base-superstructure metaphor, however, are among the most vexed and controversial questions of historical materialism. Marx's theory does not view the superstructure as an epi-phenomenon of the economic base, nor overlook the necessity of legal and political institutions. It is precisely because a superstructure is needed to organize and stabilize society that the economic structure brings about those institutions that are best suited to it. Nor are superstructure and base related like a statue and plinth; that superstructures affect or 'react back on' the base is one of the fundamental tenets of historical materialism.

Law, in particular, is necessary to 'sanction the existing order' and grant it 'independence from mere chance and arbitrariness' (Capital 111, ch. 47). This function itself gives the legal realm some autonomy since the-existing relations of production are represented and legitimated in an abstract, codified form, which in turn fosters the ideological illusion that the law is entirely autonomous with respect to the economic structure. In addition, under capitalism the 'fictio juris of a contract' between free agents obscures the real nature of production, in particular, the 'invisible threads' which bind the wage-labourer to capital (Capital I, ch. 23). In precapitalist societies, for example in feudalism, tradition and custom perform a similar stabilizing function and may also win a degree of autonomy. There, the true nature of the social relations of production is obscured by entanglement with the relations of personal domination which characterize the other spheres of feudal life.

Marx's stress on class analysis, surprisingly absent from the 'Preface', connects, with the above themes of historical materialism in several significant ways. In the social organization of production, people stand in different relations to the forces and products of production and in any given mode of production these relations will be of certain characteristic sorts. The individual's economic position as that is understood in terms of the existing social production relations establishes certain material interests in common with others and determines class membership. Hence follow the familiar definitions of the bourgeoisie and proletariat by reference to the purchase and sale, respectively, of labour power.

A central thesis of historical materialism is that class position, so defined, determines the characteristic consciousness or world view of its members. For example Marx's discussion of the Legitimists and Orleanists in 18th Brumaire emphasizes that on the basis of its socio-economic position each class creates 'an entire superstructure of distinct and peculiarly formed sentiments, illusions, modes of thought and views of life'. The differing material interests of classes divide them and lead to their struggle. Classes differ in the extent to which their members perceive themselves as a class, so that antagonisms between classes may not be discerned by the participants, or may be understood only in a mystified or ideological form.

The ultimate success or failure of a class is determined by its relation to the advance of the productive forces. In the Marx writes German

Ideology, 'the conditions under which definite productive forces can be applied are the conditions of the rule of a definite class of society'. That class which has the capacity and the incentive to introduce or preserve the relations of production required to accommodate the advance of the productive forces has its hegemony ensured. Thus Marx thought that the eventual success of the proletarian cause, like the earlier rise of the bourgeoisie, was guaranteed by the fundamental currents of history while, for example, the heroic slave revolts of the ancient world were doomed to failure. Historical materialism views class rule, hitherto, as both inevitable and necessary to force the productivity of the direct producers beyond the subsistence level. 'No antagonism, no progress', states *The Poverty of Philosophy* (ch. 1). "This is the law that civilization has followed.... Till now the productive forces have been developed by virtue of this system of class antagonism,' The productive progress brought by capitalism, however, eliminates both the feasibility of, and the historical rationale for, class rule. Since the state is primarily the vehicle by which a class secures its rule, it will wither away in post-class society.

Historical materialism contends that class conflict and the basic trajectory of human history is accounted for by the advance of the productive forces. Their advance, however, must be understood in terms of a theoretical model that reveals the character of the specific modes of production involved. Such a theory will be very abstract with regard to any particular society. Thus, for example, Marx presents the evolution of capitalism in abstraction from the specific physiognomy of any particular capitalist nation state. Marx contends that socialism is 'inevitable', but by the same token it does not empower one to predict the arrival of socialism at any particular time or place - only to affirm that the tendency of capitalist development is such as to bring it about. Nor does the specific course of each society simply repeat some universal dialectic of forces and relations of production. Societies are rarely isolated, untouched and uninfluenced by productive advances outside them. Accordingly, every social group of the globe is not fated to pass through the same stages of economic development, nor is the evolution of any particular social formation solely a matter of internal productive events. Although historical materialism permits countries to lag behind or even skip steps, their course must still be accounted for within the over-arching pattern of socio-economic evolution, and that development is due to the productive forces.

The 'Preface' designates the Asiatic, ancient, feudal, and modern bourgeois modes of production as the major epochs in humanity's advance, but these mark the general stages of socio-economic evolution as a whole- not the steps which history obliges every nation, without exception, to climb. Iri a famous letter of November 1877, Marx characteristically denied propounding 'any historico-philosophical theory of the marche generale imposed by fate upon every people"; but this oft-quoted remark does not amount to a rejection of historical determinism. Marx could consistently believe in a necessary, productive-force-determined evolution of history without holding that every social group is preordained to follow the same course. It seems likely, in fact, that Marx would have been willing to revise his particular tabulation of historical periods since he did not analyse in detail humanity's early modes of production. Modification of Marx's historical scheme as well as of his analysis of capitalism and the projected transition to socialism is in principle compatible with the basic tenets of historical materialism. It should be borne in mind that historical materialism does not pretend to explain every last detail of history. From its broad purview, many historical events, and certainly the specific forms they take, are accidental. Nor does the theory seek to explain scientifically individual behaviour, though it attempts to situate that behaviour within its historical confines. In so far as there are ineluctable tendencies in history, these result from, not despite, the choices of individuals. The explanatory ambitions of historical materialism as a social-scientific theory do not commit it to philosophical determinism.

Because historical materialism is so central to Marxism, diverse political and intellectual currents in Marxism have frequently distinguished themselves by their differing interpretations of that theory. One fairly standard interpretation has been presented above, but controversy rages over the basic concepts and theorems of the theory, and the relative importance of its various components. The task of rendering historical materialism as an empirically plausible theory without reducing it to a collection of truisms has proved very formidable. Given the far-ranging claims of the theory and the lack of an interpretative consensus, an accurate assessment of its viability is exceedingly difficult. – **Editor**

The premises from which we begin are not arbitrary ones, not dogmas, but real premises from which abstraction can be made only in the imagination. They are the real individuals, their activity and the material conditions of their life, both those which they find already existing and those produced by their activity. These premises can thus be verified in a purely empirical way.

The first premise of all human history is, of course, the existence of living human individuals. Thus the first fact to be established is the physical organisation of these individuals and their consequent relation to the rest of nature. Of course, we cannot go here either into the actual physical nature of man, or into the natural conditions in which man finds himself - geological, oro-hydrographical, climactic and so on. All historical writing must set out from these natural bases and their modification in the course of history through the action of men.

Men can be distinguished from animals by consciousness, by religion or anything else you like. They themselves begin to distinguish themselves from animals as soon as they begin to produce their means of subsistence, a step which is conditioned by their physical organisation. By producing their means of subsistence men are indirectly producing their material life.

The way in which men produce their means of subsistence depends first of all on the nature of the means of subsistence they actually find in existence and have to reproduce.

This mode of production must not be considered simply as being the reproduction of the physical existence of the individuals. Rather it is a definite form of activity of these individuals, a definite form of expressing their life, a definite mode of life on their part. As individuals express their life, so they are. What they are, therefore, coincides with their production, both with what they produce and with how they produce. Hence what individuals are depends on the material conditions of their production.

This production only makes its appearance with the increase of population. In its turn this presupposes the intercourse of individuals with one another. The form of this intercourse is again determined by production.

Since we are dealing with the Germans, who are devoid of premises, we must begin by stating the first premise of all human existence, and, therefore, of all history, the premise, namely, that men must be in a position to live in order to be able to 'make history'. But life involves before everything else eating and drinking, housing, clothing, and various other things. The first historical act is thus the production of the means to satisfy these needs, the production of material life itself. And indeed this is an historical act, a fundamental condition of all history, which today, as thousands of years ago, must daily and hourly be fulfilled merely in order to sustain human life. Therefore in any conception of history one has first of all to observe this fundamental fact in all its significance and all its implications and to accord it its due importance.

The second point is that the satisfaction of the first need, the action of satisfying and the instrument of satisfaction which has been acquired, leads to new needs; and this creation of new needs is the first historical act.

The third circumstance which, from the very outset, enters into historical development, is that men, who daily re-create their own life, begin to make other men, to propagate their kind: the relation between man and woman, parents and children, the family. The family, which to begin with is the only social relation, becomes later, when increased needs create new social relations and the increased population new needs, a subordinate one (except in Germany), and must then be treated and analysed according to the existing empirical evidence, not according to 'the concept of the family', as is the custom in Germany.

These three aspects of social activity are not of course to be taken as three different stages, but just as three aspects or, to make it clear to the Germans, three 'moments', which have existed simultaneously since the dawn of history and the first men, and which still assert themselves in history today.

The production of life, both of one's own in labour and of fresh life in procreation, now appears as a twofold relation: on the one hand as a natural, on the other as a social relation - social in the sense that it denotes the co-operation of several individuals, no matter under what conditions, in what manner and to what end. It follows from this that a certain mode of production, or industrial stage, is always combined with a certain mode of co-operation, or social stage.

This conception of history thus relies on expounding the real process of production - starting from the material production of life itself- and comprehending the form of intercourse connected with and created by this mode of production, i.e., civil society in its various stages, as the basis of all history; describing it in its action as the state, and also explaining how all the different theoretical products and forms of consciousness, religion, philosophy, morality, etc., etc., arise from it, and tracing the process of their formation from that basis; thus the whole thing can, of course, be depicted in its totality (and therefore, too, the reciprocal action of these various sides on one another). It has not, like the idealist view of history, to look for a category in every period, but constantly remains on the real ground of history; it does not explain practice from the idea but explains the formation of ideas from material practice. It shows that history does not end by being resolved into 'self-consciousness' as 'spirit of the spirit', but that each stage contains a material result, a sum of productive forces, a historically created relation to nature and of individuals to one another, which is handed down to each generation from its predecessor; a mass of productive forces, capital funds and circumstances, which on the one hand is indeed modified by the new generation, but on the other also prescribes for it its conditions of life and gives it a definite development, a special character. It shows that circumstances make just as much as men make circumstances.

My inquiry led me to the conclusion that neither legal relations nor political forms could be comprehended whether by themselves or on the basis of a so-called general development of the human mind, but that on the contrary they originate in the material conditions of life, the sum total of which Hegel, following the example of English and French thinkers of the eighteenth century, embraces within the term 'civil society'; that the anatomy of this civil society, however, has to be sought in political economy. The study of this, which I began in Paris, I continued in Brussels, where I moved owing to an expulsion order issued by My Guizot. The general conclusion at which I arrived and which, once reached, became the guiding principle of my studies can be summarisec as follows. In the social production of their existence, men inevitably enter into definite relations, which are independent of their will, namely relations of production appropriate to a given stage in the development of their material forces of production. The totality of these relations production constitutes the economic structure of society, the real foundation, on which arises a legal and political superstructure and to which correspond definite forms of social consciousness. The mode of production of material life conditions the general process of social political and intellectual life. It is not the consciousness of men that determines their existence, but their social existence that determines their consciousness. At a certain stage of development, the material productive forces of society come into conflict with the existing relations of production or this merely expresses the same thing in legal terms - with the property relations within the framework of which they have operated hitherto. From forms of development of the: productive forces these relations turn into their fetters. Then begins an era of social revolution. The changes in the economic foundation lead sooner or later to the transformation of the whole immense superstructure. In studying such transformations it is always necessary to distinguish between the material transformation of the economic conditions of production, which can be determined with the precision of natural science, and the legal, political, religious, artistic or philosophic - in short, ideological forms in which men become conscious of this conflict and fight it out. Just as one does not judge an individual by what he thinks about himself, so one cannot judge such a period of transformation by its consciousness, but, on the contrary, this consciousness must be explained from the contradictions of material life, from the conflict existing between the social forces of production and the relations of production.

No social order is ever destroyed before all the productive forces for which it is sufficient have been developed, and new superior relations of production never replace older ones before the material conditions for their existence have matured within the framework of the old society. Mankind thus inevitably sets itself only such tasks as it is able to solve, since closer examination will always show that the problem itself arises only when the material conditions for its solution are already present or at least in the course of formation. In broad outline, the Asiatic, ancient, feudal and modern bourgeois modes of production may be designated as epochs marking progress in the economic development of society. The bourgeois mode of production is the last antagonistic form of the social process of production - antagonistic not in the sense of individual antagonism but of an antagonism that emanates from the individuals' social conditions of existence - but the productive forces developing within bourgeois society create also the material conditions for a solution of this antagonism. The prehistory of human society accordingly closes with this social formation.

This sketch of the course of my studies in the domain of political economy is intended merely to show that my views - no matter how they may be judged and how little they conform to the interested prejudices of the ruling classes - are the outcome of conscientious research carried on over many years. At the entrance to science, as at the entrance to hell, the demand must be made.

(Preface to the Critique of Political Economy 1859) (From Marx: *Early Writings*, translated by Rodny Livingstone, Penguin Books, England, 1975).

11

Productive and Unproductive Labour

The polemics against Adam Smith's distinction between productive and unproductive labour were for the most part confined to the *diiminorum, gentium* (among whom moreover Storch was the most important); they are not to be found in the work of any economist of significance – of anyone of whom it can be said that he made some discovery in political economy. They are, however, the hobby-horse of the second-rate fellows and especially of the schoolmasterish compilers and writers of compendia, as well as of *dilettanti* with facile pens and vulgarisers in this field. What particularly aroused these polemics against Adam Smith was the following circumstance.

The great mass of so-called "higher grade" workers – such as state officials, military people, artists, doctors, priests, judges, lawyers, etc. – some of whom are not only not productive but in essence destructive, but who know how to appropriate to themselves a very great part of the "material" wealth partly through the sale of their "immaterial" commodities and partly by forcibly imposing the latter on other people – found it not at all pleasant to be relegated economically to the same class as clowns and menial servants and to appear merely as people partaking in the consumption, parasites on the actual producers (or rather agents of production). This was a peculiar profanation precisely of those functions which had hitherto been surrounded with a halo and had enjoyed superstitious veneration. Political economy in its classical period, like the bourgeoisie itself in its parvenu period, adopted a severely critical attitude to the machinery of the

State, etc. At a later stage it realized and – as was shown too in practice – learnt from experience that the necessary for the inherited social combination of all these classes, which in part were totally unproductive, arose from its own organization.

In so far as those "unproductive labourers" do not produce entertainment, so that their purchase entirely depends on how the agent of production cares to spend his wages or his profit – in so far on the contrary as they are necessary or make themselves necessary because of physical infirmities (like doctors), or spiritual weakness (like parsons), or because of the conflict between private interests and national interests (like statesman, all lawyers, police and soldiers) – they are regarded by Adam Smith, as by the incidental expenses of production, which are therefore to be cut down to the most indispensable minimum and provided as cheaply as possible. Bourgeois society reproduces in its own from everything against which it had fought in feudal or absolutist form. In the first place therefore it becomes a principal task for the sycophants of this society, and especially of the upper classes, to restore in theoretical terms even the purely parasitic section of these "unproductive labourers", or to justify the exaggerated claims of the section which is indispensible. The dependence of the ideological, etc., classes on the capitalists was in fact proclaimed.

Secondly, however, a section of the agents of production (of material production itself) were declared by one group of economists or another to be "unproductive". For example, the landowner, by those among the economists who represented industrial capital (Ricardo). Others (for example Carey) declared that the merchant in the true sense of the word was an "unproductive" labourer. Then even a third group came along who declared that the "capitalists" themselves were unproductive, or who at least sought to reduce their claims to material wealth to "wages", that is, to the wages of a "productive labourer". Many intellectual workers seemed inclined to share the skepticism in regard to the capitalist. It was therefore time to make a compromise and to recognize the "productivity" of all classes not directly included among the agents of material production. One good turn deserves another; and, as in the *Fable of the Bees*, it had to be established that even from the "productive", economic standpoint, the bourgeois world with all its "unproductive labourers" is the best of all worlds. This was all the more necessary because the "unproductive labourers" on their part were advancing critical observations in regard to the productivity of the classes who in general were "*fruges consumer nati*" or in regard to those agents of production, like landowners, who do nothing at all, etc. Both the do-nothings and their parasites had to be found a place in this best possible order of things.

Thirdly, as the dominion of capital extended, and in fact those spheres of production not directly related to the production of material wealth became also more and more dependent on it – especially when the positive science (natural sciences) were subordinated to it as serving material production – the sycophantic underlings of political economy felt in their duty to glorify and justify every sphere of activity by demonstrating that it was a means towards it; and they honored everyone by making him a "productive labourer" in the "primary" sense, namely, a labourer who labours in the service of capital, is useful in one way or another to the enrichment of one capitalist, etc. In this matter even such people as Malthus are to be preferred, who directly defend the necessary and usefulness of "unproductive labourers" and pure parasites.

– Editor

Adam Smith and His Views on Productive and Unproductive Labour

Before we finish with Adam Smith, we will cite two further passages, the first, in which he gives vent to his hatred of the unproductive government; the second, in which he aims to explain why the advance of industry, etc., presupposes free labour. Concerning Smith's hatred of the clergy.

The first passage runs:

It is the highest impertinence and presumption, therefore, in kings and ministers, to pretend to watch over the economy of private people, and to restrain their expense, either by sumptuary laws, or by prohibiting the importation of foreign luxuries. They are themselves always, and without any exception, the greatest spendthrifts in the society. Let them look well after their own expense, and they may safely trust private people with theirs. If their own extravagance does not ruin the State, that of their subjects never will.

And once more the following passage –

The labour of some of the most respectable orders in the society is, like that of menial servants, unproductive of any value, (it has value, and therefore costs an equivalent, but it produces no value) and does not fix or realize itself in any permanent subject, or vendible commodity. The sovereign, for example, with al the officers both of justice and war who serve under him, the whole army and navy, are unproductive labourers. They are the servants of the public, and are maintained by a part of the annual produce of the industry of other people. In the same class must be ranked churchmen, lawyers, physicians, men of letters of all kinds; players, buffoons, musicians, opera-singers, opera-dancers, etc.

This is the language of the still revolutionary bourgeoisie, which has not yet subjected to itself the whole of society, the State, etc. All these illustrations and time-honored occupations – sovereign, judge, officer, priest, etc, - with all the old ideological professions to which they give rise, their men of letters, their teachers and priests, are from an economic standpoint put on the same level as the swarm of their own lackeys and jesters maintained by the bourgeoisie and by idle wealth – the landed nobility and idle capitalists. They are mere servants of the public, just as the others are their servants. They live on the produce of other people's industry, therefore they must be reduced to the smallest possible number. State, church, etc., are only justified in so far as they are committees to superintend or administer the common interests of the productive bourgeoisie; and their costs – since by their nature these costs belong to the overhead costs of production – must be reduced to the unavoidable minimum. This view is of historical interest in sharp contrast partly to the standpoint of antiquity, when material productive labour bore the stigma of slavery and was regarded merely as a pedestal for the idle citizen, and partly to the standpoint of the absolute or aristocratic-constitutional monarchy which arose from the disintegration of the Middle Ages – as Montesquieu, still captive to these ideas, so naively expressed them in the following passage "If the rich do not spend much, the poor will perish of hunger".

When on the other hand the bourgeoisie has won the battle, and has partly itself taken over the State, partly made a compromise with its former possessors; and has likewise given recognition to the ideological professions as flesh of its and everywhere transformed them into its functionaries, of like natural; when it itself no longer confronts these as the representative of productive labour, but when the real productive labourers rise against it and moreover tell it that it lives on other people's industry; when it is enlightened enough not to be entirely absorbed in production, but to want also to assume "in an enlightened way"; when the spiritual labours themselves are more and more performed in its service and enter into the service of capitalist production – then things take a new turn, and the bourgeoisie tries to justify "economically", from its own standpoint, what at an earlier stage it had criticised and fought against. Its spokesman and conscience-slavers in this line are the Garniers', etc. in addition to this, these economists, who themselves and priests, professors, etc., are eager to prove their "productive" usefulness, to justify their wages "economically".

A philosopher produces ideas, a poet poems, a clergyman sermons, a professor compendia and so on. A criminal produces crimes. If we look a little closer at the connection between this latter branch of production and society as a whole, we shall rid ourselves of many prejudices. The criminal produces not only crimes but also criminal law, and with this also the professor who gives lectures on criminal law and in addition to this the inevitable compendium in which this same professor throws his lectures onto the general market as "commodities". This brings with it augmentation of national wealth, quite apart from the personal enjoyment which – as a competent witness, Herr Professor Roscher, tells us – the manuscript of the compendium brings to its originator himself.

The criminal moreover produces the whole of the police and of criminal justice, constables, judges, hangmen, juries, etc.; and all these different lines of business, which form equally many categories of the social division of labour, develop different capacities of the human spirit, create new needs and new ways of satisfying them. Torture alone has given rise to the most ingenious mechanical inventions, and employed many honourable craftsmen in the production of instruments.

The criminal produces an impression, partly moral and partly tragic, as the case may be, and in this way renders a "service" by arousing the moral and aesthetic feelings of the public. He produces not only compendia on Criminal Law, not only penal codes and along with them legislators in this field, but also art, belles-letters, novels, and even tragedies, as not only Mullner's Schuld and Schiller's Rauber show, but also *Oedipus and Richard the Third*. The criminal breaks the monotony and everyday security of bourgeois life. In this way he keeps it from stagnation, and gives rise to that uneasy tension and agility without which even the spur of competition would get blunted. Thus he gives a stimulus to the productive forces. While crime takes a part of the superfluous population of the labour market and thus reduces competition among the labourers – up to a certain point preventing wages from falling below the minimum – the struggle against crime absorbs another part of his population. Thus the criminal comes in as one of those natural "counterweights" which bring about a correct balance and open up a whole perspective of "useful" occupations.

The effects of the criminal on the development of productive power can be shown in detail. Would locks ever have reached their present degree of excellence had there been no thieves? Would the making of bank-notes have reached its present perfection had there been no forgers? Would the microscope have found its way into the sphere of ordinary commerce (see Babbage) but for trading frauds? Doesn't practical chemistry owe just as much to adulteration of commodities and the efforts to show it up as to the honest zeal for production? Crime, through its constantly new methods of attack on property, constantly calls into being new methods of defence, and so is as productive as strikes for the invention of machines. And if one leaves the sphere of private crime: would the world-market ever have come into being but for national crime? Indeed, would even the nations have arisen? And hasn't the Tree of Sin been at the same time the Tree of Knowledge ever since the time of Adam?

In his *Fable of the Bees* (1705) Mandeville had already shown that every possible kind of occupation is productive, and had given expression to the line of this whole argument:

That what we call Evil in this World, Moral as well as Natural, is the grand principle that makes us sociable creatures, the solid basis, the *Life and Support of all Trades and Employments* without exception, there we must look for the true origin of all arts and sciences; and the moment evil ceases, the society must be spoiled if not totally dissolved.

Only Mandeville was of course infinitely bolder and more honest than the philistine apologists of bourgeoisie society.

The first work which I undertook to dispel the doubts assailing me was a critical re-examination of the Hegelian philosophy of law, the introduction to this work being published in Paris in 1844. My inquiry led me to the conclusion that neither legal relations nor political forms could be comprehended whether by themselves or on the basis of a so-called general development of the human mind, but that on the contrary they originate in the material conditions of life, the sum total of which Hegel, following the example of English and French thinkers of the eighteenth century, embraces within the term 'civil society'; that the anatomy of this civil society, however, has to be sought in political economy. The study of this, which I began in Paris, I continued in Brussels, where I moved owing to an expulsion order issued by M. Guizot. The general conclusion at which I arrived and which, once reached, became the guiding principle of my studies can be summarized as follows. In the social production of their existence, men inevitably enter into definite relations, which are independent of their will, namely relations of production appropriate to a given stage in the development of their material forces of production. The totality of these relations of production constitutes the economic structure of society, the real foundations, on which arises a legal and political superstructure and to which correspond definite forms of social consciousness. The mode of production of material life conditions the general process of social, political and intellectual life. It is not the consciousness of men that determines their existence, but their social existence that determines their consciousness. At a certain stage of development, the material productive forces of society come into conflict with the existing relations of production or – this merely expresses the same thing in legal terms – with the property relations within the framework of which they have operated hitherto. From forms of development of the productive forces these relations turn into their fetters. Then begins an era of social revolution. The changes in the economic foundation lead sooner or later to the transformation of the whole immense superstructure. In studying such transformations it is always necessary to distinguish between the material transformation of the economic conditions of production, which can be determined destroyed before all the productive forces for which it is sufficient have been developed, and new superior relations of production never replace older ones before the material conditions for their existence have matured within the framework of the old society. Mankind thus inevitably sets itself only such tasks as it is able to solve, since closer examination will always show that the problem itself arises only when the material conditions for its solution with the precision of natural science, and the legal, political, religious, artistic or philosophic- in short, ideological forms in which men become conscious of this conflict and fight it out. Just as one does not judge an individual by what he thinks about himself, so one cannot judge such a period of transformation by its consciousness, but on the contrary, this consciousness must be explained from the contradictions of material life, from the conflict existing between the social forces of production and the relations of production. No social order is ever are already present or at least in the course of formation. In broad outline, the Asiatic, ancient, feudal and modern bourgeois modes of production may be designated as epochs marking progress in the economic development of society. The bourgeois mode of production is the last antagonistic form of the social process of production – antagonistic not in the sense of individual antagonism but of an antagonism that emanates from the individuals' social conditions of existence – but the productive forces developing within bourgeois society create also the material conditions for a solution of this antagonism. The prehistory of human society accordingly closes with this social formation.

(From *Marx and Eagles: Selected Works,* Progress Publishers, Moscow, 1975)

12

The Commodity

Marx's mature work in *Capital* (first volume) seeks to analyse the mechanisms of 19th.century capitalism which lead to the impoverishment of the many in economies that produce ever more wealth for the few. This analysis involves a critical stance towards philosophy. The dominant forms of philosophy, in Marx's view, have an ideological function. Intellectual production is bound up with the ownership of the means of production, and so with the class divisions that are characteristic of capitalism. The 'ruling ideas' are, as he put it in The German Ideology of 1845, the ideas of the 'ruling class'. This need not, though, involve conscious, deception by those who propagate the ideology which justifies their interests: ideology can function unconsciously.

Were Marx to regard his critique of ideology as a strictly philosophical matter, it would have to explain philosophies wholly in terms of power-relations and forms of production. At times, Marx seems to move in this direction, and this suggests an important problem. Capital sometimes presents itself as a scientific account of capitalism, and Marx is prone to adopt the idea that knowing the scientific truth about capitalism is the direct route to achieving the practical political goal of changing it. It is not far from this to saying that society and history are subject to natural laws, and so trying to justify as natural necessity whatever actions are deemed necessary to arrive at a better form of society Economic factors undoubtedly do create necessities which cannot be avoided: as Marx shows, once a new form of technology renders the previous way of doing things expensive and inefficient, it will generally be adopted. The distance between this historical fact, and the actual ways in which technology affects society which have ethical and political dimensions – is vital, and Marx sometimes ignores it. His main approach to these issues is via the model of the 'economic base', which causes changes in the social 'superstructure' The approach can be illustrated by the effects of the move from agrarian to industrial production, which helps bring about the end of feudalism. The specifically philosophical importance of this issue is apparent in his account of 'commodity form'.

Marx attempts to work out an objective measure of value which would allow him to claim scientific status for his theory. However, the key to his theory of value actually undermines this status and opens up what will be one of his most influential conceptions for subsequent German philosophy. In the Preface to *A Critique of Political Economy* of 1859, Marx asserts that 'it is not the consciousness of men that conditions their being, but, on the contrary, their social being that conditions their consciousness'. A tension is apparent in the word 'besthnm which can mean determines' in the sense that a natural phenomenon is causally determined by a scientific law. If the word is translated as 'conditions', however, it can mean something like 'influences'. This suggests we have a degree of autonomy; even as we are necessarily affected by the sort of society in which we live. Marx talks in this respect of language as 'practical consciousness: language both conditions our consciousness, and enables us to become in some measure self-determining. The further factor which determines conditions our consciousness is the commodity form, which, like language, reduces the particular to the general.

In capitalism, the value of something cannot be measured in terms of its intrinsic worth. The latter Marx terms 'use-value'. The highly portable computer I am using has the use-value of enabling me to write this book anywhere that I can work. Its 'exchange value' is expressed by how much I paid for it, or by how much it is worth if I re-sell it: 'As use values commodities are above all of different quality, as exchange values they only be of different quantity'. The latter value is relational and makes the computer's value equivalent to anything else of the same price. Marx seeks the real basis of value in the average socially necessary labour time required to produce something. If the owner of the means of producing something makes a profit, more of the time taken to produce the thing is worked to the worker by the owner, who therefore receives unpaid 'surplus value'. This theory has, though, not been a success as an economic tool, and is arguably a moral claim about the unfair distribution of wealth.

What makes the theory of the commodity so compelling to later philosophers, like Lukács, Heidegger, and Adorno, is its connection to the fate of metaphysics in the modern world. If the, aim of metaphysics is a system which can incorporate everything into its terms, the commodity market can be seen as a realization of such a system: any object can be grasped in terms of its exchange value. The system both enables rapid wealth creation and technical innovation, by facilitating the exchange and movement of goods, and has questionable effects on culture: like Oscar Wilde's cynic, it knows 'the price of everything and the value of nothing'. It embodies what Jacobi see Spinozism as nihilism, namely the way that in the modern world things only are what they are in relation to their conditions. Marx sees both the massive potential of capital to transform the world – he thinks capitalism is a necessary stage of the development of human production, not something to be demonized - and the need to think beyond the commodity form. Jacobi sought a theological basis for value beyond the world of 'conditioned conditions'. Marx thinks of the move beyond this world in terms of political and social revolution in which the proletariat abolishes the system that oppresses it. Whether that would bring with it the abolition of philosophy depends on how one interprets the goal of philosophy.

–Editor

The wealth of societies in which the capitalist mode of production prevails appears as an 'immense collection of commodities'; the individual commodity appears as its elementary form. Our investigation therefore begins with the analysis of the commodity. The commodity is, first of all, an external object, a thing which through its qualities satisfies human needs of whatever kind. The nature of these needs, whether they arise, for example, from the stomach, or the imagination, makes no difference. Nor does it matter here how the thing satisfies man's need, whether directly as a means of subsistence, i.e. an object of consumption, or indirectly as a means of production.

Every useful thing, for example, iron, paper, etc., may be looked at from the two points of view of quality and quantity. Every useful thing is a whole composed of many properties; it can therefore be useful in various ways. The discovery of these ways and hence of the manifold uses of things is the work of history. So also is the invention of socially recognized standards of measurement for the quantities of these useful objects. The diversity of the measures for commodities arises in part from the diverse nature of the objects to be measured, and in part from convention.

The usefulness of a thing makes it a use-value. But this usefulness does not dangle in mid-air. It is conditioned by the physical properties of the commodity, and has no existence apart from the latter. It is therefore the physical body of the commodity itself, for instance iron, corn, a diamond, which is the use-value or useful thing. This property of a commodity is independent of the amount of labour required to appropriate its useful qualities. When examining use-values, we always assume we are dealing with definite quantities, such as dozens of watches, yards of linen, or tons of iron. The use-values of commodities provide the material for a special branch of knowledge, namely the commercial knowledge of commodities. Use-values are only realized in use or in consumption. They constitute the material content of wealth, whatever its social form may be. In the form of society to be considered here they are also the material bearers of exchange-value.

Exchange-value appears first of all as the quantitative relation, the proportion, in which use-values of one kind exchange for use-values of another kind. This relation changes constantly with time and place. Hence exchange-value appears to be something accidental and purely relative, and consequently an intrinsic value, i.e. an exchange-value that is inseparably connected with the commodity, inherent in it, seems a contradiction in terms. Let us consider the matter more closely.

A given commodity, a quarter of wheat for example, is exchanged for x boot-polish, y silk or z gold, etc. In short, it is exchanged for other commodities in the most diverse proportions. Therefore the wheat has many exchange values instead of one. But x boot-polish, y silk or z gold, etc., each represent the exchange-value of one quarter of wheat. Therefore x boot-polish, y silk, z gold, etc., must, as exchange-values, be mutually replaceable or of identical magnitude. It follows from this that, firstly, the valid exchange-values of a particular commodity express something equal, and secondly, exchange-value cannot be anything other than the mode of expression, the 'form of appearance', of a content distinguishable from it.

Let us now take two commodities, for example corn and iron. Whatever their exchange relation may be, it can always be represented by an equation in which a given quantity of corn is equated to some quantity of iron, for instance 1 quarter of corn = x cvft of iron. What does this equation signify? It signifies that a common element of identical magnitude exists in two different things, in 1 quarter of corn and similarly in x cwt of iron. Both are therefore equal to a third thing, which in itself is neither the one nor the other. Each of them, so far as it is exchange-value, must therefore be reducible to this third thing.

A simple geometrical example will illustrate this. In order to determine and compare the areas of all rectilinear figures we split them up into triangles. Then the triangle itself is reduced to an expression totally different from its visible shape: half the product of the base and the altitude. In the same way the exchange values of commodities must be reduced to a common element, of which they represent a greater or a lesser quantity.

This common element cannot be a geometrical, physical, chemical or other natural property of commodities. Such properties come into consideration only to the extent that they make the commodities useful, i.e. turn them into use-values. But clearly, the exchange relation of commodities is characterized precisely by its abstraction from their use-values. Within the exchange relation, one use-value is worth just as much as another, provided only that it is present in the appropriate quantity. Or, as old Barbon says: 'One sort of wares are as good as another, if the value be equal. There is no difference or distinction in things of equal value. One hundred pounds worth of lead or iron, is of as great a value as one hundred pounds worth of silver and gold.'

As use-values, commodities differ above all in quality, while as exchange-values they can only differ in quantity, and therefore do not contain an atom of use-value.

If then we disregard the use-value of commodities, only one property remains, that of being products of labour. But even the product of labour has already been transformed in our hands. If we make abstraction from its use-value, we abstract also from the material constituents and forms which make it a use-value. It is no longer a table, a house, a piece of yarn or any other useful thing. All its sensuous characteristics are extinguished. Nor is it any longer the product of the labour of the joiner, the mason or the spinner, or of any other particular kind of productive labour. With the disappearance of the useful character of the products of labour, the useful character of the kinds of labour embodied in them also disappears; this in turn entails the disappearance of the different concrete forms of labour. They can no longer be distinguished, but are all together reduced to the same kind of labour, human labour in the abstract.

Let us now look at the residue of the products of labour. There is nothing left of them in each case but the same phantom like objectivity; they are merely congealed quantities of homogeneous human labour, i.e. of human labour-power expended without regard to the form of its expenditure. All these things now tell us is that human labour-power has been expended to produce them, human labour is accumulated in them. As crystals of this social substance, which is common to them all, they are values - commodity values.

We have seen that when commodities are in the relation of exchange, their exchange-value manifests itself as something totally independent of their use-value. But if we abstract from their use-value, there remains their value, as it has just been defined. The common factor in the exchange relation, or in the exchange-value of the commodity, is therefore its value. The progress of the investigation will lead us back to exchange-value as the necessary mode of expression, or form of appearance, of value. For the present, however, we must consider the nature of value independently of its form of appearance.

A use-value, or useful article, therefore, has value only because abstract human labour is objectified or materialized in it. How, then, is the magnitude of this value to be measured? By means of the quantity of the 'value-forming substance', the labour, contained in the article. This quantity is measured by its duration, and the labour-time is itself measured on the particular scale of hours, days etc.

It might seem that if the value of a commodity is determined by the quantity of labour expended to produce it, it would be the more valuable the more unskilful and lazy the worker who produced it, because he would need more time to complete the article. However, the labour that forms the substance of value is equal human labour, the expenditure of identical human labour-power. The total labour-power of society, which is manifested in the values of the world of commodities, counts here as one homogeneous mass of human labour-power, although composed of innumerable individual units of labour-power. Each of these units is the same as any other, to the extent that it has the character of a socially average unit of labour-power and acts as such, i.e. only needs, in order to produce a commodity, the labour time which is necessary on an average, or in other words is socially necessary. Socially necessary labour-time is the labour-time required to produce any use-value under the conditions of production normal for a given society and with the average degree of skill and intensity of labour prevalent in that society. The introduction of power-looms into England, for example, probably reduced by one half the labour required to convert a given quantity of yarn into woven fabric. In order to do this, the English hand-loom weaver in fact needed the same amount of labour-time as before; but the product of his individual hour of labour now only represented half an hour of social labour, and consequently fell to one half its former value.

What exclusively determines the magnitude of the value of any article is therefore the amount of labour socially necessary, or the labour-time socially necessary for its production.

The individual commodity counts here only as an average sample of its kind. Commodities which contain equal quantities of labour, or which can be produced in the same time, have therefore the same value. The value of a commodity is related to the value of any other commodity as the labour-time necessary for the production of the one is related to the labour-time necessary for the production of the other. As exchange-values, all commodities are merely definite quantities of congealed labour-time.

The value of a commodity would therefore remain constant, if the labour-time required for its production also remained constant. But the latter changes with every variation in the productivity of labour. This is determined by a wide range of circumstances; it is determined amongst other things by the workers' average degree of skill, the level of development of science and its technological application, the social organization of the process of production, the extent and effectiveness of the means of production,, and the conditions found in the natural environment. For example, the same quantity of labour is present in eight bushels of corn in favourable seasons and in only four bushels in unfavourable seasons. The same quantity of labour provides more metal in rich mines than in poor. Diamonds are of very rare occurrence on the earth's surface, and hence their discovery costs, on an average, a great deal of labour-time. Consequently much labour- is represented in a small volume. Jacob questions whether gold has ever been paid for at its full value. This applies still more to diamonds. According to Eschwege, the total produce of the Brazilian diamond mines for the eighty years ending in 1823 still did not amount to the price of 1 years' average produce of the sugar and coffee plantations of the same country,! although the diamonds represented much more labour, therefore more value. With richer mines, the same quantity of labour would be embodied in more diamonds, and their value would fall. If man succeeded, without much labour, in transforming carbon into diamonds, their value might fall below that of bricks. In general, the greater the productivity of labour, the less the labour-time required to produce an article, the less the mass of labour crystallized in that article, and the less its value. Inversely, the less the productivity of labour, the greater the labour-time necessary to produce an article, and the greater its value. The value of a commodity, therefore, varies directly as the quantity, and inversely as the productivity, of the labour which finds its realization within the commodity. Now we know the substance of value. It is labour. We know the measure of its magnitude. It is labour-time. The form, which stamps value as exchange-value, remains to be analysed. But before this we need to develop the characteristics we have already found somewhat more fully.

A thing can be a use-value without being a value. This is the case whenever its utility to man is not mediated through labour. Air, virgin soil, natural meadows, unplanted forests, etc. fall into this category. A thing can be useful, and a product of human labour, without being a commodity. He who satisfies his own need with the product of his own labour admittedly creates use-values, but not commodities. In order to produce the latter, he must not only produce use-values, but use-values for others, social use-values. And not merely for others. The medieval peasant produced a corn-rent for the feudal lord and a corn-tithe for the priest; but neither the corn-rent nor the corn-tithe became commodities simply by being produced for others. In order to become a commodity, the product must be transferred to the other person, for whom it serves as a use-value, through the medium of exchange. Finally, nothing can be a value without being an object of utility. If the thing is useless, so is the labour contained in it; the labour does not count as labour, and therefore creates no value.

The Dual Character of the Labour Embodied in Commodities

Initially the commodity appeared to us as an object with a dual character, possessing both use-value and exchange-value.Later on it was seen that labour, too, has a dual character: in so far as it finds its expression in value, it no longer possesses the same characteristics as when it is the creator of use-values. I was the first to point out and examine critically this twofold nature of the labour contained in commodities. As this point is crucial to an understanding of political economy, it requires further elucidation.

Let us take two commodities, such as a coat and 10 yards of linen, and let the value of the first be twice the value of the second, so that, if 10 yards of linen = Wf the coat = 2 W.

The coat is a use-value that satisfies a particular need. A specific kind of productive activity is required to bring it into existence. This activity is determined by its aim, mode of operation, object, means and result. We use the abbreviated expression 'useful labour' for labour whose utility is represented by the use-value of its product, or by the fact that its product is a use-value. In this connection we consider only its useful effect.

As the coat and the linen are qualitatively different use-values, so also are the forms of labour through which their existence is mediated - tailoring and weaving. If the use-values were not qualitatively different, hence not the products of qualitatively different forms of useful labour, they would be absolutely incapable of confronting each other as commodities. Coats cannot be exchanged for coats, one use-value cannot be exchanged for another of the same kind.

The totality of heterogeneous use-values or physical commodities reflects a totality of similarly heterogeneous forms of useful labour, which differ in order, genus, species and variety: in short, a social division of labour. This division of labour is a necessary condition for commodity production, although the converse does not hold; commodity production is not a necessary condition for the social division of labour. Labour is socially divided in the primitive Indian community, although the products do not thereby become commodities. Or, to take an example nearer home, labour is systematically divided in every factory, but the workers do not bring about this division by exchanging their individual products. Only the products of mutually independent acts of labour, performed in isolation, can confront each other as commodities. To sum up, then: the use-value of every commodity contains useful labour, i.e. productive activity of a definite kind, carried on with a definite aim. Use-values cannot confront each other as commodities unless the useful labour contained in them is qualitatively different in each case. In a society whose products generally assume the form of commodities, i.e. in a society of commodity producers, this qualitative difference between the useful forms of labour which are carried on independently and privately by individual producers develops into a complex system, a social division of labour.

It is moreover a matter of indifference whether the coat is worn by the tailor or by his customer. In both cases it acts as a use-value. So, too, the relation between the coat and the labour that produced it is not in itself altered when tailoring becomes a special trade, an independent branch of the social division of labour. Men made clothes for thousands of years, under the compulsion of the need for clothing, without a single man ever becoming a tailor. But the existence of coats, of linen, of every element of material wealth not provided in advance by nature, had always to be mediated through a specific productive activity appropriate to its purpose, a productive activity that assimilated particular natural materials to particular human requirements. Labour, then, as the creator of use-values, as useful labour, is a condition of human existence which is independent of all forms of society; it is an eternal natural necessity which mediates the metabolism between man and nature, and therefore human life itself.

Use-values like coats, linen, etc., in short, the physical bodies of commodities, are combinations of two elements, the material provided by nature, and labour. If we subtract the total amount of useful labour of different kinds which is contained in the coat, the linen, etc., a material substratum is always left. This substratum is furnished by nature without human intervention. When man engages in production, he can only proceed as nature does herself, i.e. he can only change the form of the materials.

Furthermore, even in this work of modification he is constantly helped by natural forces. Labour is therefore not the only source of material wealth, i.e. of the use-values it produces. As William Petty says, labour is the father of material wealth, the earth is its mother.

Let us now pass from the commodity as an object of utility to the value of commodities.

We have assumed that the coat is worth twice as much as the linen. But this is merely a quantitative difference, and does not concern us at the moment. We shall therefore simply bear in mind that if the value of a coat is twice that of 10 yards of linen, 20 yards of linen will have the same value as a coat. As values, the coat and the linen have the same substance, they are the objective expressions of homogeneous labour. But tailoring and weaving are qualitatively different forms of labour. There are, however, states of society in which the same man alternately makes clothes and weaves. In this case, these two different modes of labour are only modifications of the labour of the same individual and not yet fixed functions peculiar to different individuals, just as the coat our tailor makes today, and the parr of trousers he makes tomorrow, require him only to vary his own individual labour. Moreover, we can see at a glance that in our capitalist society a given portion of labour is supplied alternately in the form of tailoring and in the form of weaving, in accordance with changes in the direction of the demand for labour. This change in the form of labour may well not take place without friction, but it must take place.

If we leave aside the determinate quality of productive activity, and therefore the useful character of the labour, what remains is its quality of being an expenditure of human labour-power. Tailoring and weaving, although they are qualitatively different productive activities, are both a productive expenditure of human brains, muscles, nerves, hands etc., and in this sense both human labour. They are merely two different forms of the expenditure of human labour-power.

Of course, human labour-power must itself have attained a certain level of development before it can be expended in this or that form. But the value of a commodity represents human labour pure and simple, the expenditure of human labour in general. And just as, in civil society, a general or a banker plays a great part but man as such plays a very mean part, so, here too, the same is true of human labour. It is the expenditure of simple labour-power, i.e. of the labour-power possessed in his bodily organism by every ordinary man, on the average, without being developed in any special way. Simple average labour, it is true, varies in character in different countries and at different cultural epochs, but in a particular society it is given. More complex labour counts only as intensified, or rather multiplied simple labour, so that a smaller quantity of complex labour is considered equal to a larger quantity of simple labour. Experience shows that this reduction is constantly being made. A commodity may be the outcome of the most complicated labour, but through its value it is posited as equal to the product of simple labour, hence it represents only a specific quantity of simple labour. The various proportions in which different kinds of labour are reduced to simple labour as their unit of measurement are established by a social process that goes on behind the backs of the producers; these proportions therefore appear to the producers to have been handed down by tradition. In the interests of simplification, we shall henceforth view every form of labour-power directly as simple labour-power by this we shall simply be saving ourselves the trouble of making the reduction.

Just as, in viewing the coat and the linen as values, we abstract from their different use-values, so, in the case of the labour represented by those values, do we disregard the difference between its useful forms, tailoring and weaving. The use-values coat and linen are combinations of, on the one hand, productive activity with a definite purpose, and, on the other, cloth and yarn; the values coat and linen, however, are merely congealed quantities of homogeneous labour. In the same way, the labour contained in these values does not count by virtue of its productive relation to cloth and yarn, but only as being an expenditure of human labour-power. Tailoring and weaving are the formative elements in the use-values coat and linen, precisely because these two kinds of labour are of different qualities; but only in so far as abstraction is made from their particular qualities, only in so far as both possess the same quality of being human labour, do tailoring and weaving form the substance of the values of the two articles mentioned.

Coats and linen, however, are not merely values in general, but values of definite magnitude, and, following our assumption, the coat is worth twice as much as the 10 yards of linen. Why is there this difference in value? Because the linen contains only half as much labour as the coat, so that labour-power had to be expended twice as long to produce the second as to produce the first.

While, therefore, with reference to use-value, the labour contained in a commodity counts only qualitatively, with reference to value it counts only quantitatively, once it has been reduced to human labour pure and simple. In the former case it was a matter of the 'how and the 'what of labour, in the latter of the 'how much', of the temporal duration of labour. Since the magnitude of the value of a commodity represents nothing but the quantity of labour embodied in it, it follows that all commodities, when taken in certain proportions, must be equal in value.

If the productivity of all the different sorts of useful labour required, let us say, for the production of a coat remains unchanged, the total value of the coats produced will increase along with their quantity. If one coat represents x days' labour, two coats will represent 2x days' labour, and so on. But now assume that the duration of the labour necessary for the production of a coat is doubled or halved. In the first case, one coat is worth as much as two coats were before; in the second case two coats are only worth as much as one was before, although in both cases one coat performs the same service, and the useful labour contained in it remains of the same quality. One change has taken place, however: a-change in the quantity of labour expended to produce the article.

In itself, an increase in the quantity of use-values constitutes an increase in material wealth. Two coats will clothe two men, one coat will only clothe one man, etc. Nevertheless, an increase in the amount of material wealth may correspond to a simultaneous fall in the. magnitude of its value. This contradictory movement arises out of the twofold character of labour. By productivity' of course, we always mean the productivity of concrete useful labour; in reality this determines only the degree of effectiveness of productive activity directed towards a given purpose witliin a given period of time. Useful labour becomes, therefore, a more or less abundant source of products in direct proportion as its productivity rises or falls. As against this, however, variations in productivity have no impact whatever on the labour itself represented in value. As productivity is an attribute of labour in its concrete useful form, it naturally ceases to have any bearing on that labour as soon as we abstract from its concrete useful form. The same labour, therefore, performed for the same length of time, always yields the same amount of value, independently of any variations in productivity. But it provides different quantities of use-values during equal periods of time;

.more, if productivity rises; fewer, if it falls. For this reason, the same change in productivity which increases the fruitfulness of labour, and therefore the amount of use-values produced by it, also brings about a reduction in the value of this increased total amount, if it cuts down the total amount of labour-time necessary to produce the use-values. The converse also holds.

On the one hand, all labour is an expenditure of human labour-power, in the physiological sense, and it is in this quality of being equal, or abstract, human labour that it forms the value of commodities. On the other hand, all labour is an expenditure of human labour-power in a particular form and with a definite aim, and it is in this quality of being concrete useful labour that it produces use-values.

The Value-Form, or Exchange-Value

Commodities come into the world in the form of use-values or material goods, such as iron, linen, corn, etc. This is their plain, homely, natural form. However, they are only commodities because they have a dual nature, because they are at the same time objects of utility and bearers of value. Therefore they only appear as commodities, or have the form of commodities, in so far as they possess a double form, i.e. natural form and value form.

Not an atom of matter enters into the objectivity of commodities as values; in this it is the direct opposite of the coarsely sensuous 'objectivity of commodities as physical objects. We may twist and turn a single commodity as we wish; it remains impossible to grasp it as a thing possessing value. However, let us remember that commodities possess an objective character as values only in so far as they are all expressions of an identical social substance, human labour, that their objective character as values is therefore purely social.

Everyone knows, if nothing else, that commodities have a common value-form which contrasts in the most striking manner with the motley natural forms of their use-values. I refer to the money-form. Now, however, we have to perform a task never even attempted by bourgeois economics. That is, we have to show the origin of this money-form, we have to trace the development of the expression of value contained in the value-relation of commodities from its simplest, almost imperceptible outline to the dazzling money-form. When this has been done, the mystery of money will immediately disappear.

The simplest value-relation is evidently that of one commodity to another commodity of a different kind (it does not matter which one). Hence the relation between the values of two commodities supplies us with the simplest expression of the value of a single commodity.

(a) The simple, isolated, or accidental form of value;

x commodity A = y commodity B or: x commodity A is worth y commodity B.

(20 yards of linen = 1 coat, or: 20 yards of linen are worth 1 coat)

(1) The two poles of the expression of value: the relative form of value and the equivalent form.

The whole mystery of the form of value lies hidden in this simple form. Our real difficulty, therefore, is to analyse it.

Here two different kinds of commodities (in our example the linen and the coat) evidently play two different parts. The linen expresses its value in the coat; the coat serves as the material in which that value is expressed. The first commodity plays an active role, the second a passive one. The value of the first commodity is represented as relative value, in other words the commodity is in the relative form of value. The second commodity fulfils the function of equivalent, in other words it is in the equivalent form.

The relative form of value and the equivalent form are two inseparable moments, which belong to and mutually condition each other; but, at the same time, they are mutually exclusive or opposed extremes, i.e. poles of the expression of value. They are always divided up between the different commodities brought into relation with each other by that expression. I cannot, for example, express the value of linen in linen. 20 yards of linen = 20 yards of linen is not an expression of value. The equation states rather the contrary: 20 yards of linen are nothing but 20 yards of linen, a definite quantity of linen considered as an object of utility. The value of the linen can therefore only be expressed relatively, i.e. in another commodity. The relative form of the value of the linen therefore presupposes that some other commodity confronts it in the equivalent form. On the other hand, this other commodity, which figures as the equivalent, cannot simultaneously be in the relative form of value. It is not the latter commodity whose value is being expressed. It only provides the material in which the value of the first commodity is expressed.

The Fetishism of Commodities

A commodity appears at first sight an extremely obvious, trivial thing. But its analysis brings out that it is a very strange thing, abounding in metaphysical subtleties and theological niceties. So far as it is a use-value, there is nothing mysterious about it, whether we consider it from the point of view that by its properties it satisfies human needs, or that it first takes on these properties as the product of human labour. It is absolutely clear that, by his activity, man changes the forms of the materials of nature in such a way as to make them useful to him. The form, of wood, for instance, is altered if a table is made out of it. Nevertheless the fable continues to be wood, an ordinary, sensuous thing. But as soon as it emerges as a commodity, it is transformed into a thing which transcends sensuousness. It not only stands with its feet on the ground, but, in relation to all other commodities, it stands on its head, and evolves out of its wooden brain grotesque ideas, far more wonderful than if it were to begin dancing of its own free will.

The mystical character of the commodity does not therefore arise from its use-value. Just as little does it proceed from the nature of the determinants of value. For in the first place, however varied the useful kinds of labour, or productive activities, it is a physiological fact that they are functions of the human organism, and that each such function, whatever may be its nature or its form, is essentially the expenditure of human brain, nerves, muscles and sense organs. Secondly, with regard to the foundation of the quantitative determination of value, namely the duration of that expenditure or the quantity of labour, this is quite palpably different from its quality. In all situations, the labour-time it costs to produce the means of subsistence must necessarily concern mankind, although not to the same degree at different stages of development. And finally, as soon as men start to work for each other in any way, their labour also assumes a social form.

Whence, then, arises the enigmatic character of the product of labour, as soon as it assume the form of a commodity? Clearly, it arises from this form itself. The quality of the kinds of human labour takes on a physical form in the equal objectivity of the products of labour as values; the measure of the expenditure of human labour-power by its duration takes on the form of the magnitude of the value of the products of labour; and finally the relationships between the producers, within which the social characteristics of their labours are manifested, take on the form of a social relation between the products of labour.

The mysterious character of the commodity form consists therefore simply in the fact that the commodity reflects back the social characteristics of men's own labour as objective characteristics of the products of labour themselves, as the socio-natural properties of these things. Hence it also reflects back the social relation of the producers to the sum total of labour as a social relation between objects, a relation which leads an existence outside the producers. Through this substitution, the products of labour become commodities, sensuous things which are at the same time supra-sensible or social. In the same way, the impression made by a thing on the optic nerve is perceived not as a subjective excitation of that nerve but as the objective form of a thing outside the eye. In the act of seeing, of course, light is really transmitted from one thing, the external object, to another thing, the eye. It is a physical relation between physical things. As against this, the commodity-form, and the value-reaction of the products of labour within which it appears, have absolutely no connection with the physical nature of the commodity and the material relations arising out of this. It is nothing but the definite social relation between men themselves which assumes here, for them, the fantastic form of a relation between things. In order, therefore, to find an analogy we must take flight into the misty realm of religion. There the products of the human brain appear as autonomous figures endowed with a life of their own, which enter into relations both with each other and with the human race. So it is in the world of commodities with the products of men's hands. I call this the fetishism which attaches itself to the products of labour as soon as they are produced as commodities, and is therefore inseparable from the production of commodities.

This fetishism of the world of commodities arises from the peculiar social character of the labour which produces them. Objects of utility become commodities only because they are the products of the labour of private individuals who work independently of each other. The sum total of the labour of all these private individuals forms the aggregate labour of society. Since the producers do not come into social contact until they exchange the products of their labour, the specific social characteristics of their private labours appear only within this exchange, In other words, the labour of the private individual manifests itself as an element of the total labour of society only through the relations which the act of exchange establishes between the products, and, through their mediation, between the producers. To the producers, therefore, the. social relations between their private labours appear as what they are, i.e. they do not appear as direct social relations between persons in their work, but rather as material relations between persons and social relations between things.

It is only by being exchanged that the products of labour acquire a socially uniform objectivity as values, which is distinct from their sensuously varied objectivity as articles of utility. This division of awareness as one single social labour force. All the characteristics of Robinson's labour are repeated here, but with the difference that they are social instead of individual. All Robinson's products were exclusively the result of his own personal labour and they were therefore directly objects of utility for him personally. The total product of our imagined association is a social product. One part of this product serves as fresh means of production and remains social. But another part is consumed by the members of the association as means of subsistence. This part must therefore be divided amongst them. The way this division is made will vary with the particular kind of social organization of production and the corresponding level of social development attained by the producers. We shall assume, but only for the sake of a parallel with the production of commodities, that the share of each individual producer in the means of subsistence is determined by his labour-time. Labour-time would in that case play a double part. Its apportionment in accordance with a definite social plan maintains the correct proportion between the different functions of labour arid the various needs of the associations. On the other hand, labour-time also serves as a measure of the part taken by each individual in the common labour, and of his share in the part of the. total product destined for individual consumption. The social relations of the individual producers, both towards their labour and the products of their labour, are here transparent in their simplicity, in production as well as in distribution.

For a society of commodity producers, whose general social relation of production consists in the fact that they treat their products as commodities, hence .as values, and in this material form bring their individual, private labours into relation with each other as homogeneous human labour, Christianity with its religious cult of man in the abstract, more particularly in its bourgeois development, i.e. in Protestantism, Deism, etc., is the most fitting form of religion. In the ancient Asiatic, classical-antique, and other such modes of production, the transformation of the product into a commodity, and therefore men's existence as producers of commodities, plays a subordinate role, which however increases in importance as these communities approach nearer and nearer to the stage of their dissolution. Trading nations, properly so called, exist only in the interstices of the ancient world, like the gods of Epicurus in the intermundia, or Jews in the pores of Polish society. Those ancient social organisms of production are much more simple and transparent than those of bourgeois society. But they are founded either on the immaturity of man as an individual, when he has not yet torn himself loose from the umbilical cord of his natural species-connection with other men, or on direct relations of dominance and servitude. They are conditioned by a low stage of development of the productive powers of labour and correspondingly limited relation's between men within the process of creating and reproducing their material life, hence also limited relations between man and nature. These real limitations are reflected in the ancient worship of nature, and in other elements of tribal religions. The religious reflections of the real world can, in any case, vanish only when the practical relations of everyday life between man and man, and man and. nature, generally present themselves to him in a transparent and rational form. The veil is not removed from the countenance of the social life-process, i.e. the process of material production, until it becomes production by freely associated men, and stands under their conscious and planned control. This, however, requires that society possess a material foundation, or a series of material conditions of existence, which in their turn are the natural and spontaneous product of a long and tormented historical development.

Political economy has indeed analysed, however incompletely, value and its magnitude, and has uncovered the content concealed within these forms. But it has never once asked the question why .this content has assumed that particular form, that is to say, why labour is expressed in value, and why the measurement of labour by its duration is expressed in the magnitude of value of the product. These formulas, which bear the unmistakable stamp of belonging to a social formation in which the process of production has mastery over man, instead of the opposite, appear to the political economists' bourgeois consciousness to be as much a self-evident and nature-imposed necessity as productive labour itself. Hence the pre-bourgeois forms of the social organization of production are treated by political economy in much the same way as the Fathers of the Church treated pre-Christian religions.

The degree to which some economists are misled by the fetishism attached to the world of commodities or by the objective appearance of the social charcteristics of labour is shown, among other things, by the dull and tedious dispute over the part played by nature in the formation of exchange value. Since exchange value is a definite social manner of expressing the labour bestowed on a thing, it can have no more natural content than has, for example, the rate of exchange.

Since the commodity-form is the most general and the most undeveloped form of bourgeois production, it makes its appearance at an early date, though not in the same predominant, and therefore characteristic, manner as nowadays. Hence its fetish character is still relatively easy to penetrate. But when we come to more concrete forms, even this appearance of simplicity vanishes.

We will content ourselves here with one more example relating to the commodity-form itself. If commodities could speak, they would say this; our use-value may interest men, but it doesnot belong to us as objects. What does belong to us as objects, however, is our value. Our own intercourse as commodities proves it We relate to each other merely as exchange values. Now listen how those commodities speak through the mouth of the economist: Value (i.e. exchange-value) is a property of things, riches (i.e. use-value) of man. Value, in this sense, necessarily implies exchanges, riches do not. Riches (use-value)-are the attribute of man, value is the attribute of commodities. A man or a community is rich, a pearl or diamond is valauble. A pearl or a diamond is valuable as a pearl or diamond.

So far no chemist has ever discovered exchange-value either in a pearl or a diamond. The economists who have discovered this chemical substance, and who lay special claim to critical accumen, nevertheless find that the use-value of material objects belongs to them independently of their material properties, while their value, on the other hand, forms a part of them as objects. What confirms them in this view is the peculiar circumstance that the use-value of a thing is realized without exchange, i.e. in the direct relations between the thing and man, while, inversely, its value is realized only in exchange, i.e. in a social process.

(From *Capital Vol. 1*, 1867, tr. Ben Fowkes, 1976).

13

On the Jewish Question

In the autumn of 1843, when he was 25 years old and living with his new bride, Jenny, Marx wrote "On the Jewish Question," basing the wok on two articles on the subject of Bruno Bauer, and quoting liberally in order to establish the grounds of his own critique. Marx is already implicitly critical of his erstwhile mentor, Bauer, and finish off the job a few years later in *The Holy Family* which is a turgid diatribe against Bauer and his two brothers; however, in "On the Jewish Question," the tone is still respectful. This essay, is important as a stage in Marx's development of his overall theory, but it is also significant as showing how Marx tried to liberate himself from the Jewish Question and how he tried to liberate the Jews from the their religion.

Bauer's argument was that Jews were unrealistic and inconsistent in wanting political emancipation as Jews, while retaining their religion. Either they must seek support from liberal Germans, albeit the Christin belief, and who except the same action from the Jews for whom they are fighting; or they must appeal to the believing Christians for support, because their very belief entails an adherence to the view that only the Christian religion is the correct one for the state and will therefore oppose Jews as such from having the rights of citizens.

The solution, according to Bauer, is that the Jews renounce Judaism and that all men renounce religion in order to be citizens. The political abolition of religion, means, for him, the abolition of all religion. This is Bauer's main argument. Marx, in good Hegelian fashion, wants to transcend it critically. He starts by accepting his friend's wish to abolish religion in general. To end religious opposition between Christian and Jew, one abolishes religion. As Marx puts it, "As soon as Jew and Christian come to see in their respective religions nothing more than stages in the development of the human mind, they will no longer find themselves in religious opposition, but in a purely critical scientific and human relationship. Adding an emphasis to Bauer's idea, Marx continues, "Science will then constitute their unity. But scientific oppositions are resolved by science itself. Such a statement is very Hegelian, with a touch of Saint –Simonian positivism hanging over it, and it is evocative of Marx's own stages of development from Jew to Christian to scientist. Marx's "science" in short, can end the strife of Jew and Christian in the real, as well as personal, world. It is, for him, a liberating force.

Marx then goes well beyond Bauer. Marx states, it is not true, as Bauer asserts, that true political emancipation means the end of religion: the United States is proof that a politically free country can also have a flourishing system of private religions. Bauer's limitation is that he stops at political and religious emancipation, but does not examine the relation between political and human emancipation. In order to understand what is involved in the latter freedom, one must understand the relations of state and civil society. The motivating force of civil society, or what we would call the economic sphere, is the "egoistic life," The relation of civil society to the state bears close examination, Marx asserts, for the state sees man as living in a community and civil society sees man as being a private individual, whose interests may be opposed to the general interest.

He sees the perfected political state as representing man as a species being, above egoism, and in opposition to egoism. A contradiction, therefore, exists. In very murky fashion, Marx describes what will later become a central part of his scientific theory of social development. Material changes bring about political and intellectual changes, although the political turns at times on the civil in cannibalistic fashion as during the Reign of Terror. "At those times," he writes, "when the state is most aware of itself, political life seeks to stifle its own prerequisites – civil society and its elements – and to establish itself as the genuine and harmonious species –life of man. But it can only achieve this end by setting itself in violent contradiction with its own condition of existence, by declaring a permanent revolution.

Political life is merely a reflected, or alienated, state of man. His real life is in tangible, material existence. Thus, Marx declares, "We do not say to the Jews, Therefore, as does Bauer: you cannot be emancipated politically, without emancipating yourselves completely from Judaism.

We say rather: it is because you can be emancipated politically, without renouncing Judaism completely and absolutely, that political emancipation itself is not human emancipation. If you want to be politically emancipated, without emancipating yourselves humanly, the inadequacy and the contradiction is not entirely in yourselves but in the nature and the category of political emancipation".

Now political emancipation by itself was, Marx conceded, a form of "great progress." What he saw, however, was that this progress was the result of changes in civil society, not a cause in itself. The problem with political revolution per se is that "it dissolves civil society into its elements without revolutionizing these elements themselves or subjecting them to criticism," Bauer had stopped at religious and political criticism and revolution and had not seen that they are merely the tail on the dog.

How are we to beyond Bauer? In fact, Marx's first quote, at the very beginning of his own article, touches on this part of Baer's message. "You Jews", Bauer writes, "are egoists if you demand for yourselves Jews, a special emancipation. You should work, as Germans for the political emancipation of Germany, and as men, for the emancipation of mankind." As Bauer wrote," If they wish to become free the Jews should not embrace Christianity as such, but Christianity in dissolution, religion in dissolution; that is to say, the Enlightenment, criticism, and its outcome, a free humanity." In short, Jews should convert to atheism.

Marx, pursuing the theme of human, and not just religious, emancipation, takes another tack. "What specific social element," he asks, is it necessary to overcome in order to abolish Judaism? To find the answer, he continues, "Let us consider the real Jew: not the Sabbath Jew whom Bauer considers, but the everyday Jew." Marx's conclusion is devastating: "What is the profane basis of Judaism? Practical need, self-interest. "What is the worldly cult of the Jew? Huckstering. What is his worldly god? Money."

What is so striking is that Marx has reified individual Jews, some of whom may be engaged in monied activities, into the Jew, and thus accepted all of the streotypes placed on this entity by anti-Semites. When he adds that in Judaism we find a universal antisocial element" whose eradication – Marx's word is "emancipation"- will emancipate all mankind, we are close to the ravings of an Adolf Hitler.

We are not saying- that Marx was a Nazi, or even an anti- Semite as such. In fact, shortly before his article, Marx had supported a petition to the Rhenish Diet, the purpose of which was to do away with the remaining legal discriminations against Jews. He would probably have recoiled violently from the "practice" of his thought; however, his thought does lend itself to misuse by later doers of deeds. What Marx was saying, overtly, was that Judaism is a synonym for capitalism. At its core is money: "Money is the jealous God of Israel, beside which no other god may exist. Money abases all the alienated essence of man's work and existence; this essence dominates him and he worships it." These are the same terms Marx user to describe capitalism in his Economic and Philosophic Manuscripts.

Marx, who overtly abjured nationalism, and had no ostensible nationality of his own, wrote: "The chimerical nationality of the Jew is the nationality of the trade, and above all of the financier." Thus, he echoes the charge that Jew and capitalist are without loyalty to the nation, un-rooted in the land, and quick to take their liquid gold – money – anywhere they can make a profit.

Christianity would appear to overcome and do away with this essence of Judaism. But Marx prefers to read history as a matter of Judaism attaining "universal domination" through the very universality of Christianity, with the latter being merely "the sublime thought of Judaism," which retains its "vulgar, practical" nature. God and money are identical, as are Christianity and Judaism, in that both are sources of alienation: we create these artificial beings and then allow them to dominate us; thus we are alienated from ourselves. To abolish our alienated existence, we must do away with the existence of Judaism as well as of religion. "The social emancipation of the Jew," Marx concludes, "is the emancipation of society from Judaism."

The essay "On the Jewish Question" is an extraordinary work. It combines the embryos of many of Marx's most important and penetrating mature theories with a farrago of nonsense and almost incredibly bad reasoning. Many commentators have been content to emphasize the incipient theories, and dismiss the rest as a lapse of sorts. Others have read it as lamentable anti-Semitic utterances, and nothing more important.

By now, words such as "egoism" and "money" in Marx's writings must always alert us to their personal meanings for him. A commonplace in the culture of his time, the words and the arguments about them, have additional and special meaning for him. So does the "Jewish Question," and anything to do with Christianity and religion in general. Marx may, and does, hide this from himself; there is no reason for it to be hidden from us.

We noticed earlier Marx's use of the phrase "self-contempt" in his essay on choosing a vocation. Why and how would a seventeen – year-old boy know about such feelings? we asked. His father had accused him of being egoistic and possibly demon driven against mankind. Money was a source of discord between the two men. As a Jew, though a Christian, Marx was open to the criticism of anti-Semites that Jews were self-interested hucksters, whose interest were adverse both to the nation and to humanity. These are all matters of potential self-loathing. To restore a sense of an esteemed self, how better then to identify with the criticism, project them outward, and in a critical spirit, reject them call for their abolition.

In so doing, Karl Marx also stumbled on toward is fruitful insights about society, capitalism, and history. He who was alienated from his self, could glimpse the nature of alienation in society. He could understand that religion and the state, were to be perceived in relation to the society from which they sprang and on which they stood. He could realize that change in civil society, whose latest form was the capitalist, meant change in the rest of the social structure and culture. Alienation, religion, capitalism, these were the staples of intellectual discourse at the time; Marx's genius was to give them a new and personal twist.

In the writings that follow the "Jewish Question," the personal note grows less and less obvious. It is there, but Marx has settled a major score and can now distance himself, intellectually, from it. The introduction the "*Contribution to the Critique of Hegel's Philosophy of Right*," written in that burst of creative energy in the fall of 1843, right after his marriage, serves as a bridge to Marx's increasingly intellectualized work. The centrality of the religious question, if not the Jewish one, is still the starting point.

"The criticism of religion," Marx announce in the first sentence, "is the premise of all criticism. "Besides Hegel, Marx had now also been reading Ludwig Feuerbach –indeed, he sent a copy of his essay to him, accompanying it with a long letter of admiration and it is Feuerbach influence that can be felt in the next assertion that" man makes religion; religion does not make man." It is only a short step to the future claim that men make their history.

There are a number of reasons why Judaism is important in relation to Marx and Marxism, though its substantive content has not ; featured in debate. First, it offered Marx an opportunity to consider the role of a religion in society - other than Christianity which was then an adjunct of the state - at a time when he was moving from democratic radicalism to historical materialism. Secondly, Marx was of Jewish origin and wanted to distance himself from that association. Thirdly, Marx has often been accused of being anti-Semitic. Most of the extant and continuing literature on the subject tends to concentrate on the latter two factors.

Marx was drawn into the debate on Jews and Judaism after the Jews of Germany, with strong support from an increasingly powerful liberal lobby, had been campaigning for half a century for civil emancipation and the abolition of their special tolerated status. For Marx, the critique of religion in Germany had been completed and he supported the demand for civil rights for Jews, partly because any structural change in the organization of the Christian state would be desirable in that it would undermine the foundations of an irrelevant social order, and partly because civil rights would only confer political emancipation, an insufficient but necessary precursor of the achievement of human emancipation. Marx did not join the debate on Jews spontaneously. He had followed with interest the demystification of Christianity which began with Strauss's seminal work, *The Life of Jesus* (1837). It was followed soon after by Feuerbach's *Essence of Christianity* (1841) and Bruno Bauer's systematic critique of theology. Feuerbach added an original dimension to the debate by leaving Christian theology intact and presenting it in anthropological terms, with the Christian god as man's projection of his spiritual self onto an imaginary divinity. Moses Hess completed this line of religious critique by the Young Hegelians, rejecting their 'theological consciousness' and calling for a social analysis of the human condition.

When Bruno Bauer joined the debate on Jewish emancipation he followed the reasoning established in the German philosophical tradition. Fichte, the first to respond to the original demand for emancipation in the late eighteenth century, rejected it on the grounds that the isolation of the Jews was largely of their own making. As human beings they could claim human rights, but as dissenters in a Christian state they could not claim formal acceptance of their dissent, where Christians themselves were denied the right to dissent. Hegel, in a famous footnote in the Philosophy of Right (1821), also emphasized the human status of the Jews, but linked the question of civil rights to the acceptance of civil obligations. If, for example, Jews were willing to accept military service and Quakers were not, then Jews had a prior tight to be emancipated. Bauer, however, preferred to follow Fichtc. In two well-known essays he rejected Jewish emancipation partly because the Jews were unwilling to free themselves of their Jewishness and also because Christians could not bestow freedom on Jews while they themselves were not free.

It was at this point that Marx joined the debate with a critical analysis of Bauer's arguments. Like Hess, he called for a social analysis of religion and dismissed Bauer's contention that Jews would have to give up their Judaism to be eligible for civil equality. Religion was a private matter and the state had no right to intervene other than on issues concerning the individual as a citizen. Bauer's objections were theological and therefore invalid. There was, however, a social question and Marx agreed with Bauer that, if the Jews, who were numerically an insignicant section of the population could nevertheless exert an influence out of all proportion to their number, then this was due to their traditional concentration in trade and commerce, a position which gave them real political power.

Marx elaborated on this and emphasized the importance of financial power, which had enabled the Jews not only to demand civil rights, but also to infiltrate their social and commercial values into the organization of civil society. The state needs the commercial function of the Jews and becomes 'Judaized' in its pursuit of money. Jewish exclu-siveness, which serves their ethnocentric preoccupations is not determined, as Bauer had argued, by their refusal to accept a position in history, but, on the contrary, is a product of history which preserves the Jew as an essential element in the structure of civil society. It follows that, when Jews relinquish their social role as traders and hucksters, or the state frees itself of its need for commercialism, the Jews and their dedication to the mystical egoism of their religious tradition, will vanish.

Marx's main argument was set out in two review essays on Bauer. The first essay is an incisive presentation of the relationship between church and state in which Bauer's theological position is demolished. The second essay, which deals with the social roles of Jews and Judaism, is a short, vehement polemic, written in an aggressive, virulent style, full of assertions and assumptions, which owe little to the empirical realities of Jewish life in the first half of the nineteenth century, or to the intellectual traditions of Judaism. When they were first published, the essays made no impact and the only known review of them in a Jewish newspaper of the time, welcomed Marx's support of the Jewish claim for emancipation. The polemical character of the second essay raised no comment, probahly because the intemperate language in which it was couched was quite commonplace in the 1840s. With the advent of formal anti-semitic movements in the wake of the successful outcome of the Jewish struggle for emancipation in the last quarter of the nineteenth century, renewed attention was focusedon Marx's essays, by both protagonists and opponents of Marxism. Jews also had to take a position on Marx's essays, particularly those who were attracted by socialism in one form or another. It was in this context that a large literature was generated, which strove to resolve two questions. Was Marx Jewish in a more meaningful sense than mere biological descent and was he anti-Semitic or, more accurately, did he share the conviction of the anti-Jewish lobby that Jews and Judaism were inimical to the interests and well-being of nations, groups or social classes?

Regarding the first question, there have been many attempts to depict Marx as a 'prophet' in Old Testament tradition, as a secular Jew steeped in a Jewish ethical tradition, as a self-hating Jew or as a Jewish apostate. Marx has also frequently been described as a Jew by 'race', with all the character implications this carries in racialist theories. Marx himself did not comment on this subject except to acknowledge his origins. Apart from a literary appreciation of the Hebrew prophets, there is no evidence that Marx was, or felt himself to be, Jewish or influenced by the Judaic tradition. With the advent of the Nazi era and the mass extermination of the Jews of Europe, the question of Marx's anti-Semitism has become a more sensitive issue. As one Jewish socialist put it, the call for the emancipation of mankind from Judaism in 1843 has come too close to being a prescription for the events of 1943. Although we know that Marx was not averse to using offensive vulgarisms about some Jews, there is no basis for regarding him as having been anti-semitic. At the same time, there can be no doubt that his second essay on the Jews has been and continues to be used by those who propagate anti-Jewish views, in support of their various accusations against the Jews. It is also true that the misuse of Marx's essay began in his lifetime, without eliciting protest or comment from him.

The argument over Marx's relationship to Jews and Judaism goes on and is likely to continue but rarely touches on the most interesting problem which Marx has raised about Judaism. That is, whether Judaism has survived through history or in spite of it. This question was elaborated by Moses Hess when he revived the idea of a national solution to the Jewish problem in 1862, but did not receive a great deal of attention until the emergence of political Zionism at the end of the nineteenth century. It then gave rise to a vigorous, though largely hostile debate, which nevertheless contributed substantially to the development of Marxist analyses of nationalism generally.

– Editor

The political emancipation of the Jew, the Christian, the religious man in general, is the emancipation of the state from Judaism, from Christianity, from religion in general. The state emancipates itself from religion in a form and manner peculiar to its nature as state by emancipating itself from the state religion, i.e., by acknowledging no religion, by instead acknowledging itself as state. Political emancipation from religion is not complete and consistent emancipation from religion, because political emancipation is not the complete and consistent form of human emancipation.

The limitations of political emancipation are immediately apparent from the fact that the state can liberate itself from a restriction without man himself being truly free of it, that a state can be a free state without man himself being a free man. Bauer himself tacitly admits this when he poses the following condition for political emancipation:

'All religious privileges, including the monopoly of a privileged church, would have to be abolished and if some or many or even the overwhelming majority still considered themselves obliged to fulfil their religious duties, then this should be left to them as a purely private affair.'

Therefore the state can have emancipated itself from religion even if the overwhelming majority is still religious. And the overwhelming majority does not cease to be religious by being religious in private.

But the attitude of the state, especially the free state, to religion is still only the attitude to religion of the men who make up the state. It therefore follows that man liberates himself from a restriction through the medium of the state, in a political way, by transcending this restriction in an abstract and restricted manner, in a partial manner, in contradiction with himself. It also follows that when man liberates himself politically he does so in a devious way, through a medium, even though the medium is a necessary one. Finally it follows that even when man proclaims himself an atheist through the mediation of the state, i.e., when he proclaims the state an atheist, he still remains under the constraints of religion because he acknowledges his atheism only deviously, through a medium. Religion is precisely that: the devious acknowledgement of man, through an intermediary. The state is the intermediary between man and man's freedom. Just as Christ is the intermediary to whom man attributes all his divinity, all his religious constraints, so the state is the intermediary to which man transfers all his non-divinity, all his human unconstraint.

The political elevation of man above religion shares all the shortcomings and all the advantages of political elevation in general. For example, the state as state annuls private property, man declares in a political way that private property is abolished, immediately the property qualification is abolished for active and passive election rights, as has happened in many North American states. Hamilton interprets this fact quite correctly from the political standpoint: 'The masses have gained a victory over the property owners and financial wealth.' Is not private property abolished in an ideal sense when the propertyless come to legislate for the propertied? The property qualification is the last political form to recognize private property.

And yet the political annulment of private property does not mean the abolition of private property; on the contrary, it even presupposes it. The state in its own way abolishes distinctions based on birth, rank, education and occupation when it declares birth, rank, education and occupation to be non-political distinctions, when it proclaims that every member of the people is an equal participant in popular sovereignty regardless of these distinctions, when it treats all those elements which go to make up the actual life of the people from the standpoint of the state. Nevertheless the state allows private property, education and occupation to act and assert their particular nature in their own way, i.e., as private property, as education and as occupation. Far from abolishing these factual distinctions, the state presupposes them in order to exist, it only experiences itself as political state and asserts its universality in opposition to these elements. Hegel therefore defines the relationship of the political state to religion quite correctly when he says:

In order for the state to come into existence as the self-knowing ethical actuality of spirit, it is essential that it should be distinct from the form of authority and of faith. But this distinction emerges only in so far as divisions occur in the ecclesiastical sphere itself. It is only in this head in the minds of the political emancipators so that the end appears as the means and the means as the end. This optical illusion present in their minds would continue to pose the same problem, though in a psychological and theoretical form.

But there is a straightforward solution.

Political emancipation is at the same time the dissolution of the old society on which there rested the power of the sovereign, the political system as estranged from the people. The political revolution is the revolution of civil society. What was the character of the old society ? It can be characterized in one word: feudalism. The old civil society had a directly political character, i.e. the elements of civil life such as property, family and the mode and manner of work were elevated in the form of seignory, estate and guild to the level of elements of political life. In this form they denned the relationship of the single individual to the state as a whole, i.e. his political relationship, his relationship of separation and exclusion from the other components of society. For the feudal organization of the life of the people did not elevate property or labour to the level of social elements but rather completed their separation from the state as a whole and constituted them as separate societies within society. But the functions and conditions of life in civil society were still political, even though political in the feudal sense, i.e. they excluded the individual from the state as a whole, they transformed the particular relationship of his guild to the whole state into his own general relationship to the life of the people, just as they transformed his specific civil activity and situation into his general activity and situation. As a consequence of this organization, the unity of the state, together with the consciousness, the will and the activity of the unity of the state, the universal political power, likewise, inevitably appears as the special concern of a ruler and his servants, separated from the people.

The political revolution which overthrew this rule and turned the affairs of the state into the affairs of the people, which constituted the political state as a concern of the whole people, i.e. as a real state, inevitably destroyed all the estates, corporations, guilds and privileges which expressed the separation of the people from its community. The political revolution thereby abolished the political character of civil society. It shattered civil society into its simple components - on the one hand individuals and on the other the material and spiritual elements which constitute the vital content and civil situation of these individuals. It unleashed the political spirit which had, as it were, been dissolved, dissected and dispersed in the various cul-de-sacs of feudal society; it gathered together this spirit from its state of dispersion, liberated it from the adulteration of civil life and constituted it as the sphere of the community, the universal concern of the people ideally independent of those particular elements of civil life. A person's particular activity and situation in life sank to the level of a purely individual significance. They no longer constituted the relationship of the individual to the state as a whole. Public affairs as such became the universal affair of each individual and the political function his universal function.

But the perfection of the idealism of the state was at the same time the perfection of the materialism of civil society. The shaking-off of the political yoke was at the same tune the shaking-off of the bonds which had held in check the egoistic spirit of civil society. Political emancipation was at the same time the emancipation of civil society from politics, from even the appearance of a universal content. Feudal society was dissolved into its foundation into man. But into man as he really was its foundation - into egoistic man.This man, the member of civil society, is now the foundation, the presupposition of the political state. In the rights of man the state acknowledges him as such.

But the freedom of egoistic man and the acknowledgement of this freedom is rather the acknowledgement of the unbridled movement of the spiritual and material elements which form the content of his life.Hence man was not freed from religion – he received the freedom of religion. He was not freed from property – he received the freedom of property. He was not freed from the egoism of trade -he received the freedom to engage in trade.

The constitution of the political state and the dissolution of civil society into independent individuals – who are related by law just as men in the estates and guilds were related by privilege – are achieved in one and the same act. But man, as member of civil society, inevitably appears as unpolitical man, as natural man. The rights of man appear as natural rights, for self-conscious activity is concentrated upon the political act. Egoistic man is the passive and merely given result of the society which has been dissolved, an object of immediate certainty, and for that reason a natural object. The political revolution dissolves civil society into its component parts without revolutionizing these parts and subjecting them to criticism. It regards civil society, the world of needs, of labour, of private interests and of civil law, as the foundation of its existence, as a presupposition which needs no further grounding, and therefore as its natural basis. Finally, man as he is a member of civil society is taken to be the real man, man as distinct from citizen, since he is man in his sensuous, individual and immediate existence, whereas political man is simply abstract, artificial man, man as an allegorical, moral person. Actual man is acknowledged only in the form of the egoistic individual and true man only in the form of the abstract citizen.

Rousseau's description of the abstraction of the political man is a good one:

Whoever dares to undertake the founding of a people's institutions must feel himself capable of changing, so to speak, human nature, of transforming each individual, who in himself is a complete and solitary whole, into a part of a greater whole from which he somehow receives his life and his being, of substituting a partial and moral existence for physical and independent existence. He must take man's own powers away from him and substitute for them alien ones which he can only use with/the assistance of others.

All emancipation is reduction of the human world and of relationships to man himself. Political emancipation is the reduction of man on the one hand to the member of civil society, the egoistic, independent individual, and on the other to the citizen, the moral person.

Only when real, individual man resumes the abstract citizen into himself and as an individual man has become a species-being in his empirical life, his individual work and his individual relationships, only when man has recognized and organized his forces propres as social forces so that social force is no longer separated from him in the form of political force, only then will human emancipation be completed.

Bauer deals in this form with the relation between the Jewish and Christian religions, as well as their relation to criticism. Their relation to criticism is then relation to the capacity to become free.

His conclusion is:

The Christian has only one hurdle to overcome, namely, his religion, in order to dispense with religion altogether, and hence to become free. The Jew, on the other hand, does not only have to break with his Jewish nature; he also has to break with the development towards the completion of his religion, a development which has remained alien to him.

Thus Bauer here transforms the question of Jewish emancipation into a purely religious question. The theological problem as to who has the better chance of gaining salvation- Jew or Christian - is here repeated in a more enlightened form: who is the more capable of emancipation! The question is no longer: which gives freedom, Judaism or Christianity? Rather it is the reverse: which gives more freedom, the negation of Judaism or the negation of Christianity? If they wish to become free, the Jews should not embrace Christianity but Christianity in dissolution and more generally religion in dissolution, i.e. enlightenment, criticism and its product free humanity. It is still a matter of embracing a religion for the Jew. It is no longer a question of Christianity, but of Christianity in dissolution. Bauer demands of the Jew that he break with the essence of the Christian religion - a demand which, as he himself says, does not proceed from the development of the Jewish nature.

Since Bauer, at the end of his Jewish Question, represented Judaism as nothing more than a crude religious criticism of Christianity, and therefore gave it 'only' a religious significance, it was clear in advance that he would also transform the emancipation of the Jews into a philosophico-theological act.

Indeed, the practical domination of Judaism over the Christian world is expressed in such an unambiguous and natural fashion in North America that the very proclamation of the Gospel, Christian teaching, has become a commercial object and the bankrupt businessman is just as likely to go into evangelizing as the successful evangelist into business.

'The man you see at the head of a respectable congregation started out as a businessman; his business failed so he became a minister; the other started out as a priest, but as soon as he had saved some money he left the pulpit for business. In many people's eyes the religious ministry is a veritable industrial career.'

In Bauer's view it is 'a dishonest state of affairs when in theory the Jew is deprived of political rights while in practice he possesses enormous power and exercises a political influence in the larger sphere that is denied him as an individual'.

The contradiction between the practical political power of the Jew and his political rights is the contradiction between politics and financial power in general. Ideally speaking the former is (superior to the latter, but in actual fact it is in thrall to it.

Judaism has kept going alongside Christianity not simply as a religious critique of Christianity and an embodiment of doubts about the religious origins of Christianity but also because the practical Jewish spirit, Judaism, has managed to survive in Christian society and has even reached its highest level of development there. The Jew, who is a particular member of civil society, is only the particular manifestation of the Judaism of civil society.

Judaism has managed to survive not despite history but through it.Civil society ceaselessly begets the Jew from its own entrails.What was the essential basis of the Jewish religion? Practical need, egoism.

The monotheism of the Jew is therefore in reality the polytheism of the many needs, a polytheism that makes even the lavatory an object of divine law. Practical need, egoism, is the principle of civil society and appears as such in all its purity as soon as civil society has fully brought forth the political state. The god of practical need and self-interest is money,

Money is the jealous god of Israel before whom no other god may stand. Money debases all the gods of mankind and turns them into commodities. Money is the universal and self-constituted value of all things. It has therefore deprived the entire world - both the world of man and of nature-of its specific value. Money is the estranged essence of man's work and existence; this alien essence dominates him and he worships it.

The god of the Jews has been secularized and become the god of the world. Exchange is the true god of the Jew. His god is nothing more than illusory exchange.The view of nature which has grown up under the regime of private property and of money is an actual contempt for and practical degradation of nature which does exist in the Jewish religion but only in an imaginary form. In this sense Thomas Mtinzer declares it intolerable that creatures have been made into property, the fish in the water, the birds in the air, the plants on the earth - all living things must also become free'.

What is present in an abstract form in the Jewish religion -contempt for theory, for art, for history, for man as an end in himself - is the actual and conscious standpoint, the virtue, of the man of money. The species-relation itself, the relation between man and woman, etc., becomes a commercial object! Woman is put on the market.

The chimerical nationality of the Jew is the nationality of the merchant, of the man of money in general. The ungrounded and unfounded law of the Jew is only the religious caricature of ungrounded and unfounded morality and law in general, of the purely formal rites with which the world of / self-interest surrounds itself.

Here too the supreme relation of man is the legal relation, the relation to laws which apply to him not because they are the laws of his own will and nature but because they dominate him and because breaches of them would be avenged.

Jewish Jesuitry, the same practical Jesuitry that Bauer finds in the Talmud, is the relationship of the world of self-interest to the laws that dominate it; the wily circumvention of those laws constitutes the principal skill of that world.

Indeed, the motion of that world within its laws is necessarily a continual supersession of the law. Judaism could not develop further as a religion could not develop further theoretically, because the world-view of practical need is by nature narrow-minded and rapidly exhausted. The religion of practical need could not by its very nature find its completion in theory but only in practice precisely because its truth is practice. Judaism could not create a new world; it could only draw the new creations and conditions of the world into the province of its own activity, since practical need, whose understanding is only at the level of self-interest, is passive and incapable of extending itself in directions of its own choosing; instead, it finds itself extended in line with the development of social conditions themselves.

Judaism reaches its peak with the completion of civil society; but civil society first reaches its completion in the Christian world. Only under the rule of Christianity, which makes all national, natural, moral and theoretical relationships external to man, could civil society separate itself completely from political life, tear apart all the species-bonds of man, substitute egoism and selfish need for those bonds and dissolve the human world into a world of atomistic individuals confronting each other in enmity.

Christianity sprang from Judaism. It has now dissolved back into Judaism. The Christian was from the very beginning the theorizing Jew. The Jew is therefore the practical Christian and the practical Christian has once again become a Jew. Christianity overcame real Judaism only in appearance. It was too refined spiritual, to do away with the crudeness of practical need except by raising it into celestial space. Christianity is the sublime thought of Judaism and Judaism is e vulgar application of Christianity. But this application could not become universal until Christianity as perfected religion had heoretically completed the self-estrangement of man from himself and from nature. Only then could Judaism attain universal domination and turn alienated man and alienated nature into alienable, saleable objects subject to the slavery of egoistic need and to the market.

Selling is the practice of alienation. As long as man is restrained by religion he can objectify his essence only by making it into an alien, fantastic being. In the same way, when under the sway of egoistic need he can act practically and practically produce objects only by making his products and his activity subordinate to an alien substance and giving them the significance of an alien substance money.

Translated into practice, the Christian egoism of eternal happiness inevitably becomes the material egoism of the Jew, celestial need becomes terrestrial need and subjectivism becomes self-interest. We can explain the tenacity of the Jew not from his religion but from the human foundation of his religion, from practical need and egoism.

Since the real essence of the Jew is universally realized and secularized in civil society, civil society could not convince the Jew of the unreality of his religious essence, which is nothing more than the ideal expression of practical need. Therefore not only in the Pentateuch and the Talmud but also in present-day society we find the essence of the modern Jew not in an abstract but in a supremely empirical form, not only as the narrowness of the Jew but as the Jewish narrowness of society.

As soon as society succeeds in abolishing the empirical essence of Judaism - the market and the conditions which give rise to it Jew will have become impossible, for his consciousness will no longer have an object, the subjective basis of Judaism – practical need - will have become humanized and the conflict between man's individual sensuous existence and his species-existence will have been superseded.

The social emancipation of the Jew is the emancipation of society from Judaism.

(From *Marx and Eagles*, *Selected Works*, Progress Publishers, Moscow, 1974)

14

Critique of the Gotha Programme

Until quite recently there was little overt or extended theoretical reflection about the place that principles of justice occupy within Marxist thought. Two conflicting altitudes have been common in the tradition: on the one hand, explicit, sometimes fervent, disavowals of any reliance on considerations of justice, as being irrelevant to the case for socialism and against capitalism; on the other hand, a widespread use in practice of arguments precisely from justice, unreflectively or unknowingly yet time and again resorted to in Marxist social criticism.

From the early 1970s, however, an intensive interest among philosophers in the concept of distributive justice began to leave its imprint on the discussion of. Marx's ideas, generating a considerable exegetical literature, itself polarized in accordance with the two traditionally conflicting attitudes. Principles of distributive justice concern the proper division of benefits and burdens within a society. Did Marx condemn capitalism in the light of any such principles?

Many say that he did not. They cite:

(1) His insistence in *Capital* that the wage relation, as an exchange of equivalent values (labour power for the wage), involves no injustice to the worker;

(2) Marx's polemic in *Critique of the Gotha Programme*, against socialist appeals to notions of 'fair distribution' or 'right'

(3) His view that standards of right and justice are internal to specific modes of production and, as such, historically relative; and

(4) His characterization of morality in general as ideological, part of a dependent, changing superstructure.

Defenders of this view point argue further:

(5) that to impute to Marx a care for justice bends his meaning towards a narrow concern with reforming the sphere of distribution income differentials, wage levels and the like -where in fact his aim was more fundamental and revolutionary, the transformation of production and property relations;

(6) that the imputation denatures, also, his effort to identify the real historical forces leading to the overthrow of capitalism, substituting a project of ethical enlightenment he would himself have dubbed idealist;

(7) that, as a juridical principle, justice could not anyway be implemented in a communist society, which Marx conceived as having no juridical apparatuses of state and law; and

(8) that his vision of communism excluded those circumstances of scarcity and conflict which render norms of justice necessary, anticipating instead a distributive standard ('To each according to their needs') which lay beyond justice.

(9) If Marx did condemn capitalism, finally, he did so, on this interpretation, in the light of values other than justice: primarily, freedom and self-realization.

Other commentators believe Marx has a theory of justice and did criticize capitalism as unjust. They defend this position:

(1) that his description of the wage relation as an exchange of equivalents was merely provisional, applying to the sphere of circulation - and followed by a characterization of the production process in which he displayed that relationship as in truth exploitative, not a genuine exchange at all but appropriation by the capitalist of unpaid surplus labour;

(2) chat notwithstanding his own polemics against moralistic criticism, he presented exploitation as wrongful or unfair, calling it 'robbery' and 'theft';

(3) that by ranking, in Critique of the Gotha Programme, the principle of distribution according to need above the principle of distribution according to work and this in turn above the distributional norms of capitalism, Marx offered, implicitly, trans-historical, non-relative criteria of moral ordering, a sort of hierarchy of standards of distributive justice; and

(4) that his apparent statements of moral relativism expressed, in fact, a moral realism, specifying the material conditions necessary for

achieving 'higher' standards of fairness, rather than denying that such historically transcendent ethical judgements could be made.

In addition, these commentators contend,

(5) a concern with distribution is not intrinsically reformist, since, broadly conceived, distribution covers the most general division of social goods and burdens, including the ownership of productive resources – a revolutionary project indeed.

(6) Equally, while Marx did not think that moral criticism by itself was sufficient, still, as a complement to materialist historical analysis of the potential agencies of change, it had a place in his thought.

(7) Categorizing principles of justice as juridical is too narrow; they can be envisaged also, independently of any instruments of coercion, as simply ethical principles for evaluating and determining the allocation of social benefits and burdens.

(8) 'To each according to their needs' is such a principle, a norm of distributive justice, its aim an equal right to self-realization; even though viewed by Marx as to be achieved with the disappearance of coercive state apparatuses.

(9) The distinction made in the opposing interpretation, finally, between his views of justice and of freedom, is exegetically arbitrary: so far as Marx did sometimes belittle ethical criticism or characterize moral norms as being historically limited or relative, freedom and other values figured alongside justice amongst his targets.

Partly because he was no moral philosopher, and indeed impatient with ethical advocacy and analysis, partly because of his play with 'dialectical' contradictions in expounding the nature of the wage relation, it is not possible to render all of Marx's ideas in this area consistent with one another. A resolution of the controversy requires some effort of intellectual reconstruction, an attempt to make the best sense that can be made of his various viewpoints. The most cogent such reconstruction broadly vindicates those who say Marx did think capitalism unjust. Some sense can be made of the apparent evidence to the contrary; whereas no satisfactory answer has been given to the questions which trouble the opposing interpretation. For, first, there is no persuasive account of why Marx should have described exploitation as robbery if he did not see it as a wrong. Second, the argument that he condemned the unfreedoms rather than the injustices of capitalism poses a spurious alternative: concerned, as he was, with the distribution of freedom, his criticism in this matter was itself a critique of injustice. Third, though obscured by some of what Marx himself says, the principle 'To each according to their needs' is both a principle of moral equality and -if we construe the notion of communist "abundance' in any realistic fashion – a norm of distributive justice.

On the other hand, Marx's express refusal to offer criticism in terms of justice is explicable as being due to the narrow conception of this value which he (overtly) entertained; a conception associating justice with the prevailing norms internal to a. given social order; and with those norms, moreover, covering distribution in its most limited sense; distribution of consumption goods. But these two conceptual associations are not obligatory. There are broader notions of distributive justice than they define. Inasmuch as he did clearly regard the most general distribution of benefits and burdens under capitalism as, by some historically transcendent standards, morally objectionable, we must conclude that Marx thought capitalism unjust, on a broader conception of justice than the one he himself professed. Implicitly, his critique was a critique of social injustice. **–Editor**

Labour is the source of all wealth and culture, and since useful labour can only be performed in and through society, all members of society have an equal right to the undiminished proceeds of labour.

First part of the paragraph: 'Labour is the source of all wealth and culture'.

Labour is not the source of all wealth. Nature is just as much the source of use-values as labour. Labour is itself only the manifestation of a force of nature, human labour power. This phrase can be found in any children's primer; it is correct in so far as it is assumed that labour is performed with the objects and instruments necessary to it. A socialist programme, however, cannot allow such bourgeois formulations to silence the conditions which give them the only meaning they possess. Man's labour only becomes a source of use-values, and hence also of wealth, if his relation to nature, the primary source of all instruments and objects of labour, is one of ownership from the start, and if he treats it as belonging to him. There is every good reason for the bourgeoisie to ascribe supernatural creative power to labour, for when a man has no property other than his labour power it is precisely labour's dependence on nature that forces him, in all social and cultural conditions, to be the slave of other men who have taken the objective conditions of labour into their own possession. He needs their permission to work, and hence their permission to live.

Let us now leave this sentence as it stands, or rather hobbles. What sort of conclusion would one have expected? Obviously the following: 'Since labour is the source of all wealth, it follows that no one in society can appropriate wealth except as the product of labour. Thus, if a person does not work himself, he must live off the labour of others and his culture, too, must be acquired at the cost of other people's labour.'

Bakunin still makes me responsible, for example, not only for all the programmes, etc. of that party, but even for every step that Liebknecht has taken since the first day of his cooperation with the People's Party.

Apart from that, it is my duty not to approve, even by diplomatic silence, a programme which in my opinion is thoroughly reprehensible and demoralizing for the party.

Every step of a real movement is more important than a dozen programmes. If it was not possible, therefore, to go further than the Eisenach programme and, in the present conditions, it is not - then they should simply have concluded an agreement for action against the common enemy. Drawing up a programme of principle, however (instead of postponing this until such time as it has been prepared for by a considerable period of common activity), means erecting a milestone for all the world to see, by which the progress of the party will be measured.

Conditions forced the Lassallean leaders to come. If they had been told from the start that no haggling over principles would be tolerated, then they would have had to be satisfied with a programme of action or with an organizational plan for common action. Instead, they are being allowed to appear wielding mandates, and these mandates are being recognized as binding. This constitutes a surrender to the favour or disfavour of the people who are themselves most in need of help. To crown the matter, they turn around and hold a congress before the compromise congress, while our own party holds its congress post festum., Obviously the idea was to make all criticism ineffective, and to prevent our party from having second thoughts. It is clear that the mere fact of unification will satisfy the workers, but it is a mistake to believe that this momentary success has not been bought dearly.

Furthermore, the programme is no good, even when one disregards the hallowing of Lassalle's articles of faith.

In the near future, I shall be sending you the final instalment of the French edition of Capital The rest of the printing was held up for a long while by the French government's ban. It should all be settled by this week or the beginning of next. Did you get the earlier six instalments? Please also send me Bernhard Becker's address, for I have to send him the final instalment as well.

Instead of this the words 'and since' are used to tack on a second proposition so that a conclusion can be drawn from this one rather than the first.

Second port of the paragraph: 'Useful labour can only be performed in and through society'.

According to the first proposition, labour was the source of all wealth and culture, so that a society could not exist without labour. Now we are told the opposite: 'useful' labour cannot exist without society.

One could just as well have said that it is only in society that useless labour, or even labour harmful to the community, can become a line of business, and that only the society is it possible to live from idleness, etc., etc. in short, one could have copied down the whole of Rousseau.

And what is 'useful' labour? Surely simply labour which brings the desired useful result. A savage - and man was a savage after he ceased to be an ape - who kills an animal with a stone, gathers fruit, etc., is performing 'useful' labour.

Thirdly; the conclusion: 'And since useful labour can only be performed in and through society, all members of society have an equal right to the undiminished proceeds of labour.'

A beautiful conclusion! If useful labour can only be performed in and through society then the proceeds of labour belong to society - even if the individual worker only receives as much of them as is not required for the maintenance of the 'condition' of labour, society.

In fact, this sentence is not new: it has been used in all periods by the champions of the existing state of society. First come the claims of the government and all that goes with it, since it is the social organ for the maintenance of social order; then come the claims of the various kinds of private property, since the various kinds of private property form the foundations of society, etc. Hollow phrases such as these can clearly be twisted and turned at will.

The first and second parts of the paragraph would have some intelligible connection only if worded as follows: 'Labour becomes the source of all wealth and culture only when it is social labour,' or, which comes to the same thing, only 'in and through society'.

This proposition is indisputably correct, for although isolated labour (given its material conditions) can also create use-values, it cannot create either wealth or culture.

But this other proposition is equally indisputable: 'The social development of labour, and thus its development as a source of wealth and culture, proceeds in equal proportion to the development of poverty and destitution among the workers and of wealth and culture among the non-workers.'

Up to the present day all history has been governed by this law. What was needed here, therefore, was not generalizations about 'labour' and 'society' but concrete proof that in present capitalist society the material conditions have finally been created which enable and compel the worker to break this historical curse.

In fact, however, the sole purpose of this paragraph, a mess both in style and content, is to inscribe the Lassallean catchword of 'the undiminished proceeds of labour' as a slogan at the top of the party banner. I shall return to the 'proceeds of labour', 'equal right', etc. below, where the same things reappear in a somewhat different form.

In present society the capitalist class has a monopoly of the instruments of labour; the resultant dependence of the working class is the cause of misery and servitude in all its forms.

This sentence has been lifted from the Rules of the International but is incorrect in this 'improved' version.

In present society the instruments of labour are the monopoly of the landowners (the monopoly of landed property is even the basis of the monopoly of capital) and of the capitalists. Neither class of monopolists is mentioned by name in the relevant passage of the Rules of the International. This text speaks of the 'monopolizer of the means of labour, that is, the sources of life'; the addition of the 'sources of life' is adequate indication that land and soil are included under the instruments of labour.

The amendment was made because Lassalle, for reasons now generally known, only attacked the capitalist class and not the landowners. In England, the capitalist generally does not even own the land and soil on which his factory stands.

For the emancipation of labour the instruments of labour must be elevated to the common property of society and the whole of labour must be regulated on a cooperative basis, with a just distribution of the proceeds of labour.

'The instruments of labour must be elevated to common property'! This is probably meant to mean 'converted into common property'. But this just incidentally.

What are the 'proceeds of labour'? Are they the product of labour or its value? And in the latter case, is it the total value of the product or only that part of its value which labour has created over and above the value of the means of production consumed?

'Proceeds of labour' is a loose notion, used by Lassalle in place of definite economic concepts.

What is 'just' distribution?

Does not the bourgeoisie claim that the present system of "distribution is 'just'? And given the present mode of production is it not, in fact, the only 'just' system of distribution? Are economic relations regulated by legal concepts of right or is the opposite not the case, that legal relations spring from economic ones? Do not the socialist sectarians themselves have the most varied notions of 'just' distribution?

To discover what we are meant to understand by the phrase 'just distribution' as used here we must take the opening paragraph and this one together. The latter presupposes a society in which 'the instruments of labour are common property and the whole of labour is regulated on a cooperative basis' and from the opening paragraph we learn that 'all members of society have an equal right to the undiminished proceeds of labour'.

'All members of society'? Including people who do not work? Then what remains of the 'undiminished proceeds of labour'? Only the working members of society? Then what remains of the 'equal right' of all members of society?

'All members of society' and 'equal right', however, are obviously mere phrases. The heart of the matter is that in this communist society every worker is supposed to receive the 'undiminished' Lassallean 'proceeds of labour'.

If we start by taking 'proceeds of labour' to mean the product of labour, then the cooperative proceeds of labour are the total social product.

From this the following must now be deducted:

Firstly: cover to replace the means of production used up.

Secondly: an additional portion for the expansion of production.

Thirdly: a reserve or insurance fund in case of accidents, disruption caused by natural calamities, etc.

These deductions from the 'undiminished proceeds of labour' are an economic necessity and their magnitude will be determined by the means and forces available. They can partly be calculated by reference to probability, but on no account by reference to justice.

There remains the other part of the total product, designed to serve as means of consumption.

But before this is distributed to individuals the following further deductions must be made:

Firstly: the general costs of all administration not directly appertaining to production.

This part will, from the outset, be very significantly limited in comparison with the present society. It will diminish commensurately with the development of the new society.

Secondly: the amount set aside for needs communally satisfied, such as schools, health services, etc.

This part will, from the outset, be significantly greater than in the present society. It will grow commensurately with the development of the new society.

Thirdly: a fund for people unable to work, etc., in short, for what today comes under so-called official poor relief.

Only now do we come to that 'distribution' which, under the influence of the Lassalleans, is the only thing considered by this narrow-minded programme, namely that part of the means of consumption which is distributed among the individual producers within the cooperative.

The 'undiminished proceeds of labour' have meanwhile already been quietly 'diminished', although as a member of society the producer still receives, directly or indirectly, what is withheld from him as a private individual.

Just as the phrase 'undiminished proceeds of labour' has vanished, the phrase 'proceeds of labour' now disappears altogether.

Within the cooperative society based on common ownership of the means of production the producers do not exchange their products; similarly, the labour spent on the products no longer appears as the value of these products, possessed by them as a material characteristic, for now, in contrast to capitalist society, individual pieces of labour are no longer merely indirectly, but directly, a component part of the total labour. The phrase 'proceeds of labour', which even today is too ambiguous to be of any value, thus loses any meaning whatsoever.

We are dealing here with a communist society, not as it has developed on its own foundations, but on the contrary, just as it 'emerges from capitalist society. In every respect, economically, morally, intellectually, it is thus still stamped with the birth-marks of the old society from whose womb it has emerged. Accordingly, the individual producer gets back from society - after the deductions - exactly what he has given it. What he has given it is his individual quantum of labour. For instance, the social working day consists of the sum of the individual hours of work. The individual labour time of the individual producer thus constitutes his contribution to the social working day, his share of it. Society gives him a certificate stating that he has done such and such an amount of work (after the labour done for the communal fund has been deducted), and with this certificate he can withdraw from the social supply of means of consumption as much as costs an equivalent amount of labour. The same amount of labour he has given to society in one form, he receives back in another.

Clearly, the same principle is at work here as that which regulates the exchange of commodities as far as this is an exchange of equal values.

Content and form have changed because under the new conditions no one can contribute anything except his labour and conversely nothing can pass into the ownership of individuals except individual means of consumption. The latter's distribution among individual producers, however, is governed by the same principle as the exchange of commodity equivalents: a given amount of labour in one form is exchanged for the same amount in another.

Hence equal right is here still - in principle - a bourgeois right, although principle and practice are no longer at loggerheads, while the exchange of equivalents in commodity exchange only exists on the average and not in the individual case.

In spite of such progress this equal right still constantly suffers a bourgeois limitation. The right of the producers is proportional to the labour they do; the equality consists in the fact that measurement is by the same standard, labour. One person, however, may be physically and intellectually superior to another and thus be able to do more labour in the same space of time or work for a longer period. To serve as a measure labour must therefore be determined by duration or intensity, otherwise it ceases to be a standard. This equal right is an unequal right for unequal labour. It does not acknowledge any class distinctions, because everyone is just a worker like everyone else, but it gives tacit recognition to a worker's individual endowment and hence productive capacity as natural privileges. This right is thus in its content one of inequality, just like any other right, A right can by its nature only consist in the application of an equal standard, but unequal individuals (and they would not be different individuals if they were not unequal) can only be measured by the same standard if they are looked at from the same aspect, if they are grasped from one particular side, e.g., if in the present case they are regarded only as workers and nothing else is seen in them, everything else is ignored. Further: one worker is married, another is not; one has more children than another, etc., etc. Thus, with the same work performance and hence the same share of the social consumption fund, one will in fact be receiving more than another, one will be richer than another, etc. If all these defects were to be avoided rights would have to be unequal rather than equal.

Such defects, however, are inevitable in the first phase of communist society, given the specific form in which it has emerged after prolonged birth-pangs from capitalist society. Right can never rise above the economic structure of a society and its contingent cultural development.

In a more advanced phase of communist society, when the enslaving subjugation of individuals to the division of labour, and thereby the antithesis between intellectual and physical labour, have disappeared; when labour is no longer just a means of keeping alive but has itself become a vital need; when the all-round development of individuals has also increased their productive powers and all the springs of cooperative wealth flow more abundantly - only then can society wholly cross the narrow horizon of bourgeois right and inscribe on its banner: From each according to his abilities, to each according to needs!

(From: *The First International and After*, *Marx: Political Writings*, Volume 3, Penguin, London, 1974)

15

Colonialism

Marxist analyses of colonialism have approached it by focusing on several general issues. First, they have tried to establish that direct political control of non-capitalist societies was in some way a result of the reproductive requirements or tangential developments of European and American industrial capitalist economies in the nineteenth century. Second, they have examined the political, economic and ideological effects of industrial capitalist entry into non-capitalist societies. In this, they have been concerned primarily with the results of these effects for the development of socialism in both the industrial capitalist and colonized societies; consequently, they have tended to focus on the forms of colonial capitalist development created and perpetuated by the colonizing powers, and on the implications of this. Finally, they have assessed the possible consequences of socialist developments in colonial societies for socialist transformation in colonizing countries. These problems have been approached from within different theoretical and political perspectives in the Marxist tradition, and the varying answers given have laid down parameters for Marxist debates on the nature of post-colonial capitalist and socialist development.

Much of the writings of Marx and Engels on colonialism are commentaries on the results of British colonial rule in India and China, contained in articles and letters, the most detailed of which were written by Marx on India in 1853. At this rime Marx was working on drafts of the *Grundrisse*, one of whose sections - 'Forms that preceded capitalist production' - deals in passing with the effects of colonial rule on non-capitalist modes of production, and particularly on the Asiatic mode of production. These brief writings indicate that Marx and Engels considered the relation between industrial capitalist development and colonial control and expansion a complex one -irreducible to the "basic" economic tendencies offered as explanations by many later Marxist writers. They argued that colonial control was necessary not simply as a means for gaining access to markets and raw materials, but also as a means for excluding rival industrial nations, and in cases where the reproduction of non-capitalist economies was particularly resistant to capitalist penetration. They thus placed colonial control within a general economic context of a need for markets, raw materials, and investment outlets, to which, however, its presence and operation-was not always reducible. The analysis of the resistance of non-capitalist modes of production to industrial capitalist entry was further developed in Capital III, where Marx stressed the importance of the colonial state for transforming those non-capitalist modes whose political level was crucial for their reproduction (as, for example, in the Asiatic mode of production).

To many critics there seem to be two contradictory strands in Marx's analysis. When, for example, he analyses the effects of colonialism on Indian society, he shows how the economy is undermined by the forcible destruction of the textile industry and the neglect of state-organized public works; yet, in an apparent paradox, he also states that colonial rule is beneficial, in that it introduces an economic system which can revolutionize production, introducing technological changes which will benefit the indigenous population in the long term. This seemingly contradictory notion of the colonial impact being detrimental yet beneficial became the focus for Marxist debates on the 'colonial question'.

The analysis of the impact of colonialism in breaking down non-capitalist modes of production and transforming them in a capitalist direction was further developed by Luxemburg. From an under consumptions perspective which viewed colonial control as a means for destroying self-sufficient natural economies in the interests of a capitalism whose reproduction was hindered by a continual lack of effective demand, Luxemburg posited four destructive industrial capitalist mechanisms. Natural economies could be undermined by the introduction of a commodity economy and an internal separation of trade from agriculture, or they could be coercively undercut by a forcible possession of their fertile land, raw materials and labour power. Only colonialism could achieve this undermining successfully; it came as a last resort, when the operation of economic mechanisms such as trade, investment and monetarization had failed to restrict the reproduction of the natural economy.

The Marxist perspective on colonialism has been subjected to detailed criticism, the most important focusing on the following points: Colonialism was not particular to any specific phase in the development of the industrial capitalist economies. Although annexation and expansion did intensify in the late nineteenth century, the evidence is insufficient to establish the Marxist case in general, and Lenin's analysis in particular.

The economic arguments for the existence of a particular 'imperialist' stage of capitalist development are weak, if not unsustainable. Several authors, notably Barratt-Brown (1974), Warren (1980), and O'Connor (1970), have specified the major limitations: that 'finance capital – defined as the dominance of banking over industrial capital - only prevailed in a minority of industrial capitalist states; that the export of capital did not increase dramatically in the latter part of the nineteenth century; that it was not simply a matter of profit rates being higher in the colonies, but rather the mass of profit realizable, and this was far greater in the industrialized economies; that the decay and technological retardation of capitalist progress which Lenin associated with the need to export capital is little evidenced in the nineteenth and early twentieth centuries.

Whatever the multitude of links in the chain between the actions of the colonial state and the reproductive requirements of the industrial capitalist economies, Marxist analyses of colonialism have always ultimately reduced the former to the latter. This economic determinism has severely restricted the analysis of such aspects as the colonial class structure, with its continual reproduction of economic groupings whose existence cannot be explained simply by the reproductive needs of industrial capitalism.

Analysis of the societies that existed before the colonial impact has been either ignored or placed within all-embracing residual categories whose generality has rendered them heuristically valueless. Such categories are Luxemburg's concept of a pre-capitalist self-sufficient natural economy, or the notion that pre-colonial societies were simply equivalent to European feudal formations before the advent of capitalism.

The focus on the possibilities of a colonial capitalism creating the basis for a transition to a socialist economy has led to a political and theoretical obsession with the emergence of a national bourgeoisie. This has further restricted the possibilities of a rigorous Marxist analysis of classes and the state in colonial societies. **–Editor**

The Modern Theory of Colonization

Political economy confuses, on principle, two different kinds of private property, one of which rests on the labour of the producer himself, and the other on the exploitation of the labour of others. It forgets that the latter is not only the direct antithesis of the former, but grows on the former's tomb and nowhere else.

In Western Europe, the homeland of political economy, the process of primitive accumulation has more or less been accomplished. Here the capitalist regime has either directly subordinated to itself the whole of the nation's production, or, where economic relations are less developed, it has at least indirect control of those social layers which, although they belong to the antiquated mode of production, still continue to exist side by side with it in a state of decay. To this ready-made world of capital, the political economist applies the notions of law and of property inherited from a pre-capitalist world, with all the more anxious zeal and all the greater unction, the more loudly the facts cry out in the face of his ideology.

It is otherwise in the colonies. There the capitalist regime constantly comes up against the obstacle presented by the producer, who, as owner of his own conditions of labour, employs that labour to enrich himself instead of the capitalist. The contradiction between these two diametrically opposed economic systems has its practical manifestation here in the struggle between them. Where the capitalist has behind him the power of the mother country, he tries to use force to clear out of the way the modes of production and appropriation which rest on the personal labour of the independent producer.

The same interest which, in the mother country, compels the sycophant of capital, the political economist, to declare that the capitalist mode of production is theoretically its own opposite, this same interest, in the colonies, drives him 'to make a clean breast of it', and to proclaim aloud the antagonism between the two modes of production. To this end he demonstrates that the development of the social productivity of labour, co-operation, division of labour, application of machinery on a large scale, and so on, are impossible without the expropriation of the workers and the corresponding transformation of their means of production into capital. In the interest of the so-called wealth of the nation, he seeks for artificial means to ensure the poverty of the people. Here his apologetic armour crumbles off, piece by piece, like rotten touchwood.

It is the great merit of Wakefield to have discovered, not something new about the colonies, but, in the colonies, the truth about capitalist relations in the mother country. Just as the system of protection originally had the objective of manufacturing capitalists artificially in the mother country, so Wakefield's theory of colonization, which England tried for a time to enforce by Act of Parliament, aims at manufacturing wage-labourers in the colonies. This is what he calls 'systematic colonization'.

First of all, Wakefield discovered that, in the colonies, property in money, means of subsistence, machines and other means of production does not as yet stamp a man as a capitalist if the essential complement to these things is missing: the wage-labourer, the other man, who is compelled to sell himself of his own free will. He discovered that capital is not a thing, but a social relation between persons which is mediated through things. A Mr Peel, he complains, took with him from England to the Swan River district of Western Australia means of subsistence and of production tothe amount of £50,000. This Mr Peel even had the foresight to bring besides, 3,000 persons of the working class, men, women and children. Once he arrived at his destination, 'Mr Peel was left without a servant to make his bed or fetch him water from the river.' Unhappy Mr Peel, who provided for everything except the export of English relations of production to Swan River!

For the understanding of the following discoveries of Wakefield, let us make two preliminary remarks: We know that the means of production and subsistence, while they remain the property of .the immediate producer, are not capital. They only become capital under circumstances in which they serve at the same time as means of exploitation of, and domination over, the worker. But this, their capitalist soul, is so intimately wedded, in the mind of the political economist, to their material substance, that he christens them capital under all circumstances, even where they are its exact opposite. Thus it is with Wakefield. Further he describes the splitting-up of the means of production into the individual property of many mutually independent and self-employed workers as equal division of capital. The political economist is like the feudal jurist, who used to attach the labels supplied by feudal law even to relationships which were purely monetary.

'If' says Wakefield, 'all the members of the society are supposed to possess equal portions of capital... no man would have a motive for accumulating more capital than he could use with his own hands. This is to some extent the case in new American settlements, where a passion for owning land prevents the existence of a class of labourers for hire.' So long, therefore, as the worker can accumulate for himself - and this he can do so long as he remains in possession of his means of production - capitalist accumulation and the capitalist mode of production are impossible. The class of wage-labourers essential to these is lacking. How then, in old Europe, was the expropriation of the worker from his conditions of labour brought about? In other words, how did capital and wage-labour come into existence? By a social contract of a quite original kind. 'Mankind have adopted a simple contrivance for promoting the accumulation of capital,' which, of course, had dangled in front of them since the time of Adam as the ultimate and only goal of their existence, 'they have divided themselves into owners of capital and owners of labour. This division was the result of concert and combination.' In short: the mass of mankind expropriated itself in honour of the 'accumulation of capital'. Now one would think that this instinct of self-denying fanaticism would especially run riot in the colonies, the only places where the men and the conditions exist to turn a social contract from a dream into a reality. So why should 'systematic colonization' be called in. to replace its opposite, spontaneous and unregulated colonization? Here is one reason: 'In the Northern States of the American Union, it may be doubted whether so many as a tenth of the people would fall under the description of hired labourers. In England the labouring class compose the bulk of the people.' Indeed, the drive to self-expropriation for the glory of capital exists so little in the case of working humanity, that slavery, according to Wakefield himself, is the sole natural basis of colonial wealth. His systematic colonization is a mere makeshift, resulting from the fact that he has free men, not slavtes, to deal with. "The first Spanish settlers in Saint Domingo did not obtain labourers from Spain. But, without labourers', (i.e. without slavery) 'their capital must have perished, or, at least, must soon have been diminished to that small amount which each individual could employ with his own hands. This has actually occurred in the last colony founded by Englishmen - the Swan River Settlement - where a great mass of capital, of seeds, implements, and cattle, has perished for want of labourers to use it, and where no settler has preserved much more capital than he can employ with his own hands.'

We have seen that the expropriation of the mass of the people from the soil forms the basis of the capitalist mode of production. The essence of a free colony, on the contrary, consists in this, that the bulk of the soil is still public property, and every settler on it can therefore turn part of it into his private property and his individual means of production, without preventing later settlers from performing the same operation. This is the secret both of the prosperity of the colonies and of their cancerous affliction -their resistance to the establishment of capital.

'Where land is very cheap and all men are free, where every one who so pleases can easily obtain a piece of land for himself, not only is labour very dear, as respects the labourer's share of the produce, but the difficulty is to obtain combined labour at any price.'

In the colonies the separation of the worker from the conditions of labour and from the soil, in which they are rooted, does not yet exist, or only sporadically, or on too limited a scale. Hence the separation of agriculture from industry does not exist either, nor have any of the domestic industries of the countryside been destroyed. Whence then is to come the home market for capital? 'No part of the population of America is exclusively agricultural, excepting slaves and their employers who combine capital and labour in particular works. Free Americans, who cultivate the soil, follow many other occupations. Some portion of the furniture and tools which they use is commonly made by themselves. They frequently build their own houses, and carry to market, at whatever distance, the produce of then' own industry. They are spinners and weavers, they make soap and candles, as well as, in many cases, shoes and clothes for their own use. In America the cultivation of land is often the secondary pursuit, of a blacksmith, a miller or a shopkeeper.' Where, among such curious characters, is the 'field of abstinence' for the capitalists?

The great beauty of capitalist production consists in this, that it not only constantly reproduces the wage-labourer as a wage-labourer, but also always produces a relative surplus population of wage-labourers in proportion to the accumulation of capital. Thus the law of supply and demand as applied to labour is kept on the right lines, the oscillation of wages is confined within limits satisfactory to capitalist exploitation, and lastly, the social dependence of the worker on the capitalist, which is indispensable, is secured. At home, in the mother country, the smug deceitfulness of the political economist can turn this relation of absolute dependence into a free contract between buyer and seller, between equally independent owners of commodities, the owner of the commodity capital on one side, the owner of the commodity labour on the other. But in the colonies this beautiful illusion is torn aside. There, the absolute numbers of the population increase much more quickly than in the mother country, because many workers enter the colonial world as ready-made adults, and still the labour-market is always under stocked.

The law of the supply and demand of labour collapses completely. On the one hand, the old world constantly throws in capital, thirsting after exploitation and 'abstinence'; on the other, the regular reproduction of the wage-labourer as a wage-labourer comes up against the most mischievous obstacles, which are in part insuperable. And what becomes of the production of redundant wage-labourers, redundant, that is, in proportion to the accumulation of capital? Today's wage-labourer is tomorrow's independent peasant or artisan, working for himself. He vanishes from the labour-market - but not into the workhouse. This constant transformation of wage-labourers into independent producers, who work for themselves instead of for capital, and enrich themselves instead of tie capitalist gentlemen, reacts in its turn- very adversely on the conditions of the labour-market. Not only does the degree of exploitation of the wage-labourer remain indecently low. The wage-labourer also loses, along with the relation of dependence, the feeling of dependence on the abstemious capitalist. Hence all the inconveniences depicted so honestly, so eloquently and so movingly by our friend Wakefield.

The supply of wage-labour, he complains, is neither constant, nor regular, nor sufficient. 'The supply of labour is always, not only small, but uncertain.' "Though the produce divided between the capitalist and the labourer be large, the labourer takes so great a share that he soon becomes a capitalist.., Few, even of those whose lives are unusually long, can accumulate great masses of wealth. The workers most emphatically refuse to let the capitalist abstain from paying for the greater part of their labour. It is of no assistance to him if he cunningly imports his own wage-labourers from Europe, with his own capital. They soon 'cease ... to be labourers for hire; they ... become independent landowners, if not competitors with their former masters in the labour-market.' Horror of horrors! The excellent capitalist has imported bodily from Europe, with his own good money, his own competitors! The end of the world has come! No wonder Wake-field laments the absence both of relations of dependence and feelings of dependence on the part of the wage-labourers in the colonies. On account of the high wages, says his disciple Merivale, there is in the colonies an urgent desire for cheaper and more sub-servant workers, for a class of people to whom the capitalist may dictate his terms, instead of having his terms dictated by them ... In the old civilized countries the worker, although free, is by a law of nature dependent on the capitalist; in colonies this dependence must be created by artificial means.

What now is the consequence of this regrettable state of affairs in the colonies, according to Wakefield? A 'barbarizing tendency of dispersion' of producers and of the wealth of the nation. The fragmentation of the means of production among innumerable owners, working on their own account, annihilates, along with the centralization of capital, all the foundations of combined labour. Every lengthy undertaking, extending over several years and demanding the outlay of fixed capital, is prevented from being carried out. In Europe, capital does not hesitate for a moment, for the working class forms its living appendage, always present in excess, always at its disposal. But not in the colonies! Wakefield recounts the following exceedingly painful anecdote. He was talking with some capitalists of Canada and the state of New York, where moreover the wave of immigration often sticks, depositing a sediment of 'redundant' workers. 'Our capital says one of the characters in the melodrama', was ready for many operations which require a considerable period of tune for their completion; but we could not begin such operations with labour which, we knew, would soon leave us. If we had been sure of retaining the labour of such emigrants, we should have been glad to have engaged it at once, and for a high price: and we should have engaged it, even though we had been sure it would leave us, provided we had been sure of a fresh supply whenever we might need it'

After Wakefield has contrasted English capitalist agriculture and its 'combined' labour with the scattered cultivation of American peasants, he unwittingly shows us the obverse of the medal. He depicts the mass of the American people as well-to-do, independent, enterprising and comparatively cultured, whereas the English agricultural labourer is a miserable wretch, a pauper ... In what country, except North America and some new colonies, do the wages of free labour employed in agriculture, much exceed a bare subsistence for the labourer? Undoubtedly, farm-horses in England, being a valuable property, are better fed than English peasants.' But never mind, the wealth of the nation is once again, by its very nature, identical with the misery of the people.

How then can the anti-capitalist cancer of the colonies be healed? If men were willing to turn the whole of the land from public into private property at one blow, this would certainly destroy the root of the evil, but it would also destroy - the colony. The trick is to kill two birds with one stone. Let the government set an artificial price on the virgin soil, a price independent of the law of supply and demand, a price that compels the immigrant to work a long time for wages before he can earn enough money to buy land and turn himself into an independent farmer. The fund resulting from the sale of land at a price relatively prohibitory for the wage-labourers, this fund of money extorted from the wages of labour by a violation of the sacred law of supply and demand, is to be applied by the government, in proportion to its growth, to the importation of paupers from Europe into the colonies, so as to keep the wage-labour market full for the capitalists. Under these circumstances, 'everything will be for the best in the best of all possible worlds'. This is the great secret of 'systematic colonization'. Under this plan, Wakefield exclaims triumphantly, 'the supply of labour must be constant and regular, because, first, as no labourer would be able to procure land until he had worked for money, all immigrant labourers, working for a time for wages and in combination, would produce capital for the employment of more labourers; secondly, because every labourer who left off working for wages and became a landowner, would, by purchasing land, provide a fund for bringing fresh labour to the colony.' The land-price laid down by the state must of course be 'sufficient', i.e. it must be high enough 'to prevent the labourers from becoming independent landowners until others had followed to take their place'. This 'sufficient price for the land' is nothing but a euphemistic circumlocution for the ransom which the worker must pay to the capitalist in return for permission to retire from the wage-labour market to the land. First, he must create for the capitalist the 'capital' which enables him to exploit more workers; then, at his own expense, he must put a 'substitute' in the labour-market, who is dispatched across the sea by the government, again at the worker's expense, for his old master, the capitalist.

It is extremely characteristic that the English government for years practised this method of 'primitive accumulation' prescribed by Mr. Wakefield expressly for use in the colonies. The resulting fiasco was of course as ignominious as the fate of Peel's Bank Act. The stream of emigration was simply diverted from the English colonies to the United States. Meanwhile, the advance of capitalist production in Europe, accompanied by increasing government pressure, has rendered Wakefield's recipe superfluous. On the one hand, the enormous and continuous flood of humanity, driven year in, year out, onto the shores of America, leaves behind a stationary sediment in the East of the United States, since the wave of immigration from Europe throws men onto the labour-market there more rapidly than the wave of immigration to the West can wash them away. On the other hand, the American Civil War has brought in its train a colossal national debt and, with it, a heavy tax-burden, the creation of a finance aristocracy of the vilest type, and the granting of immense tracts of public land to speculative companies for the exploitation of railways, mines, etc. In short, it has brought a very rapid centralization of capital. The great republic has therefore ceased to be the promised land for emigrating workers. Capitalist production advances there with gigantic strides, even though the lowering of wages and dependence of the wage-labourer has by no means yet proceeded so far as to reach the normal European level. The shameless squandering of uncultivated colonial land on aristocrats and capitalists by the English government, so loudly denounced even by Wakefield, has, especially in Australia, in conjunction with the stream of men attracted by the gold-diggings, and the competition from imported English commodities which affects everyone down to the smallest artisan, produced an ample 'relative surplus population of workers', so that almost every mail-boat brings ill tidings of a 'glut of the Australian labour-market', and prostitution flourishes there in some places as exuberantly as in the Haymarket in London.

However, we are not concerned here with the condition of the colonies. The only thing that interests us is the secret discovered in the New World by the political economy of the Old World, and loudly proclaimed by it: that the capitalist mode of production and accumulation, and therefore capitalist private property as well, have for their fundamental condition the annihilation of that private property which rests on the labour of the individual himself; in other words, the expropriation of the worker.

(From *Capital*, Volume 1, translated by Ben Fowkes, 1976)

The British Rule in India

London, Friday, June 10, 1853

...Hindostan is an Italy of Asiatic dimensions, the Himalayas for the Alps, the Plains of Bengal for the Plains of Lombardy, the Deccan for the Apennines, and the Isle of Ceylon for the Island of Sicily. The same rich variety in the products of the soil, and the same dismemberment in the political configuration. Just as Italy has, from, time to time, been compressed by the conqueror's sword into different national masses, so do we find Hindostan, when not under the pressure of the Mohammedan, or the Mogul, or the Briton, dissolved into as many independent and conflicting States as it numbered towns, or even villages. Yet, in a social point of view, Hindostan is not the Italy, but the Ireland. of the East. And this strange combination of Italy and of Ireland, of a world of voluptuousness and of a world of woes, is anticipated in the ancient traditions of he religion of Hindostan. That religion is at once a religion of sensualist exuberance, .and a religion of self-torturing asceticism; a religion of the Lingam and of the Juggernaut; the religion of the Monk, and of the Bayadere.

I share not the opinion of those who believe in a golden age of Hindostan, without recurring, however, like Sir Charles Wood, for the confirmation of my view, to the authority of Khuli-Khan, But take, for example, the tunes of Aurung-Zebe; or the epoch, when the Mogul appeared in the North, and the Portuguese in the South; or the age of Mohammedan invasion, and of the Heptarchy in Southern India; or, if you will, go still more back to antiquity, take the mythological chronology of the Brahmin himself, who places the commencement of Indian misery in an epoch even more remote than the Christian creation of the world.

There cannot, however, remain any doubt but that the misery inflicted by the British on Hindostan is of an essentially different and infinitely more intensive kind than all Hindostan had to suffer before. I do not allude to European despotism, planted upon Asiatic despotism, by the British East India' Company, forming a more monstrous combination than any of the divine monsters startling us in the Temple of Salsette. This is no distinctive feature of British colonial rule, but only an imitation of the Dutch, and so much so that in order to characterize the working of the British East India Company, it is sufficient to literally repeat what Sir Stamford Raffles, the English Governor of Java, said of the old Dutch East India Company;

"The Dutch Company, actuated solely by the spirit of gain, and viewing their subjects with less regard or consideration than a West India planter formerly viewed a gang upon his estate, because the latter had paid the purchase money of human property, which the other had not, employed all the existing machinery of despotism to squeeze from the people their utmost mite of contribution, the last dregs of their labour, and thus aggravated the evils of a capricious and semi-barbarous Government, by working it with all the practiced ingenuity of politicians, and all the monopolizing selfishness of traders."

All the civil wars, invasions, revolutions, conquests, famines, strangely complex, rapid and destructive as the successive action in Hindostan may appear, did not go deeper than its surface. England has broken down the entire framework of Indian society, without any symptoms of reconstitution yet appearing. This loss of his old world, with no game of a' new one, imparts a particular kind of melancholy to the present misery of the Hindoo, and separates Hindostan, ruled by Britain, from all its ancient traditions, and from the whole of its past history.

There have been in Asia, generally, from immemorial times, but three departments of Government: that of Finance, or the plunder of the interior; that of War, or the plunder Of the exterior; and, finally, the department of Public Works, Climate and territorial conditions, especially the vast tracts of desert, extending from the Sahara, through Arabia, Persia, India and Tartary, to the most elevated Asiatic highlands, constituted artificial irrigation by canals and waterworks the basis of Oriental agriculture. As in Egypt and India, inundations are used for fertilizing the soil of Mesopotamia, Persia, etc.; advantage is taken of a high level for feeding irrigative canals. This prime necessity of an economical and common use of water, which, in the Occident, drove private enterprise to voluntary association, as in Flanders and Italy, necessitated, in the Orient where civilization was too low and the territorial extent too vast to call into life voluntary association, the interference of the centralizing power of Government. Hence an, economical function devolved upon all Asiatic Governments, the function of providing public works. This artificial fertilization of the soil, dependent on a Central Government, and immediately decaying with the neglect of irrigation and drainage, explains the otherwise strange fact that we now find whole territories barren and desert that were once brilliantly cultivated, as Palmyra, Petra, the ruins in Yemen, and large provinces of Egypt, Persia and Hindostan; it also explains how a single war of devastation has been able to depopulate a country for centuries, and to strip it of all its civilization.

Now, the British in East India accepted from their predecessors the department of finance and of war, but they have neglected entirely that of public works. Hence the deterioration of an agriculture which is not capable of being conducted on the British principle of free competition, of laissez-faire and laissez-aller. But in Asiatic empires we are quite accustomed to see agriculture deteriorating under one government and reviving again under some other government. There the harvests correspond to good or bad government, as they change in Europe with good or bad seasons. Thus the oppression and neglect of agriculture, bad as it is, could not be looked upon as the final blow dealt to Indian society by the British intruder, had it not been attended by a circumstance of quite different importance, a novelty in the annals of the whole Asiatic world, However changing the political aspect of India's past must appear, its social condition has remained unaltered since its remotest antiquity, until the first decennium of the 19th century. The hand-loom and the spinning-wheel, producing their regular myriads of spinners and weavers, were the pivots of the structure of that society. From immemorial times, Europe received the admirable textures of Indian labor, sending in return for them her precious metals, and furnishing thereby his material to the goldsmith, that indispensable member of Indian society, whose love of finery is so great that even the lowest class, those who go about nearly naked, have commonly a pair of golden earrings and a gold ornament of some kind hung round their necks. Rings on the fingers and toes have also been common. Women as well as children frequently wore massive bracelets and anklets of gold or silver, and statuettes of divinities in gold and silver were met with in the households. It was the British intruder who broke up the Indian hand-loom and destroyed the spinning-wheel. England began with depriving the Indian cottons from the Europea market; it then introduced twist into Hindostan and in the end inundated the very mother country of cotton with cottons. From 1818 to 1836 the export of "Grant freedom of action" (the motto of the bourgeois economists, free traders, who insisted of free trade and non-interference by the state in the sphere of economic relations–Ed) twist from Great Britain to India rose in the proportion of 1 to 5,200. In 1824 the export of British muslins to India hardly amounted to 1,000,000 yards, while in 1837 it surpassed 64,000,000 of yards. But at the same time the population of Dacca decreased from 150,000 inhabitants to 20,000. This decline of Indian towns celebrated for their fabrics was by no means the worst consequence. British steam and science uprooted, over the whole surface of Hindostan, the union between agriculture, and manufacturing industry.

These two circumstances–the Hindoo, on the one hand, leaving, like all Oriental peoples, to the central government the care of the great public works, the prime condition of his agriculture and commerce, dispersed, on. the other hand, over the surface of the country, and agglomerated in small centers by the domestic union of agricultural and manufacturing pursuits–these two circumstances had brought about, since the remotest times, a social system of particular features–the so-called village system, which gave to each of these small unions their independent organization and distinct life. The peculiar character of this system may be judged from the following description, contained in an old official report of the British House of Commons on Indian affairs:

"A village, geographically considered, is a tract of country comprising some hundred or thousand acres of arable and waste lands; politically viewed it resembles a corporation or township. Its proper establishment of officers and 'servants consists of the following descriptions: The potail, or head inhabitant, who has generally the superintendence of the affairs of the village, settles the disputes of the inhabitants, attends to the police, and performs the duty of collecting the revenue within his village, a duty which his personal influence and minute acquaintance with the situation and concerns of the people render him the best qualified for this charge. The kurnum keeps the accounts of cultivation, and registers everything connected with it. The tallier and the totie, the duty of the former of which consists in gaining information of crimes and offenses, and in escorting and protecting persons travelling from one village to another; the province of the latter appearing to be more immediately confined to the village, consisting, among other duties, in guarding the crops and assisting in measuring them. The boundary man, who preserves the limits of the village, or gives evidence respecting them in cases of dispute. The Superintendent of Tanks and Watercourses distributes the water for the purposes of agriculture. The Brahmin, who performs the village worship. The schoolmaster, who is seen teaching the children in a village to read and write in the sand. The calendar-Brahmin, or astrologer, etc. These officers and servants generally constitute the establishment of a village; but in some parts of the country it is of less extent; some of the duties and functions above described being united in the same person; in others it exceeds the above-named number of individuals. Under this simple form of municipal government, the inhabitants of the country have lived from time immemorial. The boundaries of the villages have been but seldom altered; and though the villages themselves have been sometimes injured, and even desolated by war, famine or disease, the same name, the same limits, the same interests, and even the same families, have continued for ages. The inhabitants gave themselves no trouble about the breaking up and divisions of kingdoms; while the village remains entire, they care not to what power it is transferred, or to what sovereign it devolves; its internal economy remains unchanged. The potail is still the head inhabitant, and still acts as the petty judge or magistrate, and collector or renter of the village."

These small stereotype forms of social organism have been to the greater part dissolved, and are disappearing, not so much through the brutal interference of the British tax-gatherer and the British soldier, as to .the working of English steam and English Free Trade. Those family-communities were based on domestic industry, in that peculiar combination of hand-weaving, hand-spinning and hand-tilling agriculture which gave them self-supporting power. English interference having placed the spinner in Lancashire and the weaver in Bengal, or sweeping away both Hindoo spinner and weaver, dissolved these small semi-barbarian, semi-civilized communities, by blowing up their economical basis, and thus produced the greatest, and to speak the truth, the only social revolution ever heard of in Asia. Now, sickening as it must be to human feeling to witness those myriads of industrious patriarchal and inoffensive social organizations disorganized and dissolved into their units, thrown into a sea of woes, and their individual members losing at the same time then 'ancient form of civilization, and their hereditary means of subsistence, we must not forget that these idyllic village communities, inoffensive though they may appear, had always been the solid foundation of' Oriental despotism, that they restrained the human mind within the smallest possible compass, making it the unresisting tool of superstition, enslaving it beneath traditional rules, depriving it of all grandeur and historical energies. We must not forget the barbarian egotism which, concentrating on some miserable patch of land, had quietly witnessed the ruin of empires, the perpetration of unspeakable cruelties, the massacre of the population of large towns, with no other consideration bestowed upon them than on natural events, itself the helpless prey of any aggressor who deigned to notice it at all. We must not forget that this undignified, stagnatory, and vegetative life, that this passive sort of existence evoked on the other part, in contradistinction, wild, aimless, unbounded forces of destruction and rendered murder itself a religious rite in Hindostan. We must not forget that these little communities were contaminated by distinctions of caste and by slavery, that they subjugated man to external circumstances instead of elevating man to be the sovereign of circumstances, that they transformed a self-developing social state into never changing natural destiny, and thus brought about a brutalizing worship of nature, exhibiting its degradation in the fact that man, the sovereign of nature, fell down on his knees in adoration of Kanuman, the monkey, and Sabbala, the cow.

England, it is true, in causing a social revolution in Hindostan, was actuated only by the vilest interests, and was stupid in her manner of enforcing them. But that is not the question. The question is, can mankind fulfil its destiny without a fundamental revolution in the social state of Asia? If not, whatever may have been the crimes of England she was the unconscious tool of history in bringing about that revolution.

(*Marx and Engles – Selected Works, Vol. 1.* Progress Publishers, Moscow, 1973)

The Future Results of British Rule in India

London, Friday, July 22, 1853

I propose in this letter to conclude my observations on India. How came it that English supremacy was established in India? The paramount power of the Great Mogul was broken by the Mogul Viceroys. The power of the Viceroys was broken by the Mahrattas. The power of the Mahrattas was broken by the Afghans, and while all were struggling against all, the Briton rushed in and was enabled to subdue them all. A country not only divided between Mohammedan and Hindoo, but between tribe and tribe, between caste and caste; a society whose framework was based on a sort of equilibrium, resulting from, a general repulsion and constitutional exclusiveness between all its members. Such a country and such a society, were they not the predestined prey of conquest? If we knew nothing of the past history of Hindostan, would there not be the one great and incontestable fact, that even at this moment India; is held in English thralldom by an Indian army maintained at the cost of India? India, then, could not escape the fate of being conquered, and the whole of her past history, if it be anything, is a history of the successive conquests she has undergone. Indian society has no history at all, at least no known history. What we call its history, is but the history of the successive intruders who founded their empires on the passive basis of that unresisting and unchanging society. The question, therefore, is not whether the English had a right to conquer India, but whether we are to prefer India conquered by the Turk, by the Persian, by the Russian, to India conquered by the Briton.

England has to fulfill a double mission in India: one destructive, the other regenerating – the annihilation of old Asiatic society, and the laying of the material foundations of Western society in Asia.

Arabs, Turks, Tartars', Moguls, who had successively overrun India, soon became Hindooized, the barbarian conquerors being, by an eternal law of history, conquered themselves by the superior civilization of their subjects. The British were the first conquerors superior, and therefore, inaccessible to Hindoo civilization. They destroyed it by breaking up the native communities, by uprooting the native industry, and by leveling all that was great and elevated in the native society. The historic pages of their rule in

India report hardly anything beyond that destruction. The work of regeneration hardly transpires through a heap of ruins. Nevertheless it has begun.

The political unity of India, more consolidated, and extending farther than it ever did under the Great Moguls, was the first condition of its regeneration. That unity, imposed by the British sword, will now be strengthened and perpetuated by the electric telegraph. The native army, organized and trained by the British drill-sergeant, was the sine qua nan of Indian self-emancipation, and of India ceasing to be the prey of the first foreign intruder. The free press, introduced for the first time into Asiatic society, and managed principally by the common offspring of Hindoo and Europeans, is a new and powerful agent of reconstruction. The Zemindaree and Ryotwar"1 themselves, abominable as they are, involve two distinct forms of private property in land—the great desideratum of Asiatic society. From the Indian natives, reluctantly and sparingly educated at Calcutta, under English superintendence, a fresh class is springing up, endowed with the requirements for government and imbued with European science. Steam has brought India into regular and rapid communication with Europe, has connected its chief ports with those of the whole south-eastern ocean, and has revindicated it from the isolated position which was the prime law of its stagnation. The day is not far distant when, by a combination of railways and steam vessels, the distance between England and India, measured by tune, will be shortened to eight days, and when that once fabulous country will thus be actually annexed to the Western world.

The ruling classes of Great Britain Have had, till now, but an accidental, transitory and exceptional interest in the progress of India. The aristocracy wanted to conquer it, the moneyocracy to plunder it, and the millocracy to undersell it. But now the tables are turned. The millocracy have discovered that the transformation of India into a reproductive country has become of vital importance to them, and that, to that end, it is necessary, above all, to gift her with means of irrigation and of internal communication. They intend now drawing a net of railways over India. And they will do it. The results must he inappreciable.

It is notorious that the productive powers of India are para1-lyzed by the utter want of means for conveying and exchanging its various produce. Nowhere, more than in India, do we meet with social destitution in the midst of natural plenty, for want of the means of exchange. It was proved before a Committee of the British House of Commons which sat in 1848, that "when grain was selling from 6s. to 8s. a quarter at Kandeish, it was Sold at 64s. to 70s. at Poonah, where the people were dying in the streets of famine, without the possibility of gaining supplies from Kandeish, because the clay-roads were impracticable."

The introduction of railways may be easily made to subserve agricultural purposes by the formation of tanks, where ground is required for embankment, and by the conveyance of water along the different lines. Thus irrigation, the sine qua nan of farming in the East, might be greatly extended, and the frequently recurring local famines, arising from the want of water, would be averted. The general importance of railways, viewed under this head, must become evident, when we remember that irrigated lands, even in the districts near Ghauts, pay three times as much in taxes, afford ten or twelve times as much employment, and yield twelve or fifteen times as much profit, as the same area without irrigation.

Railways will afford the means of diminishing the amount and the cost of the military establishments. Col. Warren, Town Major of the Fort St. William, stated before a Select Committee of the House of Commons:

> "The practicability of receiving intelligence from distant parts of the country in as many hours as at present it requires days and even weeks, and of sending instructions with troops and stores, in the more brief period, are considerations which cannot be too highly estimated. Troops could be kept at more distant and healthier stations than at present, and much loss of life from sickness would by this means be spared, Stores could not to the same extent be required at the various depots, and the loss toy decay, and the destruction incidental to the climate, would also be avoided. The number of troops might be diminished in direct proportion to their effectiveness."

We know that the municipal organization and the economical basis of the village communities have been broken up, but their worst feature, the dissolution of society into stereotype and disconnected atoms, has survived their vitality. The village isolation produced the absence of roads in India, and the absence of roads perpetuated the village isolation. On this plan a community existed with a given scale of low conveniences, almost without intercourse with other villages, without the desires and efforts indispensable to social advance. The British having broken up this self-sufficient inertia of the villages, railways will provide the new want of communication and intercourse. Besides, "one of the effects of the railway system will be to bring into every village affected by it such knowledge of the contrivances and appliances of other countries, and such means of obtaining them, as will first put the hereditary and stipendiary village artisanship of India to full proof of its capabilities, and then supply its defects." (Chapman, The Cotton, and Commerce of India).

I know that the English millocracy intend to endow India with railways with the exclusive view of extracting at diminished expenses the cotton and other raw materials for their manufactures. But when you have once introduced machinery into the locomotion of a country, which possesses iron and coals, you are unable to withhold it from its fabrication. You cannot maintain a net of railways over an immense country without introducing all those industrial processes necessary to meet the immediate and current wants of railway locomotion, and out of which there must grow the application of machinery to those branches of industry not immediately connected with railways. The railway system will therefore become, in India, truly the forerunner of modern industry. This is the more certain as the Hindoos are allowed by British' authorities themselves to possess particular aptitude for accommodating themselves to entirely new labor, and acquiring the requisite knowledge of machinery. Ample proof of this fact is afforded by the capacities and expertness of the native engineers in the Calcutta mint, where they have been for years employed in working the steam machinery, by the natives attached to the several steam-engines in the Hurdwar coal districts, and by other instances. Mr. Campbell himself, greatly influenced as he is by the prejudices of the East India Company, is obliged to avow "that the great mass of the Indian people possesses a great industrial energy, is well fitted to accumulate capital, and remarkable for a mathematical clearness of head, and talent for figures and exact sciences." "Their intellects," he says, "are excellent."

Modern industry, resulting from the railway system, will dissolve the hereditary divisions of labor, upon which rest the Indian castes, those decisive impediments to Indian progress and Indian power.

All the English bourgeoisie may he forced to do will neither emancipate nor materially mend the social condition of the mass of the people, depending not only on the development of the productive powers, but on their appropriation by the people. But what they will not fail to do is' to lay down the material premises for both. Has the bourgeoisie ever done more? Has it ever effected a progress without dragging individuals and peoples through blood and dirt, through misery and degradation?

The Indians will not reap the fruits of the new elements of society scattered among them by the British bourgeoisie, till in Great Britain itself the now ruling classes shall have been supplanted by the industrial proletariat, or till the Hindoos themselves shall have grown strong enough to throw off the English yoke altogether. At all events, we may safely expect to see, at a more or less remote period, the regeneration of that great and interesting country, whose gentle natives are, to use the expression of Prince Saltykov, even in the most inferior classes, "plus fins et plus adroits gue les Italiens" whose submission even is counterbalanced by a, certain calm nobility,,who, notwithstanding their natural languor, have astonished the British officers by their bravery, whose country has been the source of our languages, our religions, and who represent the type of the ancient German in the Jat and the type of the ancient Greek in the Brahmin.

I cannot part with the subject of India without some concluding remarks.

The profound hypocrisy and inherent barbarism of bourgeois civilization lies unveiled before our eyes, turning from its home, where it assumes respectable forms, to the colonies, where it goes naked. They are the defenders of property, but did any revolutionary party ever originate agrarian revolutions like those in Bengal, in Madras, and in Bombay? Did they not, in India, to borrow an expression of that great robber, Lord Clive himself, resort to atrocious extortion, when simple corruption could not keep pace with their rapacity? While they prated in Europe about the inviolable sanctity of the national debt, did they not confiscate in India the dividends of the fayahs, who had invested their private savings in the Company's own funds? While they combated the French revolution under the pretext of defending "our holy religion," did they not forbid, at the same time, Christianity to be propagated in India, and did they not, in order to make money out of the pilgrims streaming to the temples of Orissa and Bengal, take up the trade in the murder and prostitution perpetrated in the temple of Juggernaut? These are the men of "Property, Order, Family, and Religion."

The devastating effects of English industry, when contemplated with regard to India, a country as vast as Europe, and containing 150 millions of acres, are palpable and confounding. But we must not forget that they are only the organic results of the whole system of production as it is now constituted. That production rests on the supreme rule of capital. The centralization of capital is essential to the existence of capital as an independent power. The destructive influence of that centralization upon the markets of the world does but reveal, in the most gigantic dimensions, the inherent organic laws of political economy now at work in every civilized town. The bourgeois period of history has to create the material basis of the new world – on the one hand the universal intercourse founded upon the mutual dependency of mankind, and the means of that intercourse; on the other hand the development of the productive powers of man and the transformation of material production into a scientific domination of natural agencies. Bourgeois industry and commerce create these material conditions of a new world in the same way as geological revolutions have created the surface of the earth. When a great social revolution shall have mastered the results of the bourgeois epoch, the market of the world and the modern powers of production, and subjected them to the common control of the most advanced peoples, then only will human progress cease to resemble that hideous pagan idol, who would not drink the nectar but from the skulls of the slain.

(From *Marx and Eagles*: *Selected Works*, Progress Publishers, Moscow, 1973)

16

The Eighteenth Brumaire of Louis Bonaparte

In the writings of Marx and Engels this refers to a form of regime in capitalist society in which the executive part of the state, under the rule of one individual, achieves dictatorial power over all other parts of the state, and over society. Bonapartism thus constitutes an extreme manifestation of what, in recent Marxist writing on the state, has been called its 'relative autonomy'. The main instance of this form of regime in Marx's lifetime was that of Louis Bonaparte, the nephew of Napoleon I, who became Napoleon III after his coup d'etat of 2 December 1851. That episode inspired one of Marx's most important and glittering historical writings, 18th Brumaire. For his part, Engels also paid considerable attention to the rule of Bismarck in Germany, and found in the Bismarckian regime many parallels with Bonapartism.

For Marx and Engels, Bonapartism is the product of a situation where the ruling class in capitalist society is no longer able to maintain its rule by constitutional and parliamentary means; but where the working class is not able to affirm its own hegemony either. In The Civil War, after Napoleon Ill's Second Empire had collapsed-under the impact of defeat in the Franco-Prussian War, Marx said that Bonapartism 'was the only form of government possible at a time when the bourgeoisie had already lost, and the working class had not yet acquired, the faculty of ruling the nation'. Similarly, Engels said in The Origin of the Family that while the state was generally the state of the ruling class, 'by way of exception, however, periods occur in which the warring classes balance each other so nearly that the state power, as ostensible mediator, acquires, for the moment, a certain degree of independence of both'. These formulations stress the high degree of independence of the Bonapartist state; but its dictatorial character merits equal emphasis.

The independence of the Bonapartist state, and its role as 'ostensible mediator' between warring classes, do not leave it, in Marx's phrase, 'suspended in mid air'. Louis Bonaparte, he also said, 'represented' the small-holding peasantry, the most numerous class in France, by which he may be taken to have meant that Louis Bonaparte claimed to speak for that class, and was supported by it. But Louis Bonaparte, Marx also said, claimed to speak for all other classes in society as well. In fact, the real task of the Bonapartist state was to guarantee the safety and stability of bourgeois society, and to make possible the rapid development of capitalism.

In their writings on the state of the Bonapartist type, Marx and Engels also articulate an important concept about the state, namely the degree to which it represents the interest of those who actually run it. In 18th Brumaire, Marx speaks of 'this executive power with its enormous bureaucratic and military organization, with its extensive and artificial state machinery, with a host of officials numbering half million, besides an army of another half million, this appalling parasitic body, which envelops the body of French society like a caul and chokes all it spores.' The Bonaparist state all of France's pores, as Marx acknowledged in The Civil War; for it was under its way, he wrote then, that 'bourgeois society, freed from political cares, attained a development unexpected even by itself. Out of this does not detract from the point that the quasi-autonomous Bonapartist state seeks to serve its own interest as well as that of capital. **–Editor**

The Eighteenth Brumaire of Louis Bonaparte

Hegel remarks somewhere that all facts and personages of great importance in world history occur, as it were, twice. He forgot to add: the first time as tragedy, the second as farce. Caussidiere for Danton, Louis Blanc for Robespierre, the Montagne of 1848 to 1851 for the Montagne of 1793 to 1795, the Nephew for the Uncle. And the same caricature occurs in the circumstances attending the second edition of the eighteenth Brumaire!

Men make their own history, but they do not make it just as they please; they do not make it under circumstances chosen by themselves, but under circumstances directly encountered, given and transmitted from the past. The tradition of all the dead generations weighs like a nightmare on the brain of the living. And just when they seem engaged in revolutionising themselves and things, in creating something that has never yet existed, precisely in such periods of revolutionary crisis they anxiously conjure up the spirits of the past to their service and borrow from them names, battle cries and costumes in order to present the new scene of world history in this time-honoured disguise and this borrowed language. Thus Luther donned the mask of the Apostle Paul, the Revolution of 1789 to 1814 draped itself alternately as the Roman republic and the Roman empire, and the Revolution of 1848 knew nothing better to do than to parody, now 1789, now the revolutionary tradition of 1793 to 1795. In like manner a beginner who has learnt a new language always translates it back into his mother tongue, but he has assimilated the spirit of the new language and can freely express himself in it only when he finds his way in it without recalling the old and forgets his native tongue in the use of the new.

Consideration of this conjuring up of the dead of world history reveals at once a salient difference. Camille Desmoulins, Danton, Robespierre, Saint-Just, Napoleon, the heroes as well as the parties and the masses of the old French Revolution, performed the task of their time in Roman costume and with Roman phrases, the task of unchaining and setting up modern bourgeois society. The first ones knocked the feudal basis to pieces and mowed off the feudal heads which had grown on it. The other created inside France the conditions under which alone free competition could be developed, parcelled landed property exploited and the unchained industrial productive power of the nation employed; and beyond the French borders he everywhere swept the feudal institutions away, so far as was necessary to furnish bourgeois society in France with a suitable up-to-date environment on the European Continent. The new social formation once established, the antediluvian Colossi disappeared and with them resurrected Romanity–the Brutuses, Gracchi, Publicolas, the tribunes, the senators, and Caesar himself. Bourgeois society in its sober reality had begotten its true interpreters and mouthpieces in the Says, Cousins, Royer-Collards, Benjamin Constants and Guizots; its real military leaders sat behind the office desks, and the hogheaded Louis XVIII was its political chief. Wholly absorbed in the production of wealth and in peaceful competitive struggle, it no longer comprehended that ghosts from the days of Rome had watched over its cradle. But unheroic as bourgeois society is, it nevertheless took heroism, sacrifice, terror, civil war and battles of peoples to bring it into being. And in the classically austere traditions of the Roman republic its gladiators found the ideals and the art forms, the self-deceptions that they needed in order to conceal from themselves the bourgeois limitations of the content of their struggles and to keep their enthusiasm on the high plane of the great historical tragedy. Similarly, at another stage of development, a century earlier, Cromwell and the English people had borrowed speech, passions and illusions from the Old Testament for their bourgeois revolution. When the real aim had been achieved, when the bourgeois transformation of English society had been accomplished, Locke supplanted Habakkuk.

Thus the awakening of the dead in those revolutions served the purpose of glorifying the new struggles, not of parodying the old; of magnifying the given task in imagination, not of fleeing from its solution in reality; of finding once more the spirit of revolution, not of making its ghost walk about again.

From 1848 to 1851 only the ghost of the old revolution walked about, from Marrast, the republican who disguised himself as the old Bailly, down to the adventurer, who hides his commonplace repulsive features under the iron death mask of Napoleon. An entire people, which had imagined that by means of a revolution it had imparted to itself an accelerated power of motion, suddenly finds itself set back into a defunct epoch and, in order that no doubt as to the relapse may be possible, the old dates arise again, the old chronology, the old names, the old edicts, which had long become a subject of antiquarian erudition, and the old minions of the law, who had seemed long decayed. The nation feels like that mad Englishman in Bedlam who fancies that he lives in the times of the ancient Pharaohs and daily bemoans the hard labour that he must perform in the Ethiopian mines as a gold digger, immured in this subterranean prison, a dimly burning lamp fastened to his head, the overseer of the slaves behind him with a long whip, and at the exits a confused welter of barbarian mercenaries, who understand neither the forced labourers in the mines nor one another, since they speak no common language. "And all this is expected of me," sighs the mad Englishman, "of me, a freeborn Briton, in order to make gold for the old Pharaohs." "In order to pay the debts of the Bonaparte family," sighs the French nation. The Englishman, so long as he was in his right mind, could not get rid of the fixed idea of making gold. The French, so long as they were engaged in revolution, could not get rid of the memory of Napoleon, as the election of December 10 proved. They hankered to return from the perils of revolution to the flesh-pots of Egypt, and December 2, 1851 was the answer. They have not only a caricature of the old Napoleon, they have the old Napoleon himself, caricatured as he must appear in the middle of the nineteenth century. The social revolution of the nineteenth century cannot draw its poetry from the past, but only from the future. It cannot begin with itself before it has stripped off all superstition in regard to the past. Earlier revolutions required recollections of past world history in order to drug themselves concerning then-own content. In order to arrive at its own content, the revolution of the nineteenth century must let the dead bury their dead. There the phrase went beyond the content; here the content goes beyond the phrase.

The February Revolution was a surprise attack, a taking of the old society unawares, and the people proclaimed this unexpected stroke as a deed of world importance, ushering in a new epoch. On December 2 the February Revolution is conjured away by a cardsharper's trick, and what seems overthrown is no longer the monarchy but the liberal concessions that were wrung from it by centuries of struggle. Instead of society having conquered a new content for itself, it seems that the state only returned to its oldest form, to the shamelessly simple domination of the sabre and the cowl. This is the answer to the coup de mom of February 1848, given by the coup fie tete of December 1851. Easy come, easy go. Meanwhile the interval of time has not passed by unused. During the years 1848 to 1851 French society has made up, and that by an abbreviated because revolutionary method, for the studies and experiences which, in a regular, so to speak, textbook course of development, would have had to precede the February Revolution, if it was to be more than a ruffling of the surface. Society now seems to have fallen back behind its point of departure; it has in truth first to create for itself the revolutionary point of departure, the situation, the relations, the conditions under which -alone modern revolution becomes serious.

Bourgeois revolutions, like those of the eighteenth century; storm swiftly from success to success; their dramatic effects outdo each other; men and things seem set in sparkling brilliants; ecstasy is the everyday spirit; but they are short-lived; soon they have attained their zenith, and a long crapulent depression lays hold of society before it learns soberly to assimilate the results of its siorm-and-stress period. On the other hand, proletarian revolutions, like those of the nineteenth century, criticise themselves constantly, interrupt themselves continually in their own course, come back to the apparently accomplished in order to begin it afresh, deride with unmerciful thoroughness the inadequacies, weaknesses and paltrinesses of their first attempts, seem to throw down their adversary only in order that he may draw new strength from the earth and rise again, more gigantic, before them, recoil ever and anon from the indefinite prodigiousness of their own aims, until a situation has been created which makes all turning back impossible, and the conditions themselves cry out:

Here is the rose, here dance!

For the rest, every fairly competent observer, even if he had not followed the course of French development step by step, must have had a presentiment that an unheard-of fiasco was in store for the revolution. It was enough to hear the self-complacent howl of victory with which Messieurs the Democrats congratulated each other on the expected gracious consequences of the second Sunday in May 1852. In their minds the second Sunday in May 1852 had become a fixed idea, a dogma, like the day on which Christ should reappear and the millennium begin, in the minds of the Chiliasts. As ever, weakness had taken refuge in a belief in miracles, fancied the enemy overcome when he was only conjured away in imagination, and it lost all understanding of the present in a passive glorification of the future that was in store for it and of the deeds it had in petto but which it merely did not want to carry out as yet. Those heroes who seek to disprove their demonstrated incapacity by mutually offering each other their sympathy and getting together in a crowd had tied up their bundles, collected their laurel wreaths in advance and were just then engaged in discounting on the exchange market the republics in partibus for which they had already providently organised the government personnel with all the calm of their unassuming disposition. December struck them like a thunderbolt from a clear sky, and the peoples that in periods of pusillanimous depression gladly let their inward apprehension be drowned out by the loudest bawlers will perchance have convinced themselves that the times are past when the cackle of geese could save the Capital.

The Constitution, the National Assembly, the dynastic parties, the blue and the red republicans, the heroes of Africa, the thunder from the platform, the sheet lightning of the daily press, the entire literature, the political names and the intellectual reputations, the civil law and the penal code, the liberte, egalite, fraternite and the second Sunday in May 1852 – all has vanished like a phantasmagoria before the spell of a man whom even his enemies do not make out to be a magician. Universal suffrage seems to have survived only for a moment, in order that with its own Jiand it may make its last will and testament before the eyes of all the world and declare in the name of the people itself: All that exists deserves to perish.

It is not enough to say, as the French do, that their nation was taken unawares. A nation and a woman are not forgiven the unguarded hour in which the first adventurer that came along could violate them. The riddle is not solved by such turns of speech, but merely formulated differently. It remains to be explained how a nation of thirty-six millions can be surprised and delivered unresisting into captivity by three swindlers.

Let us recapitulate in general outline the phases that the French Revolution went through from February 24, 1848 to December 1851.

Three main periods are unmistakable: the February period; May 4, 1848, to May 28, 1849: the period of the constitution of the republic, or of the Constituent National Assembly; May 28, 1849 to December 2, 1851: the period of the constitutional republic or of the Legislative National Assembly.

The first period, from February 24, or the overthrow of Louis Philippe, to May 4, 1848, the meeting of the Constituent Assembly, the February period proper, may be described as the prologue to the revolution. Its character was officially expressed in the fact that the government improvised by it itself declared that it was provisional and, like the government, everything that was mooted, attempted or enunciated during this period proclaimed itself to be only provisional. Nothing and nobody ventured to lay claim to the right of existence and of real action. All the elements that had prepared or determined the revolution, the dynastic opposition, the republican bourgeoisie, the democratic-republican petty bourgeoisie and the social-democratic workers, provisionally found their place in the February government.

It could not be otherwise. The February days originally intended an electoral reform, by which the circle of the politically privileged among the possessing class itself was to be widened and the exclusive domination of the aristocracy of finance overthrown. When it came to the actual conflict, however, when the people mounted the barricades, the National Guard maintained a passive attitude, the army offered no serious resistance and the monarchy ran away, the republic appeared to be a matter of course. Every party construed it in its own way. Having secured it arms in hand, the proletariat impressed its stamp upon it and proclaimed it to be a social republic. There was thus indicated the general content of the modern revolution, a content which was in most singular contradiction to everything that, with the material available, with the degree of education attained by the masses, under the given circumstances and relations, could be immediately realised in practice. On the other hand, the claims of all the remaining elements that had collaborated in the February Revolution were recognised by the lion's share that they obtained in the government. In no period do we, therefore, find a more confused mixture of high-flown phrases and actual uncertainty and clumsiness, of more enthusiastic striving for innovation and more deeply-rooted domination of the old routine, of more apparent harmony of the whole of society and more profound estrangement of its elements. While the Paris proletariat still revelled in the vision of the wide prospects that had .opened before it and indulged in seriously-meant discussions on social problems, the old powers of society had grouped themselves, assembled, reflected and found unexpected support in the mass of the. nation, the peasants and petty bourgeois, who all at once stormed on to the political stage, after the barriers of the July monarchy had fallen

The second period, from May 4, 1848, to the end of May 1849, is the period of the constitution, the foundation, of the bourgeois republic. Directly after the February days not only had the dynastic opposition been surprised by the republicans and the republicans by the Socialists, but all France by Paris. The National Assembly, which met on May 4, 1848, had emerged from the national elections and represented the nation. It was a living protest against the pretensions of the February days and was to reduce the results of the revolution to the bourgeois scale. In vain the Paris proletariat, which immediately grasped the character of this National Assembly, attempted on May 15, a few days after it met, forcibly to negate its existence, to dissolve it, to disintegrate again into its constituent parts the organic form in which the proletariat was threatened by the reacting spirit of the nation. As is known, May 15 had no other result save that of removing Blanqui and his comrades, that is, the real leaders of the proletarian party, from the public stage for the entire duration of the cycle we are considering.

The bourgeois monarchy of Louis Philippe can be followed only by a bourgeois republic, that is to say, whereas a limited section of the bourgeoisie ruled in the name of the king, the whole of the bourgeoisie will now rule on behalf of the people. The demands of the Paris proletariat are Utopian nonsense, to which an end must be put. To this declaration of the Constituent National Assembly the Paris proletariat replied with the June Insurrection the most colossal event in the history of European civil wars. The bourgeois republic triumphed. On its side stood the aristocracy of finance, the industrial bourgeoisie, the middle class, the petty bourgeois, the army, the lumpenproletariat organised as the Mobile Guard, the intellectual lights, the clergy and the rural population. On the side of the Paris proletariat stood none but itself. More than three thousand insurgents were butchered after the victory, and fifteen thousand were transported without trial. With this defeat the proletariat passes into the background of the revolutionary stage. It attempts to press forward again on every occasion, as soon as the movement appears to make a fresh start, but with ever decreased expenditure of strength and always slighter results. As soon as one of the. social strata situated above it gets into revolutionary ferment, the proletariat enters into an alliance with it and so shares all the defeats that the different parties suffer, one after another. But these subsequent blows become the weaker, the greater the surface of society over which they are distributed. The more important leaders of the proletariat in the Assembly and in the press successively fall victims to the courts, and ever more equivocal figures come to head it. In part it throws itself into doctrinaire experiments, exchange banks and workers' associations, hence into a movement in which it renounces the revolutionising of the old world by means of the latter's own great, combined resources, and seeks, rather, to achieve its salvation behind society's back, in private fashion, within its limited conditions of existence, and hence necessarily suffers shipwreck. It seems to be unable either to rediscover revolutionary greatness in itself or to win new energy from the connections newly entered into, until all classes with which it contended in June themselves lie prostrate beside it. But at least it succumbs with the honours of the great, world-historic struggle; not only France, but all Europe trembles at the June earthquake, while the ensuing defeats of the upper classes are so cheaply bought that they require barefaced exaggeration by the victorious party to be able to pass for events at all, and become the more ignominious the further the defeated party is removed from the proletarian party.

The defeat of the June insurgents, to be sure, had now prepared, had levelled the ground on which the bourgeois republic could be founded and built up, but it had shown at the same time that in Europe the questions at issue are other than that of "republic or monarchy." It had revealed that here bourgeois republic signifies the unlimited despotism of one class over other classes. It had proved that in countries with an old civilisation, with a developed formation of classes, with modern conditions of production and with an intellectual consciousness in which all traditional ideas have been dissolved by the work of centuries, the republic signifies in general only the political form of revolution of bourgeois society and not its conservative form of life, as, for example, in the United States of North America, where, though classes already exist, they have not yet become fixed, but continually change and interchange their elements in constant flux, where the modern means of production, instead of coinciding with a stagnant surplus population, rather compensate for the relative deficiency of heads and hands, and where, finally, the feverish, youthful movement of material production, which has to make a new world its own, has left neither time nor opportunity for abolishing the old spirit world.

During the June days all classes and parties had united in the party of Order against the proletarian class as the party of Anarchy, of socialism, of communism. They had "saved" society from "the enemies of society." They had given out the watchwords of the old society, "property, family, religion, order to their army as passwords and had proclaimed to the counterrevolutionary crusaders: "By this sign thou shalt conquer!" From that moment, as soon as one of the numerous parties which had gathered under this sign against the June insurgents seeks to hold the revolutionary battlefield in its own class interest, it goes down before the cry: "Property, family, religion, order." Society is saved just as often as the circle of its rulers contracts, as a more exclusive interest is maintained, against a wider one. Every demand of the simplest bourgeois financial reform, of the most ordinary liberalism, of the most formal republicanism, of, the most shallow democracy, is simultaneously castigated as an "attempt on society" and stigmatised as "socialism." And, finally, the high priests of "the religion of order" themselves are driven with kicks from their Pythian tripods, hauled out of their beds in the darkness of night, put in prison-vans, thrown into dungeons or sent into exile; their temple is razed to the ground, their mouths are sealed, their pens broken, their law torn to pieces in the name of religion, of property, of the family, of order. Bourgeois fanatics for order are shot down on their balconies by mobs of drunken soldiers, their domestic sanctuaries profaned, their houses bombarded for amusement–in the name of property, of the family, of religion and of order. Finally, the scum of bourgeois society forms the holy phalanx of order and the hero Crapulinski installs himself in the Tuileries as the "saviour of society" resentatives in the Chambers and a considerable sphere of influence in the press.

Its Paris organ, the National, was considered just as respectable in its way as the Journal des Debats. Its character corresponded to this position under the constitutional monarchy. It was not a faction of the bourgeoisie held together by great common interests and marked off by specific conditions of production. It was a clique of republican-minded bourgeois, writers, lawyers, officers and officials that owed its influence to the personal antipathies of the country against Louis Philippe, to memories of the old republic, to the republican faith of a number of enthusiasts, above all, however, to French nationalism, whose hatred of the Vienna treaties and of the alliance with England it stirred up perpetually. A large part of the following that the National had under Louis Philippe was due to this concealed imperialism, which could consequently confront it later under the republic, as a deadly rival in the person of Louis Bonaparte, It fought the aristocracy of finance, as did all the rest of the bourgeois opposition. Polemics against the budget, which were closely connected in France with fighting the aristocracy of finance, procured popularity too cheaply and material for puritanical leading articles too plentifully, not to be exploited. The industrial bourgeoisie was grateful to it for its slavish defence of the French protectionist system, which it accepted, however, more on national grounds than on grounds of national economy; the bourgeoisie as a whole, for its vicious denunciation of communism and socialism. For the rest, the party of the National was purely republican, that is, it demanded a republican instead of a monarchist form of bourgeois rule and, above all, the lion's share of this rule. Concerning the conditions of this transformation it was by no means clear in its own mind. On the other hand, what was clear as daylight to it and was publicly acknowledged at the reform banquets in the last days of Louis Philippe, was its unpopularity with the democratic petty bourgeois and, in particular, with the revolutionary proletariat. These pure republicans, as is, indeed, the way with pure republicans, were already on the point of contenting themselves in the first instance with a regency of the Duchess of Orleans, when the February Revolution broke out and assigned their best-known representatives a place in the Provisional Government. From the start, they naturally had the confidence of the bourgeoisie and a majority in the Constituent National Assembly. The socialist elements of the Provisional Government were excluded forthwith from the Executive Commission which the National Assembly formed when it met, and the party of the National took advantage.

On the threshold of the February Revolution, the social republic appeared as a phrase, as a prophecy. In the June days of 1848, it was drowned in the blood of the Paris proletariat, but it haunts the subsequent acts of the drama like a ghost. The democratic republic announces its arrival. On June 13, 1849, it is dissipated together with its petty bourgeois, who have taken to their heels, but in its flight it blows its own trumpet with redoubled boastfulness. The parliamentary republic, together with the bourgeoisie, takes possession of the entire stage; it enjoys its existence to the full, but December 2, 1851 buries it to the accompaniment of the anguished cry of the royalists in coalition; "Long live the Republic!"

The French bourgeoisie balked at the domination of the working proletariat; it has brought the lumpenproletariat to domination, with the chief of the Society of December 10 at the head. The bourgeoisie kept France in breathless fear of the future terrors of red anarchy; Bonaparte discounted this future for it when, on December 4, he had the eminent bourgeois of the Boulevard Montmartre and the Boulevard des Italians shot down at their windows by the liquor-inspired army of order. It apotheosized the sword; the sword rules it. It destroyed the revolutionary press; its own press has been destroyed. It placed popular meetings under police supervision; its salons are under the supervision of the police. It disbanded the democratic

National Guards; its own National Guard is disbanded. It imposed a state of siege; a state of siege is imposed upon it, It supplanted the juries by military commissions; its juries are supplanted by military commissions. It subjected public education to the sway of the priests; the priests subject it to their own education. It transported people without trial; it is being transported without trial. It repressed every stirring in society by means of the state power; every stirring in its society is suppressed by means of the state power. Out of enthusiasm for its purse, it rebelled against its own politicians and men of letters; its politicians and men of letters are swept aside, but it purse is being plundered now that its mouth has been gagged and its pen broken. The bourgeoisie never wearied of crying out to the revolution what Saint Arsenius cried out to the Christians: "Fuge, tace, quiesce! Flee, be silent, keep still!" Bonaparte cries to the bourgeoisie: "Fuge, face, quiescel Flee, be silent, keep still!"

The French bourgeoisie had long ago found the solution to Napoleon's dilemma: "It had found the solution to it in the "republique cosaque." No Circe, by means of black magic, has distorted that work of art, the bourgeois republic, into a monstrous shape. That republic has lost nothing but the semblance i of respectability. Present-day France was contained in a finished state within the parliamentary republic. It only required a bayonet thrust for the bubble to burst and the monster to spring; forth before our eyes.

Why did the Paris proletariat not rise in revolt after December 2?

The overthrow of the bourgeoisie had as yet been only decreed: the decree had not been carried out. Any serious insurrection of the proletariat would at once have put fresh life into the bourgeoisie, would have reconciled it with the army and ensured a second June defeat for the workers.

On December 4 the proletariat was incited by bourgeois and epicure to fight. On the evening of that day several legions of the National Guard promised to appear, armed and uniformed, on the scene of battle. For the bourgeois and the epicure had got wind of the fact that in one of his decrees of December 2 Bonaparte abolished the secret ballot and enjoined them to record their "yes" or' "no" in the official registers after their names. The resistance of December 4 intimidated Bonaparte. During the night he caused placards to be posted on all the street corners of Paris, announcing the restoration of the secret ballot. The bourgeois and the Spicier believed that they had gained their end. Those who failed to appear next morning were the bourgeois and the epicure.

By a coup de during the night of December 1 to 2, Bonaparte had robbed the Paris proletariat of its leaders, the barricade commanders. An army without officers, averse to fighting under the banner of the Montagnards because of the memories of June 1848 and 1849 and May 1850, it left to its vanguard, the secret societies, the task of saving the insurrectionary honour of Paris, which the bourgeoisie had so unresistingly surrendered to the soldiery that, later on, Bonaparte could sneeringly give as his motive for disarming the National Guard – his fear that its arms would be turned against it itself by the anarchists!

But if the overthrow of the parliamentary republic contains within itself the germ of the triumph of the proletarian revolution, its immediate and palpable result was the victory of Bonaparte over parliament, of the executive power over the legislative power, of force without phrases over the force of phrases. In parliament the nation made its general will the law, that is, it made the law of the ruling class its general will. Before the executive power it renounces all will of its own and submits to the superior command of an alien will, to authority. The executive power, in contrast to the legislative power, expresses the heteronomy of a nation, in contrast to its autonomy. France, therefore, seems to have escaped the despotism of a class only to fall back beneath the despotism, of an individual, and, what is more, beneath the authority of an individual without authority. The struggle seems to be settled in such a way that all classes, equally impotent and equally mute, fall on their knees before the rifle butt.

But the revolution is thorough going. It is still journeying through purgatory. It does its work methodically. By December 2, 1851, it had completed one half of its preparatory work; it is now completing the other half. First it perfected the parliamentary power, in order to be able to overthrow it. Now that it has attained this, it perfects the executive power, reduces it to its purest expression, isolates it, sets it up against itself as the sole target, in order to concentrate all its forces of destruction against it. And when it has done this second half of its preliminary work, Europe will leap from its seat and exultantly exclaim: Well grubbed, old mole!

This executive power with its enormous bureaucratic and military organisation, with its ingenious state machinery, embracing wide strata, with a host of officials numbering half a million, besides an army of another half million, this appalling parasitic body, which enmeshes the body of French society like a net and chokes all its pores, sprang up in the days of the absolute monarchy, with the decay of the feudal system, which it helped to hasten. The seigniorial privileges of the landowners and towns became transformed into so many attributes of the state power, the feudal dignitaries into paid officials and the motley pattern of conflicting mediaeval plenary powers into the regulated plan of a; state authority whose work is divided and centralised as in a factory. The first French Revolution, with its task of breaking all separate local, territorial, urban and provincial powers in order to create the civil unity of the nation, was bound to develop what the absolute monarchy had begun: centralisation, but at the same time the extent, the attributes and the agents of governmental power. Napoleon perfected this state machinery. The Legitimist monarchy and the July monarchy added nothing but a greater division of labour, growing in the same measure as the division of labour within bourgeois society created new groups of interests, and, therefore, new material for state administration. Every common interest was straightway severed from society, counterposed to it as a higher, general interest, snatched from the activity of society's members themselves arid made an object of government activity, from a bridge, a schoolhouse and the communal property of a village community to the railways, the national wealth and the national university of France. Finally, in its struggle against the revolution, the parliamentary republic found itself compelled to strengthen, along with the repressive measures, the resources and centralisation of governmental power. All revolutions perfected this machine instead of smashing it. The parties that contended in turn for domination regarded the possession of this huge state edifice as the principal spoils of the victor.

But under the absolute monarchy, during the first Revolution, under Napoleon, bureaucracy was only the means of preparing the class rule of the bourgeoisie. Under the Restoration, under Louis Philippe, under the parliamentary republic, it was the instrument of the ruling class, however much it strove for power of its own.

Only under the second Bonaparte does the state seem to have made itself completely independent. As against civil society, the state machine has consolidated its position so thoroughly that the chief of the Society of December 10 suffices for its head, an adventurer blown in from abroad, raised on the shield by a drunken soldiery, which he has bought with liquor and sausages, and which he must continually ply with sausage-anew. Hence the downcast despair, the feeling of most dreadful humiliation and degradation that oppresses the breast of France and makes her catch her breath. She feels dishonoured.

And yet the state power is not suspended in mid air. Bonaparte represents a class, and the most numerous class of French society at that, the small-holding' peasants.

Just as the Bourbons were the dynasty of big landed property and just as the Orleans were the dynasty of money, so the Bonartes are the dynasty of the peasants, that is, the mass of the rench people. Not the Bonaparte who submitted to the bourgeois parliament, but the Bonaparte who dispersed the bourgeois parliament is the chosen of the peasantry. For three years the towns had succeeded in falsifying the meaning of the election of December 10 and in cheating the peasants out of the restoration of the empire. The election of December 10, 1848, has been consummated only by the coup d'etat of December 2, 1851.

The small-holding peasants form a vast mass, the members of which live in similar conditions but without entering into manifold relations with one another. Their mode of production isolates them from one another instead of bringing them into mutual intercourse. The isolation is increased by France's bad means of communication and by the poverty of the peasants. Their field of production, the small holding, admits of no division of labour in its cultivation, no application of science and, therefore, no diversity of development, no variety of talent, no wealth no social relationships. Each individual peasant family is almost self-sufficient; it itself directly produces the major part of its consumption and thus acquires its means of life more through exchange with nature than in intercourse with society, A small holding, a peasant and his family; alongside them another small holding, another peasant and another family. A few score of these make up a village, and a few score of villages make up a Department. In this way, the great mass of the French nation is formed by simple addition of homologous magnitudes, much as potatoes in a sack form a sack of potatoes. In so far as millions of families live under economic conditions of existence that separate their mode of life, their interests and their culture from those of the other classes, and put them in hostile opposition to the latter, they form a class. In so far as there is merely a local interconnection among these small-holding peasants, and the identity of their interests begets no community, no national bond and no political organisation among them, they do not! form a class. They are consequently incapable of enforcing their. class interests in their own name, whether through a parliament or through a convention. They cannot represent themselves, they must be represented. Their representative must at the same time appear as their master, as an authority over them, as an unlimited governmental power that protects them against the other classes and sends them rain and sunshine from above. The political influence of the small-holding peasants, therefore, finds its final expression in the executive power subordinating society to itself.

Historical tradition gave rise to the belief of the French peasants in the miracle that a man named Napoleon would bring all the glory back to them. And an individual turned up who gives himself out as the man because he bears the name of Napoleon, in consequence of the Code Napoleon. After a vagabondage of twenty years and after a series of grotesque adventures, the legend finds fulfilment and the man becomes Emperor of the French. The fixed idea of the Nephew was realised, because it coincided with the fixed idea of the most numerous class of the French people.

But, it may be objected, what about the peasant risings in half of France, the raids on the peasants by the army, the mass incarceration and transportation of peasants?

Since Louis XIV, France has experienced no similar persecution of the peasants "on account of demagogic practices."

But let there be no misunderstanding. The Bonaparte dynasty represents not the revolutionary, but the conservative peasant; not the peasant that strikes out beyond the condition of his social existence, the small holding, but rather the peasant who wants to consolidate this holding; not the country folk who, linked up with the towns, want to overthrow the old order through their own energies, but on the contrary those who, in stupefied seclusion within this old order, want to see themselves and their small holdings saved and favoured by the ghost of the empire. It represents not the enlightenment, but the superstition of the peasant; not his judgement, but his prejudice; not his future, but his past; not his modern Cevennes, but his modern Vendee.

The three years' rigorous rule of the parliamentary republic had freed a part of the French peasants from the Napoleonic illusion and had revolutionised them, even if only superficially; but the bourgeoisie violently repressed them, as often as they set themselves in motion. Under the parliamentary republic the modern and the traditional consciousness of the French, peasant contended for mastery. This progress took the form of an incessant struggle between the school-masters and the priests. The bourgeoisie struck down the schoolmasters. For the first time the peasants made efforts to behave independently in the face of the activity of the government. This was shown in the continual conflict between the znaires and the prefects. The bourgeoisie deposed the maires. Finally, during the period of the parliamentary republic, the peasants of different localities rose against their own offspring, the army. The bourgeoisie punished them with states of siege and punitive expeditions. And this same bourgeoisie now cries out about the stupidity of the masses, the vile multitude, that has betrayed it to Bonaparte. It has itself forcibly strengthened the empire sentiments of the peasant class, it conserved the conditions that form the birthplace of this peasant religion. The bourgeoisie, to be sure, is bound to fear the stupidity of the masses as long as they remain conservative, and the insight of the masses as soon as they become revolutionary.

In the risings after the coup d'etat, a part of the French peasants protested, arms in hand, against their own vote of December 10, 1848. The school they had gone through since 1848 had sharpened their wits. But they had made themselves over to the underworld of history; history held them to their word, and the majority was still so prejudiced that in precisely the reddest Departments the peasant population voted openly for Bonaparte. In its view, the National Assembly had hindered his progress. He had now merely broken the fetters that the towns had imposed on the will of the countryside. In some parts the peasants even entertained the grotesque notion of a convention side by side with Napoleon.

After the first revolution had transformed the peasants from semi-villeins into freeholders, Napoleon confirmed and regulated the conditions on which they could exploit undisturbed the soil of France which had only just fallen to their lot and slake their youthful passion for property. But what is now causing the ruin of the French peasant is his small holding itself, the division of the land, the form of property which Napoleon consolidated in France. It is precisely the material conditions which made the feudal peasant a small-holding peasant and Napoleon an emperor. Two generations have sufficed to produce the inevitable result: progressive deterioration of agriculture, progressive indebtedness of the agriculturist. The "Napoleonic" form of property, which at the beginning of the nineteenth century was the condition for the liberation and enrichment of the French country folk, has developed in the course of this century into the law of their enslavement and pauperisation. And precisely this law is the first of the "idles napoleoniennes" which the second Bonaparte has to uphold. If he still shares with the peasants the illusion that the cause of their ruin is to be sought, not in this small-holding-property itself, but outside it, in the influence of secondary circumstances, his experiments will burst like soap bubbles when they come in contract with the relations of production.

The economic development of small-holding property has radically changed the relation of the peasants to the other classes of society. Under Napoleon, the fragmentation of the land in the countryside supplemented free competition and the beginning of big industry in the towns. The peasant class was the ubiquitous protest against the landed aristocracy which had just been overthrown. The roots that small-holding property struck in French soil deprived feudalism of all nutriment. Its landmarks formed the natural fortifications of the bourgeoisie against any surprise attack on the part of its old overlords. But in the course of the nineteenth century the feudal lords were replaced by urban usurers; the feudal obligation that went with the land was replaced by the mortgage; aristocratic landed property was replaced by bourgeois capital. The small holding of the peasant is now only the pretext that allows the capitalist to draw profits, interest and rent from the soil, while leaving it to the tiller of the soil himself to see how he can extract his wages. The mortgage debt burdening the soil of France imposes on the French peasantry payment of an amount of interest equal to the annual interest on the entire British national debt. Small-holding property, in this enslavement by capital to which its development inevitably pushes forward, has transformed the mass of the French nation into troglodytes. Sixteen million peasants (including women and children) dwell in hovels, a large number of which have but one opening, others only two and the most favoured only three. And windows are to a house what the five senses are to the head. The bourgeois order, which at the beginning of the century set the state to stand guard over the newly arisen small holding and manured it with laurels, has become a vampire -that sucks out its blood and brains and throws them into the alchemistic cauldron of capital. The Code Napoleon is now nothing but a codex of distraints, forced sales and compulsory auctions. To the four million (including children, etc.) officially recognised paupers, vagabonds, criminals and prostitutes in France must be added five million who hover on the margin of existence and either have their haunts in the countryside itself or, with their rags and their children, continually desert the countryside for the towns and the towns for the countryside. The interests of the peasants, therefore, are no longer, as under Napoleon, in accord with, but in opposition to the interests of the bourgeoisie, to capital. Hence the peasants find their natural ally and leader in the urban, proletariat, whose task is the overthrow of the bourgeois order. But strong and unlimited government–and this is the second "idee napoleonienne," which the second Napoleon has to carry out–is called upon to defend this "material" order by force. This "ordre materiel" also serves as the catchword in all of Bonaparte's proclamations against the rebellious peasants.

Besides the mortgage which capital imposes on it, the small holding is burdened by taxes. Taxes are the source of life for the bureaucracy, the army, the priests and the court, in short, for the whole apparatus of the executive power. Strong government and heavy taxes are identical. By its very nature, small-holding property forms a suitable basis for an all-powerful and innumerable bureaucracy. It creates a uniform level of relationships and persons over the whole surface of the land. Hence it also permits of uniform action from a supreme centre on all points of this uniform mass. It annihilates the aristocratic intermediate grades between the mass of the people and the state power. On all sides, therefore, it calls forth the direct interference of this state power and the interposition of its immediate organs. Finally, it produces an unemployed surplus population for which there is no place either on the land or in the towns, and which accordingly reaches out for state offices as a sort of respectable alms, and provokes the creation of state posts. By the new marilkets which he opened at the point of the bayonet, by the plundering of the Continent, Napoleon repaid the compulsory taxes with interest. These taxes were a spur to the industry of the peasant, whereas now they rob his industry of its last resources and complete his inability to resist pauperism. And an enormous bureaucracy, well-gallooned and well-fed, is the "idee napoleonienne" which is most congenial of all to the second Bonaparte. How could it be otherwise, seeing that alongside the actual classes of society he is forced to create an artificial caste, for which the maintenance of his regime becomes a bread-and-butter question? Accordingly, one of his first financial operations was the raising of officials' salaries to their old level and the creation of new sinecures.

Another "idee napoleonienne" is the domination of the priests as an instrument of government. But while in its accord with society, in its dependence on natural forces and. its submission to the authority which protected it from above, the small holding that had newly come into being was naturally religious, the small holding that is ruined by debts, at odds with society and authority, and driven beyond its own limitations naturally becomes irreligious. Heaven was quite a pleasing accession to the narrow strip of land just won, more particularly as it makes the weather; it becomes an insult as soon as it is thrust forward as substitute for the small holding. The priest' then appears as only the anointed bloodhound of the earthly police–another "idee napoleonienne." On the next occasion, the expedition against Rome will take place in France itself, but in a sense opposite to that of M. de Montalembert.

Lastly, the culminating point of the "idees napoleoniennes" is the preponderance of the army. The army was the point d'hoimeur of the small-holding peasants, it was they themselves transformed into heroes, defending then - new possessions against the outer world, glorifying then - recently won nationhood, plundering and revolutionising the world. The uniform was their own state dress; war was their poetry; the small holding, extended and rounded off in imagination, was their fatherland, and patriotism the ideal form of the sense of property. But the enemies against whom the French peasant has now to defend his property are not the Cossacks; they are the huissiers and the tax collectors. The small holding lies no longer in the so-called fatherland, but in the register of mortgages. The army itself is no longer the flower of the peasant youth; it is the swamp-flower of the peasant lumpenproletariat. It consists in large measure of remplacants, of substitutes, just as the second Bonaparte is himself only a remplafont, the substitute for Napoleon. It now performs its deeds of valour by hounding the peasants in masses like chamois, by doing gendarme duty, and if the internal contradictions of his system chase the chief of the Society of December 10 over the French border, his army, after some acts of brigandage, will reap, not laurels, but thrashings.

One sees: all "idees napoteoniennes" are ideas of the undeveloped small holding in the freshness of its youth; for the small holding that has - outlived its day they are an absurdity. They are only the hallucinations of its death struggle, words that are transformed into phrases, spirits transformed into ghosts. But the parody of the empire [des Imperialismus] was necessary to free the mass of the French nation from the weight of tradition and to .work out in pure form the opposition between the state power and society. With the progressive undermining of smallholding property, the state structure-erected upon it collapses. The centralisation of the state that modern society requires arises only on the ruins of the military-bureaucratic government machinery which was forged in opposition to feudalism.

The condition of the French peasants provides us with the answer to the riddle of the general elections of December 20 and 21, which bore the second Bonaparte up Mount Sinai, not to receive laws, but to give them.

Manifestly, the bourgeoisie had now no choice but to elect Bonaparte. When the puritans at the Council of Constance complained of the dissolute lives of the popes and wailed about the necessity of moral reform, Cardinal Pierre d'Ailly thundered at them: "Only the devil in person can still save the Catholic Church, and you ask for angels." In like manner, after the coup d'etat, the French bourgeoisie cried: Only the chief of the Society of December 10 can still save bourgeois society! Only, theft can still save property; only perjury, religion; bastardy, the family; disorder, order!

As the executive authority which has made itself an independent power, Bonaparte feels it to be his. mission to safeguard "bourgeois order." But the strength of this bourgeois order lies in the middle class. He looks on himself, therefore, as the representative of the 'muffle' class and issues decrees in this sense. Nevertheless, he is somebody solely due to the fact that he has broken the political power, of this middle class and daily breaks it a new. Consequently, he looks on himself as the adversary of the political and literary power of the middle class. But by protecting its material power, he generates its political power anew. The cause must accordingly be kept alive; but the effect, where it manifests itself, must be done away with. But this cannot pass off without slight confusions of cause and effect, since in their interaction both lose their distinguishing features. New decrees that obliterate the border line. As against the bourgeoisie, Bonaparte looks on himself, at the same time as representative of the peasnts and of the people in general, who wants to make the lower classes of "the people happy within the frame of bourgeois society. New decrees that cheat the "True Socialists" of their statecraft in advance. But, above all, Bonaparte looks on himself as the chief of the Society of December 10, as the representative of the lumpenproletariat to which he himself, his entourage, "his" government-and his army belong, and whose prime consideration is to benefit itself and draw California lottery prizes from the state treasury. And he vindicates his position as chief of the Society of December 10 with decrees, without decrees and despite decrees.

This contradictory task of the man explains the contradictions of his government, the confused groping about which seeks now to win, now to humiliate first one class and then another and arrays all of them uniformly against him, whose practical uncertainty forms a highly comical contrast to the imperious, categorical style of the government decrees, a style which is faithfully copied from the Uncle.

(From *Marx and Engles: Selected Works, Vol.1*, Progress Publishers, Moscow, 1973).

17

The Civil War in France

The centralized state machinery which, with its ubiquitous and complicated military, bureaucratic, clerical and judiciary organs, entoils the living civil society like a boa-constrictor, was first forged in the days of absolute monarchy as a weapon of nascent modern society in its struggle of emancipation from feudalism. The seigniorial privileges of the medieval lords and cities and clergy were feudal dignitaries by salaried state functionaries, transferring the arms from medieval retainers of the landlords and the corporations of townish citizens to a standing army, substituting for the checkered (party coloured) anarchy of conflicting "medieval powers the regulated plan of a state power, with a systematic and hierarchic division of labour. The First French Revolution (1789) with its task to found national unity (to create a nation) had to break down all local, territorial, townish and provincial independence. It was, therefore, forced to develop, what absolute monarchy had commenced, the centralization and organization of state power, and to expand the circumference and the attributes of the state power, the number of its tools, its independence of, and its supernatural its sway of real society which in fact took the place of the medieval super naturalist heaven with its saints. Every minor solitary interest engendered by the relations of social groups was separated from society itself, fixed and made independent of it and opposed to it in the form of state interest, administered by state priests with exactly determined hierarchical functions.

This parasitical civil society, pretending to be its ideal counterpart, grew to its full development under the sway of the first Bonaparte. The restoration and the monarchy of July added nothing to it but a greater division of labour, growing at the same measure in which the division of labour in civil society created new groups of interest, and, therefore, new material for state action.

In their struggle against the Revolution of 1848, the parliamentary republic of France and the governments of all continental Europe, were forced to strengthen, with their measures of repression against the popular movement, the means of action and the centralization of that governmental power. All revolutions thus perfected the state machinery instead of throwing off this deadening incubus. The fractions and parties of the ruling classes which alternately struggled for supremacy, considered the occupancy (control) (seizure) and the direction of this immense machinery of government as the main booty of the victor. It centered in the creation of immense standing armies, a host of state vermin, and huge national debts. During the time of the absolute monarchy it was a means of the struggle of modern society against feudalism, crowned by the French revolution, and under the first Bonaparte it served not only to subjugate the Revolution and annihilate all popular liberties, it was an instrument of the French revolution to strike abroad, to create for France on the Continent instead of feudal monarchies more or less slates after the image of France.

Under the Restoration and the Monarchy of July it became not only a means of the forcible class domination of the middle class, and a means of adding to the direct economic exploitation a second exploitation of the people by assuring to their families all the rich places of the State household. During the time of the Revolutionary struggle of 1848 at last it served as a means of annihilating that Revolution and all aspirations at the emancipation of the popular masses. But the state parasite received only its last development during the second Empire. The governmental power with its standing army, its all directing bureaucracy, its stultifying clergy and its servile tribunal hierarchy, had grown so independent of society itself, that a grotesquely mediocre adventurer Napoleon III with a hungry band of desperadoes behind him sufficed to wield it. It did no longer want the pretext of an armed coalition of old Europe against the modern world founded by the Revolution of 1789. It appeared no longer as a means of class domination, subordinate to its parliamentary ministry or legislature. Humbling under its sway even the interests of the ruling classes, whose parliamentary show-work it supplanted by self-elected Corps Legislatifs and self-paid senates, sanctioned in its absolute sway by universal suffrage, the acknowledged necessity for keeping up 'order', that is the rule of the capitalist and the landlord over the producer, cloaking under the tatters of a maskerade of the past, the orgies of the corruption of the present and the victory of the most parasitic faction, the financial swindler, the debauchery of all the reactionary influences of the past let loose - a pandemonium of infamies the state power had received its last and supreme expression in the Second Empire. Apparently the final victory of this governmental power over society, it was in fact the orgy of all the corrupt elements of that society. To the eye of the uninitiated it appeared only as the victory of the Executive over the legislative, as the final defeat of the form of class rule pretending to be the autocracy of society under its form pretending to be a superior power to society. But in fact it was only the last degraded and the only possible form of that class rule, as humiliating to those classes themselves as to the working classes which they kept fettered by it.

The 4th of September 1870: the proclamation of the republic, following Napoleon III's defeat and capture by the Prussians at Sedan was only the vindication of the Republic against the grotesque adventurer that had assassinated it. The true antithesis to the Empire itself - that is to the state power, the centralized executive, of which the Second Empire was only the exhausting formula - was the Commune. This state power forms in fact the creation of the middle class, first a means to break down feudalism, then a means to crush the emancipatory aspirations of the producers, of the working class. All reactions and all revolutions had only served to transfer that organised power - the organised force of the slavery of labour - from one hand to the other, from one fraction of the ruling classes to the other. It had served the ruling classes as a means of subjugation. It had sucked new forces from every new change. It had served as the instrument of breaking down every popular rise and served it to crush the working classes after they had fought and been ordered to secure its transfer from one part of its oppressors to the others. This was, therefore, a Revolution not against this or that, legitimate constitutional, republican or imperialist form of state power. It was a revolution against the State itself, this supernatural abortion of society, a resumption by the people for the people, of its own social life. It was not a revolution to transfer it from one fraction of the ruling classes to the other, but a Revolution to break down this horrid machinery of class domination itself.

It was only the working class that could formulate by the word 'Commune' and initiate by the fighting Commune of Paris - this new aspiration. Even the last expression of that state power in the Second Empire although humbling for the pride of the ruling classes and casting to the winds their parliamentary preventions of self-government, had been only the last possible form of their class rule. While politically dispossessing them, it was the orgy under which all the economic and social infamies of their regime got full sway. The middling bourgeoisie and the petty middle class were by their economical conditions of life excluded from initiating a new revolution and induced to follow in the tracks of the ruling classes or be the followers of the working class. The peasants were the passive economical basis of the Second Empire, of that last triumph of a State separate of and independent from society. Only the Proletarians, fired by a new social task to accomplish by them for all society, to do away with all classes and class rule, were the men to break the instrument of that class rule - the State, the centralized and organized governmental power usurping to be the master instead of the servant of society. In the active struggle against them by the ruling classes, supported by the passive adherence of the peasantry, the Second Empire, the last crowning at the same time as the most signal prostitution of the State - which had taken the place of the medieval church - had been engendered. It had sprung into life against them. By them it was broken, not as a peculiar form of centralized governmental power, but as its most powerful, elaborated into seeming independence from society expression, and, therefore, also its most prostitute reality, covered by infamy from top to bottom, having centered in absolute corruption at home and absolute powerlessness abroad.

The Commune - the reabsorption of the State power by society, as its own living forces instead of as forces controlling and subduing it, by the popular masses themselves, forming their own force instead of the organized force of their suppression - the political form of their social emancipation, instead of the artificial force appropriated by their oppressors their own force opposed to and organized against them of society wielded for their oppression by their enemies. The form was simple like all great things. The Commune first displaced the army by the National Guard. The people had only to organize this militia on a national scale to have done away with the standing armies; the first economical conditio sine qua non for all social improvements, discarding at once this source of taxes and state debt, and this constant danger to government usurpation of class rule - of the regular class rule or an adventurer pretending to save all classes at the same time the safest guarantee against foreign aggression and making in fact the costly military apparatus impossible in all other states; the emancipation of the peasant from the blood tax and the most fertile source of all state taxation and state debts. Here already the point in which the Commune is a bait for the peasant, the first word of his emancipation. With the 'independent police abolished, and its ruffians supplanted by servants of the Commune. The general suffrage, till now abused either for the parliamentary sanction of the Holy State power, or a play in the hands of the ruling classes, only employed by the people to choose the instruments of parliamentary class rule once in many years, adapted to its real purposes, to choose by the communes their own functionaries of administration and initiation.

Gone is the Delusion as if administration and political governing were mysteries, transcendent functions only to be trusted to the hands of a trained caste, state parasites, richly paid sycophants and sinecurists, in the higher posts, absorbing the intelligences of the masses and turning them against themselves in the lower places of the hierarchy. Doing away with the state hierarchy altogether and replacing the haughteous masters of the people by its always removable servants, a mock responsibility by a real responsibility, as they act continuously under public supervision. Paid like skilled workmen, 12 pounds a month. The whole sham of state mysteries and state pretensions was done away with by a Commune, mostly consisting of simple working men, organizing the defence of Paris, carrying war against the Pretorians of Bonaparte, securing the approvisionment of that immense town, filling all the posts hitherto divided between Government, police, and Prefecture, doing their work publicly, simply, under the most difficult and complicated circumstances, and doing it, as Milton did his Paradise Lost, for a few pounds, acting in bright daylight, with no pretensions to infallibility, not hiding itself behind circumlocution office, not ashamed to confess blunders by correcting them. Making in one order the public functions - military, administrative, political - real workmen's functions, instead of the hidden attributes of a trained caste; keeping order in the turbulence of civil war and revolution initiating measures of general regeneration. Whatever the merits of the single measures of the Commune, its greatest measure was its own organization.

With all the great towns organized into Communes after the model of Paris no government could repress the movement by the surprise of sudden reaction. All France organized into self-working and self-governing communes, the standing army replaced by the popular militias, the army of state parasites removed, the clerical hierarchy displaced by the schoolmaster, the state judges transformed into communal organs, the suffrage for the National representation not a matter of sleight of hand for an all powerful government, but the deliberate expression of organized communes, the state functions reduced to a few functions for general national purposes.

Such is the Commune - the political form of the social emancipation, of the liberation of labour from the usurpation of the slave holding monopolists of the means of labour, created by the labourers themselves or forming the gift of nature. As the state machinery and parliamentarism are not the real life of the ruling classes, but only the organized general organs of their dominion, the political guarantees and forms and expressions of the old order of things, so the Commune is not the social movement of the working class and therefore of a general regeneration of mankind but the organized means of action. The Commune does not do away with the class struggles, through which the working classes strive for the abolition of all classes and, therefore, of all class rule because it does not represent a particular interest. It represents the liberation of 'labour', that is the fundamental and natural condition of individual and social life which only by usurpation, fraud, and artificial contrivances can be shifted from the few upon the many, but it affords the rational medium in which that class struggle can run through its different phases in the most rational and human way. It could start violent reactions and as violent revolutions. It begins the emancipation of labour - its great goal - by doing away with the unproductive and mischievous work of the state parasites, by cutting away the springs which sacrifice an immense portion of the national produce to the feeding of the state-monster, on the one side, by doing, on the other, the real work of administration, local and national, for workingmen's wages. It begins therefore with an immense saving, with economical reform as well as political transformation.

The working class know that they have to pass through different phases of class struggle. They know that the superseding of the economical conditions of the slavery of labour by the conditions of free and associated labour can only be the progressive work of time, (that economical transformation) that they require not only a change of distribution, but a new organization of production, or rather the delivery (setting free) of the social forms of production in present organized labour (engendered by present industry) of the trammels of slavery, of their present class character, and their harmonious national and international coordination. They know that this work of regeneration will be again and again relented and impeded by the resistances of vested interests and class egotisms. They know that the present 'spontaneous action of the natural laws of capital and landed property' can only be superseded by 'the spontaneous action of the laws of the social economy of free and associated labour', by a long process of development of new conditions, as was the 'spontaneous action of the economic laws of slavery' and the 'spontaneous action of the economical laws of serfdom'. But they know at the same time that great strides may be taken at once through the Communal form of political organization and that the time has come to begin that movement for themselves and mankind.

(From *Marx and Eagles: Selected Works, Vol.2*, Progress Publishers, Moscow, 1973)

18

Communist Manifesto

Written in December 1847 and January 1848 at the behest of a small and mainly German revolutionary group, the Communist League, founded in the summer of 1847, it was published in London in February 1848 under the title Manifesto of the Communist Party. Although it appeared under the names of both Marx and Engels, its main author was Marx, but a number of its ideas and formulations are to be found in Engels's *Principles of Communism*, written in October 1847.

The first English translation of the Communist Manifesto, by Helen Mactarlane, was published in the Chartist journal, The Red Republican, whose editor was Julian Harney, between June and November 1850. A new translation by Samuel Moore in 1888 was edited and supplied with notes by Engels. To mark the centenary of the Manifesto, the National Executive Committee of the Labour party decided in 1947 on the publication of a new edition. This appeared in 1948 with a lengthy introduction by Harold J. Laski.

The Manifesto is the product of a period of intense intellectual and political activity for Marx and Engels, during which they fashioned a new 'world-view'. Much was added by both men in subsequent years to that 'world-view'; but the Manifesto nevertheless forms the essential framework for what later came to be known as Marxism – a term which Marx himself never used.

One of the most remarkable features of the Manifesto is its perception, at a time when industrial capitalism was still in its early stages, of the revolutionary impact it was bound to have for the whole world, and of 'the most revolutionary part' which the bourgeoisie was called upon to play. 'The bourgeoisie', Marx and Engels wrote, 'cannot exist without constantly revolutionizing the instruments of production, and thereby the relations of production, and with them the whole relations of society.

Constant revolutionizing of production, uninterrupted disturbance of all social conditions, everlasting uncertainty and agitation distinguish the bourgeois epoch from all earlier ones.' However, the Manifesto proclaimed, the bourgeoisie had also brought into being its 'gravediggers', the modern proletariat. In due course, and as a result of many struggles over objectives large and small, the working class would assume a revolutionary role and liberate itself and the whole of society from minority rule and class domination, For whereas 'all previous historical movements were movements of minorities, or in the interests of minorities', the proletarian movement 'is the self-conscious, independent movement of the immense majority, in the interests of the immense majority'. Nor was this emancipation conceived in national terms alone; on the contrary it would encompass the whole world, a notion encapsulated in the closing words of the Manifesto: 'Working Men of All Countries, Unite!'

One section of the Manifesto concerns the role of communists in this process; and it is noteworthy that, despite its title, the document affirms that 'the communists do not form a separate party opposed to other working-class parties.' Their role was rather to be 'the most advanced and resolute section of the working-class parties of every country'.

The final section of the Manifesto consists of a sharp critique of contemporary currents of thought which, though critical of the existing social order, proposed alternatives to it which Marx and Engels denounced as spurious or inadequate. They readily acknowledged that what they called 'Critical-Utopian Socialism and Communism' was full of the most valuable insights for the enlightenment of the working class; but they also condemned it for its repudiation of class struggle and its rejection of revolutionary activity.

In prefaces which they wrote for later editions, Marx and Engels said that some aspects of the Manifesto needed amendment, notably the immediate programme of reforms which it proposed; but they also said that they stood by the 'general principles' laid down in the document. In the preface of 1872 to like third German edition of the Manifesto, they also emphasized that the experience of the revolution of 1848, and particularly of the Paris Commune of 1871, had shown that 'the working class cannot simply lay hold of the ready-made state machinery, and wield it for its own purposes'; and this was repeated by Engels in the 1888 preface to the English edition. The point was to be given central importance in Lenin's '*State and Revolution*', published in 1917.

The Communist Manifesto is the most influential political pamphlet ever written. It has been translated into dozens of languages and it has been an inspiration to successive generations throughout the world. Its appearance in 1848 was a major landmark in the history of socialism; and for all the amendments and qualifications which it requires, the passage of time has scarcely dimmed the sweep and power of its message.

The Communist Manifesto published in February, 1848, the single most influential text written in the nineteenth century. Our theme in other words, is anything but antiquarian. We are interested in the Manifesto now, to see both why it was such a uniquely influential text, and what light it can still throw on our situation today.

The Manifesto was a radically new kind of political document, breaking entirely new ground rhetorically as well as analytically, and in its conception of the relation between theory and practice; but it was also a product of much more than the genius of one man. Its subsequent fame and influence have tended to obscure the fact that it was very much the product of a political movement, at the time far from strong or even popular.

Marx and his fellow activists had been living through a period of reaction, as we are; the defiant language of the Manifesto bears no relation to the actual strength of the social forces they sought to mobilise and represent. What it does testify to is their determination not to be intimidated by the strength of the forces ranged against them, their capacity to look beyond that strength to the contradictions undermining it, and – above all – their acceptance of responsibility for trying to bring about change. People have either to organise themselves to carry out joint actions or to reconcile themselves to their fates'. No document has ever made this clearer than the Manifesto.

As for the light that the Manifesto throws on contemporary problems, two things stand out. One is how much of the global expansion of capitalism, now reaching something of a climax, is not merely foreshadowed, but analysed with phenomenal precision in the Manifesto. So far from Marx being a 'deal dog' (as he himself in his postscript to Capital complained people were making Hegel out to be) he is very much alive and biting. Not to avow oneself a pupil of Marx, in the same sense that he avowed himself 'the pupil' of Hegel – i.e. to distance oneself clearly from the condescensions of 'post Marxism' would be petty and absurd. One the other hand, even where the

Manifesto was wrong, or left problems unresolved, or where contemporary problems fall outside its scope, its way of approaching problems has stood the test of time.

Why Manifesto of the Communist Party? Why not 'programme', 'platform', or 'declaration of principles'? Why not 'decree' or 'proclamation'? The noun 'manifesto' has the currency it enjoys today, and not just in English, largely because of Marx's own choice of the word. Even though he did not invent it he is likely to have adopted it from an important source, it is Marx who bears much or even most of the responsibility for putting the word on our lexicological map.

Not just in English: this gives us an important clue. Manifestation in French means 'demonstration shading over into 'protest'. Manifestant is the French or German, manifestante the Spanish or Italian, for 'demonstrator'. 'Manifestant' was sometimes used in English after the 1860s, but was duly supplanted by the word 'demonstrator' or 'protester'. The German verb manifestieren means 'to declare'; the Italian nouns manifestazione and manifestino mean 'performance' and 'leaflet, pamphlet or broadside' respectively.

Thus far 'manifesto' seems to mean that which makes manifest, or demonstrates – demonstrates in the additional sense in scientific truth is demonstrated, by being made public or visible. A manifesto can have nothing arcane or recondite about it. It has to be accessible. One could of course say the same about decrees or edicts. Yet a manifesto cannot be equated with a proclamation because it is not necessarily issued from a position of power, on the contrary, demonstrations or manifestations are generally protests, public protests, against what those in positions of power get up to, or away with. They involve that we make our voices heard, and that we be willing to put ourselves, our bodily safety, on the line. Manifestos in Latin literally means 'struck by the hand' but came to have the meaning of 'evident, clear or plain'. But this is only part of its meaning in English too, as a glance at historical dictionaries will reveal. Webster's gives us for the verb 'to manifest' the following, to be sure: 'to reveal, make appear, show plainly, make public, disclose to the eye or understanding': Webster's goes on to give us 'to reveal, show, exhibit, display, declare, or discover'. In keeping with this, the only non-obselete usage of 'manifest' as a noun in English means a list of a ship's cargo, an invoice that is to be shown or exhibited at the customhouse. Accordingly, the OED adds to Webster's inventory of meaning of the verb 'to manifest' these others: 'to be evidence of, prove or attest; to expound or unfold; to display, to give evidence of possessing, to reveal the presence of, to evince'.

Yet, intriguingly, these apparently anodyne listings are not the synonyms of 'manifest' they might appear to' be at first glance. To see this we must turn again to Webster's characterization of 'manifest', this time as an adjective: 'What is clear can be seen in all its bearings; what is plain can be seen by any man without study or reflection what is obvious lies directly in the way, and must be seen by everyone; what is evident is seen forcibly, and leaves no hesitation in the mind; what is manifest is evident in a very high degree, striking upon the mind at once with overpowering conviction'. This hits the nail on the head. If anything is to be manifest, it has to be made manifest. And making manifest is precisely what Marx is up to in the Communist Manifesto, in a variety of different, though interdependent, senses. Making manifest, so understood, is not just a form of words. It is a kind of action as Marx, was perfectly well aware.

First we must undertake a detour, for there is another understanding of 'manifestation,' not touched on above, that has enjoyed some recent intellectual currency for all the wrong reasons. This is its understanding as 'apparition'. In some ways regrettably, it has become impossible to write about Marx's Manifesto during the 1990s without invoking Jacques Derrida's *Specter of Marx*, which is itself an invocation of Marx. Derrida, to be brief, wants the 'spectre haunting Europe' in the Manifesto's opening line be haunting Marx too – as an instance of the uncanny much as Freud had understood the term. The reasons why Derrida wants to make this move, indeed the reasons why has become so suddenly fashionable for the first time, can only briefly occupy us here., Derrida wants the spectre haunting Europe to be haunting Marx too for reasons having much more to do with 'spectrality as such than with Marx. Derrida gives 'spectrality' a great deal of work to do; he believes that a world purged or cleansed of 'spectrality' – much as he assigns this understanding of 'spectrality' to Marx would be a world of pure presence, immediacy, materiality, objectivity, facticity, a reified world of things that lack a past dimension. Such a world would correspond to Fukuyama's notorious 'end of history', which Derrida nicely, and correctly, terms 'apocalyptic'. Without 'spectrality', Derrida claims, philosophy would be displaced by a bland Anglo-American anti-speculative positivism and empiricism. Whether or not 'spectraiity', so understood, is the legitimate counterpart to the very globalizing tendencies Derrida is surely right to detest depends on whether more is made to hang on the hook of the concept of 'specrrattfy' than it can reasonably be expected to bear. Overload seems distinctly likely: but over and above this question, a fairly obvious interjection - one which seems not to have occurred to Derrida - imposes itself. This is that twentieth-century 'spectrality' can be imposed by technological means. The Walter Benjamin that Derrida invokes calls upon us to preserve and sustain a 'weak messianic' power in dark patches of our history, but we should remember that this same Walter Benjamin also wrote '*The Work of Art in the Age of Mechanical Reproduction*', for reproduction these days can, and commonly does, include the reproduction of 'spectrality' itself.

Derrida reads Marx's spectre as what French term a revenant, that which comes or comes again from beyond the grave to haunt and horrify the living. While this interpretation - and all translation is interpretation, as Derrida is only too well aware – enables Derrida to inscribe Marx within a 'hauntology' by which Derrida himself is evidently ensorcelled, there are problems with it.

The first is that Marx's spectre may not be a revenant in the above sense at all. It is noteworthy that the most recent, and most accomplished, translation into English of the Manifesto 'A spectre stalks the land of Europe'. 'Stalks' as a verb of motion is a much more likely translation of the German verb umgehen in than is 'haunts', and was so in Marx's day as in our own. In view of the entire, immense, superstructure Derrida erects on the basis of a much less orthodox translation of Marx's celebrated opening outline a second problem. Who is supposed to be afraid of Marx's spectre? Marx himself immediately specifies the 'holy alliance' the real-life Holy Alliance of the 'Congress System', 'of Pope and Tsar, Metternich and Guizot, French radicals and German Police'. While these may have recoiled in various degrees of horror, feigned or otherwise, at the spectre they themselves had invented and invoked, it is more to the point that they were bent on seeing to it, with every power at their disposal, that others should quake in their boots at the onset of this apparition. The Holy Alliance, after all, was not made up holy innocents; they were an instance of full-fledged reaction with blood on their hands. If 'all that is holy is profaned,' why should the self-proclaimed Holy Alliance, of all people, be exempt? The 'spectre of communism' was one they conjured up to make people afraid of it.

Witches may never have existed they too were 'apparitions' – but witchhunts invariably found them all the same. Witchhunts accuse others, those their perpetrators call witches, of conjuring up evil spirits; but, in a neat ideological inversion, witchhunts themselves conjure up witches on? evil spirits. They willfully mischaractertize the objects of their concern to the point of inventing them out of thin air, or of callimg them into being.

Witchhunts had needed witchcraft to the extent of inventing it, of calling their adversaries, witches, into being. So too anti-communist witchhunts, their heirs and successors, need their own spectral communists, to the point of finding these where none exist, producing real victims who are likely to be guilty of nothing at all. Examples, sad to say, abound.

Marx, whatever Derrida may think, is unafraid of the spectre the Holy Alliance and its lackeys had conjured up. His object in the Manifesto is in large part to dispel such fears. 'It is high time for communists to lay before the world their perspectives, their goals, their principles and to counterpose to the horror stories of communism a manifesto of the party itself'. Marx wished to instill - which means that if the spectre stalking the land is spirit not made flesh, this is to be understood as meaning spirit not yet made flesh. It is unsubstantiated, perhaps, but this is to say that it awaits its substantiation, a substantation that only Marx and his readers can give it.

Marx's spectre does not hark back to anything that came before it. It doesn't come from beyond the grave to plague or torment us. It is not a reminder of some past or primordial existence. It is meant to point forwards, protectively and prospectively, not backwards and retroactively. And this is to say that there is, quite simply, nothing uncanny about it at all, whatever Derrida and others may think. Quite to the contrary, Marx's spectre sets us the task of finding it a home or making it a home in the world. It is not dreadful save to those who have prior cause to dread its advent. To the rest of us it is a tocsin, a call to action. As Frederic Jameson has pointed out, the Hamlet Marx's spectre suggested to Derrida was itself 'not a ghost story'; 'it did not merely tell about some grisly hold of the past on the present... but rather showed the apparition of the past in the act of provoking future action and calling for retribution by the living'. To extend Jameson's point, the 'spectriality' of the future differs in kind from that of the past (or of the revenant). While it too may not be at one with the present, this is the case only to the extent that 'its blurred lineaments... announce or foretell themselves'. Because Marx's Manifesto is in this sense proleptic in its argumentation, the spectriality Derrida misprises is in fact a 'form of the most radical politicization far from being locked into the repetitions of neurosis and obsession it is energetically future-oriented and active. And in this way, as Jameson proceeds to indicate, 'the spectrality of the future... answers to the haunting spectrality of the past, which is historicity itself.

The spectre circulating, then in Europe and later elsewhere, may have been in a certain sense wraithlike - but not, surely 'not, in the sense of being a revenantor reminder. It was then something originary and unprecedented. It seemed wraithlike and threatening because the Holy Alliance and its minions, in their outrage and condemnation, could not give it form, could not even see or identify it clearly, but their rhetoric created a space in which Marx could etch this notoriously bold outlines. Why else could Marx have insisted so only that people were 'compelled to face with sober senses' something that, to others presented to the world as sheer delirium or nightmare? The disembodiment of Marx's spectre is purely provisional; it awaits the embodiment that the Manifesto - that the Manifestos very language – proceeded, with no small flourish, to given it. In its pages Marx is openly, publicly, ostentatiously, brazenly declaring himself and his collaborators to be communists, in so doing he is naming communism itself, identifying it as a doctrine, movement and method of social analysis. He is pulling it together, fusing and synthesizing tendencies which, but for his efforts, might have remained fissiarous or even contradictory. He is seizing the time, giving substance to something that appeared to the cowed and craven to be frightening as mere form. Marx's writing the Manifesto of the Communist Party was an act of unexampled and audacious theoretical originality.

No doubt what Marx accomplished in the Manifesto is almost immesurable. It has to be his most engage book to date. But the dimensions of Marx's accomplishment cannot be gauged or even approached if we isolate the Manifesto, as though it were a set-piece, from the body of Marx's thought and action as a whole. Far from wishing to underestimate or misprize one of Marx's most engage writings under the impress of current events, we propose to raise the stakes of my argument by proposing that even a hundred and fifty years after its composition, we have not even begun to think through the enormity of what Marx achieved as a theorist when he wrote it.

Marx may have been guilty of a certain hubris when he wrote in *The German Ideology* that 'where speculation ends, in real life ... real, positive science begins. My point is that Marx's claim had a real content to it, and that having advanced it he did not rest content, 'blissfully satisfied with his own construction'. He proceeded to act it out, to put it into practice, and to give it bodily form. Marx's insight was simply - that theory, to be effective, can no longer rest content with producing empty, abstract nostrums of the kind that would put the world to rights by virtue of their very elaboration, or their intellectual elegance. If people fail to act on the basis of their beliefs – as Marx proceeded to act on the basis of his - they might as well be whistling in the dark in propounding or expounding such beliefs, or indulging themselves in what Marx had already, archly.

Sheldon Wolin has pointed out, Marx founded a new conception of politics, revolutionary in intent, proletarian in concern, and internationalist in scope and organization'. This new conception of what politics could, and should become involved a new conception of theory with which we still need to come to terms. The point here is not that Marx was alone in devoting his life to a revolutionary cause he regarded as an urgent agenda. The merest glance at the wonderland of nineteenth-century revolutionary theorizing would show that Marx did not lack for company, or even companionship, in this quest. Yet there is something singular about Marx's project that lodges in the mind. In 1857 we find him writing to Engels: 'I am working madly through the nights so that, before the deluge, I shall at least have the outlines clear'. Small wonder, perhaps that Prometheus was the most inspiring 'saint' on Marx's calendar. But it is a matter, surely, not just of Prometheus, the bringer of fire, but also of Archimedes: Marx views theorizing as a lever with which to move the world. And whatever we may think of the movement he effected, it did move the world.

The Marxian enterprise was in the fullest sense of the term of a political enterprise. The Manifesto in particular gave expression to a wish that the scope of politics, and of theory, be extended, given more meaning and greater resonance than politics or theory had ever had heretofore. Only such an expansion, we should still remember, can render the 'revolutionary unity of theory and practice' anything other than an empty phrase. Such a unity of the theoretical and the practical, the Manifesto could also remind us, cannot be an arbitrary juxtaposition, but only a genuine convergence or confluence of forces that could otherwise remain as antagonistic in perpetuity as they still are today.

The Manifesto of the Communist Party may be the most widely read political pamphlet in human history, but it is the most misleadingly titled: no such party existed. Nor, was it conceived as a manifesto. What the members of the Communist League wanted in 1847 was a 'profession of faith', and an early draft written by Engels in June 1847 shows that they were still wedded to the initiation rituals favoured by the French underground sects:

Engels's catechism might have been appropriate for a secret society such as the old League of Outlaws or the League of the just – but this was the furtive, conspiratorial tradition from which Marx wanted to rescue the new Communist League. Why, he demanded, should revolutionaries hide their views and intentions?

Marx was a born leader of the people. His speech was brief, convincing and compelling in is logic. He never said a superfluous word; every sentence was a thought and every thought was a necessary link in the chain of his demonstration. Marx had nothing of dreamer about him. Marx represented the manhood socialist thought.

By the end of the ten-day marathon, Marx and Engels had carried all before them. The June congress, which Marx had not attended, had declared merely that the League aims at the emancipation of humanity by spreading the theory of the community of property and its speediest possible practical introduction. The rules adopted at the second congress were far more combative and robust: 'The aim of the League is the overthrow of the old bourgeoisie, the rule of the proletariat, the abolition of the old bourgeois society which rests on the antagonism of classes, and the foundation of a new society without classes and without private property.' The delegates agreed these basic principles unanimously, and Marx and Engels were commissioned to draw up a manifesto summarising the new doctrine as soon as possible. Marx seemed in no great hurry to comply.

Kierkegaard says somewhere that life must be lived forwards but can only be understood backwards. This applies also to eras and epochs: the reality of a particular age many not become apparent until it is drawing to a close. Or, as Hegel wrote in his *Philosophy of Right*, 'the owl of Minerva spreads his wings only with the falling of the dusk'. When Marx wrote the Communist Manifesto, in January 1848, he imagined he could see the wise owl once more preparing for flight: the brief but brilliant era of bourgeois capitalism had served its transitional purpose and would soon be buried under its own contradictions. By driving hitherto isolated workers into mills and factories, modern industry had created the very conditions in which the proletariat could associate and combine into a dominant force. What the bourgeoisie, therefore, produces, above all, is its own grave-diggers, he noted with satisfaction at the end of the Manifesto's first section. Its fall and the victory of the proletariat are equally inevitable.

Perhaps because he thought he was rehearsing a funeral oration, he could afford to be generous to his vanquished foe. Those who have never read Marx, but know of him merely as some kind of blood-thirsty bogeyman whose name is invoked to terrify the middle classes, are often surprised to discover how much praise he lavished on the bourgeoisie. He was not a man to underestimate the enemy's achievement.

The bourgeoisie, historically, has played a most revolutionary part. The bourgeoisie, wherever it has got the upper land, has put an end to all feudal, patriarchal, idyllic relation. It has pitilessly torn asunder the motley feudal ties that bound man to his 'natural superiors', and has left remaining no other nexus between man and man than naked self–interest, than callous 'cash payment'. It has drowned the most heavenly ecstasies of religious fervour, of chivalrous enthusiasm, philistine sentimentalism, in the icy water of egotistical calculation. It has resolved personal worth into exchange value, and in place of the numberless indefeasible chartered freedoms has set up that single, unconscionable freedom- Free Trade. In one word, for exploitation, veiled by religious and political illusions, it has substituted naked, shameless, direct, brutal exploitatio.

The bourgeoisie has disclosed how it came to pass that the brutal display of vigour in the Middle Ages, which reactionists so much admire, found its fitting complement in the most slothful indolence. It has been the first to show what man's activity can bring about. It has accomplished wonders far surpassing Egyptian pyramids, Roman aqueducts and Gothic cathedrals; it has conducted expeditions that put in the shade all former Exoduses of nations and crusades.

One modern critic has described the Manifesto as 'a lyrical celebration of bourgeois works'. And so it is, after a fashion: Marx was celebrating capitalism as a temporary phenomenon, as the harbinger of a true revolution. But what he took to be its death throes were in fact nothing more than birth pangs. The signs he misinterpreted – the howls, the thrashing limbs, the blood- spattered sheets – are even more conspicuous today than in his own time, though he is seldom given any credit for noting them. The bourgeoisie has through its exploitation of the world market given a cosmopolitan character to production and consumption in every country, he pointed out. In place of the old wants, satisfied by the productions of the country, we find new wants, requiring for their satisfaction the products of distant lands and climes. Anyone surveying the fruit and veg counter in a supermarket – piled high with mangoes, avocados, sugar-snap peas and out-of- season strawberries – will see what he meant.

While importing exotica, the bourgeoisie foists its own products, tastes and habits on everyone else: 'In one word, it creates a world after its own image'. To recognise the truth of this, one need only visit Beijing – the capital of an avowedly communist state- where the city centre nor looks verily like Main Street, USA, with McDonald's , Kentucky Fried Chicken, Haagen – Dazs and Pizza Hut, plus several branches of Chase Manhattan and Citibank in which to deposit the profits.

'As in material, so also in intellectual production,' the Manifesto continued. 'The intellectual creation of individual nations become common property. The bourgeoisie, by the rapid improvement of all instruments of production, by the immensely facilitated means of communication, draws all, even the most barbarian nations, into civilisation'. One can argue about whether Arnold Schwarzenegger, John Grisham and non-stop MTV really constitute 'civilisation', but the essential truth of his perception can't be denied. He also understood that the pace of technological change would become ever more frantic, creating a sort of permanent revolution where any computer software bought more than a couple of years ago is all but obsolete. **–Editor**

A spectre is haunting Europe – the spectre of communism. All the powers of old Europe have entered into a holy alliance to exorcise this spectre: Pope and Tsar, Metternich and Guizot, French Radicals and German police-spies.

The history of all hitherto existing society is the history of class struggles.

Freeman and slave, patrician and plebeian, lord and serf, guild-master and journeyman, in a word, oppressor and oppressed stood in constant opposition to one another, carried on an interrupted, now hidden, now open fight, a fight that each time ended, either in a revolutionary reconstruction of society at large, or in the common ruin of the contending classes.

The bourgeoisie, historically, has played a most revolutionary part.... It has been the first to show what man's activity can bring about It has accomplished wonders far surpassing Egyptian pyramids, Roman aqueducts, and Gothic cathedrals; it has conducted expeditions that put in the shade all former Exoduses of nations and crusades.

The bourgeoisie cannot exist without constantly revolutionising the instruments of production, and thereby the relations of production, and with them the whole relations of society. Conservation of the old modes of production in unaltered form was, on the contrary, the first condition of existence for all earlier industrial classes. Constant revolutionising of production, uninterrupted disturbance of all social conditions, everlasting uncertainty and agitation distinguish the bourgeois epoch from all earlier ones. All fixed, fast-frozen relations, with their train of ancient and venerable prejudices and opinions, arc swept away, all new-formed ones become antiquated before they can ossify. All that is solid melts into air all that is holy is profaned, and man is at last compelled to face with sober senses, his real conditions of life, and his relations us with his kind.

The need of a constantly expanding market for its products chases the bourgeoisie over the whole surface of the globe. It must nestle everywhere, settle everywhere, establish connections everywhere.

The bourgeoisie has through its cosmopolitan character given a cosmopolitan character to production and consumption in every country. To the great chagrin of Reactionists, it has drawn from under the feet of industry the national ground on which it stood. All old-established national industries have been destroyed or are daily being destroyed. They are dislodged by new industries, whose introduction becomes a life and death question for all civilised nations by industries that no longer work up indigenous raw materials, but raw material drawn from the remotest zones; industries whose products are consumed, not only at home, but in every quarter of the globe. In place of the old wants, satisfied by the productions of the country, we find new wants, requiring for their satisfaction the products of distant lands and climes. In place of the old local and national seclusion and self-sufficiency, we have intercourse in every direction, universal interdependence of nations. And as in material, so also in intellectual production. The intellectual creations of individual nations become common property. National one-sidedness and narrow-mindedness become more and more impossible, and from the numerous national and local literatures, there arises a world literature.

The bourgeoisie, by the rapid improvement of all instruments of production, by the immensely facilitated means of communication, draws all, even the most barbarian, nations into civilisation. The cheap prices of its commodities are the heavy artillery with which it batters down all Chinese walk with which it forces the barbarians obstinate haired of foreigners to capitulate. It compels all nations, on pain of extinction, to adopt the bourgeois mode of production; it compels them to introduce what it calls civilisation into their midst, i.e., to become bourgeois themselves. In one word, it creates a world after its own image.

The bourgeoisie has subjected the country to the rule of the towns. It has created enormous cities, has greatly increased the urban population as compared with the rural, and has thus rescued a considerable part of the population from the idiocy of rural life. Just as it has made the country dependent on the towns, so it has made barbarian and semi-barbarian countries dependent on the civilised ones, nations of peasants on nations of bourgeois, the East on the West.

The bourgeoisie keeps more and more doing away with the scattered state of the population, of the means of production, and of property. It has agglomerated population, centralised means of production, and' has concentrated property in a few hands. The necessary consequence of this was political centralisation. Independent, or but loosely connected provinces with separate interests, laws, governments and systems of taxation, became lumped together into one nation, with one government, one code of laws, one national class-interest, one frontier and one customs-tariff.

The bourgeoisie, during its rule of scarce one hundred years, has created more massive and more colossal productive forces than have all preceding generations together. Subjection of Nature's forces to man, machinery, application of chemistry to industry and agriculture, steam-navigation, railways, electric telegraphs, canalisation of rivers, whole imputations conjured out of the ground what earlier century had even a presentiment that such productive forces slumbered in the lap of social labour?

A similar movement is going on before our own eyes. Modern bourgeois society with its relations of production, of exchange and of property, a society that has conjured up such gigantic means of production and of exchange, is like the sorcerer who is no longer able to control the powers of the nether world whom he has called up by his spells. For many a decade past the history of industry and commerce is but the history of the revolt of modern productive forces against modern conditions of production, against the property relations that are the conditions for the existence of the bourgeoisie and of its rule.

The bourgeoisie itself therefore, supplies the proletariat with its own elements of political and general education, in other words, it furnishes the proletariat with weapons for fighting the bourgeoisie.

Further, as we have already seen, entire sections of the ruling classes are, by the advance of industry, precipitated into the proletariat, or are at least threatened in their conditions of existence. These also supply the proletariat with fresh elements of enlightenment and progress.

Finally, in times when the class struggle nears the decisive hour, the dissolution going on within the ruling class, in fact within whole range of old society, assumes such a violent, glaring character, that a small section of the ruling class cuts itself adrift, and joins the revolutionary class, the class that holds the future in its hands. Just as, therefore, at an earlier period, a section of the nobility went over to the bourgeoisie, so now a portion of the bourgeoisie goes over the proletariat, and in particular, a portion of the bourgeois ideologists, who have raised themselves to the level of comprehending theoretically the historical movement as a whole.

Of all the classes that stand face to face with the bourgeoisie today, the proletariat alone is a really revolutionary class. The other classes decay and finally disappear in the face of modern industry; the proletariat is its special and essential product.

The lower middle class, the small manufacturer, the shopkeeper, the artisan, the peasant, all these fight against the bourgeoisie, to save from extinction their existence as fractions of the middle class. They are therefore not revolutionary, but conservative. Nay more, they are reactionary, for they try to roll back the wheel of history. If by chance they are revolutionary, they are so only in view of their impending transfer into the proletariat; they thus defend not their present, but their future interests; they desert their own standpoint to place themselves at that of the proletariat.

The 'dangerous class,' the social scum, that passively rotting mass thrown off by the lowest layers of old society, may, here and there, be wept into the movement by a proletarian revolution; its conditions of life, however, prepare it far more for the part of a bribed tool of reactionary intrigue.

The modern labourer, on the contrary, instead of rising with the progress of industry, sinks deeper and deeper below the conditions of existence of his own class. He becomes a pauper, and pauperism develops more rapidly than population and wealth. And here it becomes evident, that the bourgeoisie is unfit any longer to be the ruling class in society, and to impose its conditions of existence upon society as an over-riding law. It is unfit to rule because it is incompetent to assure an existence to its slave within his slavery because it cannot help letting him sink into such a state, that it has to feed him, instead of being fed by him. Society can no longer live under this bourgeoisie, in other words, its existence is no longer compatible with society.

The advance of industry, whose involuntary promoter is the bourgeoisie, replaces the isolation of the labourers, due to competition, by their revolutionary combination, due to association. The development of modern industry, therefore, cuts from under its feet the very foundation on which the bourgeoisie produces and appropriates products. What the bourgeoisie therefore produces, above all, are its own grave-diggers. Its fall and the victory of the proletariat are equally inevitable.

The Communists do not form a separate party opposed to other working class parties.

They have no interests separate and apart from those of the proletariat as a whole.

They do not set up any sectarian principles of their own by which to shape and mould the proletarian movement.

The distinguishing feature of communism is not the abolition of property generally, but the abolition of bourgeois property But modern bourgeois private property is the final and most complete expression of the system of producing and appropriating products that is based on class antagonisms, on the exploitation of the many by the few.

We Communists have been reproached with the desire of abolishing the right of personally acquiring property as the fruit of a man's own labour, which property is alleged to be the groundwork of all personal freedom, activity and independence.

Hard-won, self-acquired, self-earned property! Do you mean the property of the petty artisan and of the small peasant, a form of property that proceeded the bourgeois form? There is no need to abolish that; the development of industry has to a great extent already destroyed it, and is still destroying it daily.

Or do you mean modern bourgeois private property?

But does wage labour create any property for the labourer? Not a bit. It creates capital, i.e., that kind of property which exploits wage labour, and which cannot increase except upon condition of begetting a new supply of wage labour for fresh exploitation. Property, in its present form, is based on the antagonism of Capital and wage labour. Let us examine both sides of this antagonism.

To be a capitalist, is to have not only a purely personal, but a social, status in production. Capital is a collective product, and only by the n y members, nay, in the last resort, only by the united action of all members of society, can it be set in motion.

Capital is therefore not a personal, it is a social power.

Communism deprives no man of the power to appropriate the of society; all that it does is to deprive him of the power to subjugate the labour of others by means of such appropriation.

It has been objected that upon the abolition of property all work will cease, an universal laziness will overtake us.

According to this, bourgeois society ought long ago to have gone to the dogs through sheer idleness; for those of its members who work, acquire nothing, and those who acquire anything, do not work. The whole of this objection is but another expression of the tauology. There family can no longer be any wage labour when there is no longer any capital.

Abolition of the family! Even the most radical flare up at this infamous proposal of the Communists.

On what foundation is the present family, the bourgeois family based? On capital, on private gain. In its completely developed form this family exists only among the bourgeoisie. But this state of things finds its complement in the practical absence of the family among the proletrains, and in public prostitution.

And your education! Is not that also social, and determined by the social conditions under which you educate, by the intervention direct or indirect, of society, by means of schools, etc.? The Communists have not invented the intervention of society in education; they do but seek to alter the character of that intervention, and to rescue education from the influence of the ruling class.

The bourgeois claptrap about the family and education, about the hallowed correlation of parent and child, becomes all the more disgusting, the more, by the action of modern industry, all family ties among the proletarians are torn asunder, and their children transformed into simple articles of commerce and instruments of labour.

But you Communists would introduce community of women, screams the whole bourgeoisie in chorus. The bourgeois sees in his wife a mere instrument of production. He hears that the instruments of production are to be exploited in common, and, naturally, can come to no other conclusion than that the lot of being common to all will likewise fall to the women. He has not even a suspicion that the real point aimed at is to do away with the status of women as mere instruments of production.

For the rest, nothing is more ridiculous than the virtuous indignation of our bourgeois at the community of women which, they pretend, is to be openly and officially established by the Communists. The Communists have no need to introduce community of women; it has existed almost from time immemorial. Our bourgeois, not content with having the wives and daughters of their proletarians at their disposal, not to speak of common prostitutes, take the greatest pleasure in seducing each other's wives.

Bourgeois marriage is in reality a system of wives in common and thus, at the most, what the Communists might possibly be reproached with is that they desire to introduce in substitution for a hypocritically concealed, an openly legalise community of women. For the rest, it is self-evident, that the abolition of the present system of production must bring with it the abolition of the community of women springing from that system, i.e. of prostitution both public and private.

The Communists are further reproached with desiring to abolish countries and nationality. The workingmen have no country. We cannot take from them what they have not 'got. Since the proletariat must first of all acquire political supremacy must rise to be the leading class of the nation, must constitute itself the nation, it is, so far, itself national, though not in the bourgeois sense of the word.

National differences and antagonisms between peoples are daily more and more vanishing, owing to the development of the bourgeoisie, to freedom of commerce, to the world market, to uniformity in the mode of production and in the conditions of life corresponding thereto. The supremacy of the proletariat will cause them to vanish still faster. United action of the leading civilised countries at least, is one of the first conditions for the emancipation of the proletariat. In proportion as the exploitation of one individual by another is put an end to, the exploitation of one nation by another will also be put an end to. In proportion as the antagonism between classes within the nation vanishes, the hostility of one nation to another will come to an end.

The charges against communism made from a religious, a philosophical and, generally, from an ideological standpoint, are not deserving of serious examination.

The Communists disdain to conceal their views and aims. They openly declare that their ends can be attained only by the forcible overthrow of all existing social conditions. Let the ruling classes tremble at a communist revolution. The proletarians have nothing to lose but their chains. They have a world to win. Workingmen of all countries, Unite!

(From *Marx and Egles: Selected Works,* Volume 1, Progress Publishers, Moscow, 1973)

19

Future Society

Communism is the positive abolition of private property, of human self-alienation, and thus, the real appropriation of human nature, through and for man. It is therefore the return of man himself as a social, that is, really human, being, a complete and conscious return which assimilates all the wealth of previous development. Communism as a complete naturalism is humanism, and as a complete humanism is naturalism. It is the definitive resolution of the antagonism between man and Nature, and between man and man. It is the true solution of the conflict between existence and essence, between objectification and self-affirmation, between freedom and necessary, between individual and species. It is the solution of the riddle of history and knows itself to be this solution.

Religion, the family, the State, law, morality, science, art, etc, are particular forms of production and come under its general law. The positive abolition of private property, as the appropriation of human life, it thus the positive abolition of all alienation, and thus the return of man from religion, the family, the State, etc, to his human, i.e. social, life. Religious alienation only occurs in the sphere of consciousness, in the inner life of man, but economic alienation is that of real life, and its abolition therefore affects both aspects. Of course, the development in different nation has a different origin according to whether the actual life the people is more in the realm of mind of in the external world, whether it is a real or ideal life.

We have seen how, on the assumption that private property has been positively abolished, man produces man, himself and then other men, how the object, which is the direct activity of his personality, is at the same time his existence for other men, and their existence for him. Similarly, the material of labour, and man himself as a subject, are the point of origin as well as the result of this movement and because there must be this point of origin, private property is a historical necessity. Therefore, the social character is the universal character of the whole movement; as society itself produces man as man, so it is produced by him. Activity and mind are social in their content, as well as in their origin; they are social activity and social mind. The human significance of Nature only exists for social man, because only in this case is Nature a bond with other men, the basis of his existence for others and of their existence for him. Only then is Nature the basis of his own human existence, and a vital part of human reality. The natural existence of man has become his human existence and Nature itself has become, for him, human. Thus society is the accomplished union of man with Nature, the veritable resurrection of Nature, the realized naturalism of man and the realized humanism of Nature. (*Economic and Philosophical Manuscripts,* 1844).

The realm of freedom only begins, in fact, where that labour which is determined by need and external purposes ceases; it is therefore, by its very nature, outside the sphere of material production proper. Just as the savage must wrestle with Nature in order to satisfy his wants, to maintain and reproduce his life, so also must civilized man, and he must do it in all forms of society and under any possible mode of production. With his development the realm of natural necessity expands, because his wants increase; but at the same time the forces of production, by which these wants are satisfied, also increase. Freedom in this field cannot consist of anything else but the fact that socialized mankind, the associated producers, regulate their interchange with Nature rationally, bring it under their common control, instead of being ruled by it as by some blind power, and accomplish their task with the least expenditure of energy and under such conditions as are proper and worthy for human beings. Nevertheless, this always remains a realm of necessity. Beyond it begins that development of human potentiality for its own sake, the true realm of freedom, which however can only flourish upon that realm of necessity as its basis. The shortening of the working day is its fundamental prerequisite. (*Capital III*)

The 'Free State'- What is This?

It is by no means the aim of the workers, who have freed themselves from the narrow outlook of humble subjects, to set the State free. In the German Empire the State is almost as free as in Russia. Freedom consists in transforming the State from an organ dominating society into one completely subordinate to it, and even at the present time the forms of State are more or less free to the extent that they restrict the 'freedom of the State'.

'Present day society' is capitalist society, which exists in all civilized countries, more or less free from medieval adjuncts, more or less modified by the special historical development of each country, and more or less developed. On the other hand, the 'present day State' changes with a country's frontier. It is different in the Prusso-German Empire from what it is in Switzerland, it is different in England from what it is in the United States. 'The present-day State' is therefore, a fiction. Nevertheless, the different States of the different civilized countries' in spite of their manifold diversity of form, all have this in common , that they are based on modern bourgeois society, only one more or less capitalistically developed. They have, therefore, also certain essential features in common. In this sense it is possible to speak of the present day State in contrast with the future, in which its present root, bourgeois society, will have died away.

The question then arises: What charges will the State undergo in communist society? In other words, what social functions will remain there which are analogous to the present functions of the State? This question can only be answered scientifically, and one does not get a flea-hop nearer to the problem by any number of juxta positions of the word people with the word State. Between capitalist and communist society lies the period of the revolutionary transformation of the one into the other. There corresponds to this also a political transition period in which the State can be nothing but the revolutionary dictatorship of the proletariat.

What we have to deal with here is a communist society, not as it has developed on its own foundation, but on the contrary, just as it emerges from capitalist society; and which is thus in every respect, economically, morally, and intellectually, still stamped with the birth-marks of the old society from whose womb it emerges. Accordingly, the individual producer receive back from society – after the deductions have been made – exactly what he contributes to it. What he has contributed to it is his individual quantum of labour. For example, the social working day consists of the sum of the individual hours of work; the individual labour time of the individual producer is the part of the social working day contributed by him, his share in it. He receives a certificate from society that he has furnished such an amount of labour after deducting his labour for the common funds, and with this certificate he draws from the social stock of means of consumption as much as costs the same amount of labour. The same amount of labour which he has given to society in one form he receives back in another form.

Hence, equal right here is still, in principle, bourgeois right, although principle and practice are no longer at loggerheads, whereas the exchange of equivalents in commodity exchange only exists on the average and not in the individual case. In spite of this advance, equal right is still burdened with bourgeois limitations. The right of the producers is proportional to the labour they supply; the equality consists in the fact that measurement is made with an equal standard, labour.

But one man is superior to another physically or mentally and so supplies more labour in the same time, or can labour for a longer time; and labour, to serve as a measure, must be defined by its duration or intensity, otherwise it ceases to be a standard of measurement. The equal right is an unequal right for unequal labour. It recognizes no class differences, because everyone is only a worker like everyone else; but it tacitly recognizes unequal individual endowment, and thus natural privileges in respect of productive capacity. It is, therefore, in its content, a right of inequality, like every right. Right by its very nature can consist only in the application of an equal standard; but unequal individuals (and they would not be different individuals if they were not unequal) can only be assessed by an equal standard in so far as they are regarded from a single aspect, from one particular side only, as for instance, in the present case, they are regarded only as workers, and nothing more is seen in them, everything else being ignored. Further, one worker is married, another not; one has more children than another, and so on. This, with an equal performance of labour, one individual will in fact receive more than another, one will be richer than another, and so on. To avoid all these defects, right, instead of being equal, would have to be unequal.

But these defects are inevitable in the first phase of communist society as it is when it has just emerged after prolonged birth- pangs from capitalist society. Right can never be higher than the economic structure of society and the cultural development conditioned by it.

In the higher phase of communist society, when the enslaving subordination of the individual to the division of labour, and with it the antithesis between mental and physical labour, has vanished; when labour is no longer merely a means of life but has became life's principal need; when the productive forces have also increased with the all round development of the individual, and all the springs of cooperative wealth flow more abundantly – only then will it be possible completely to transcend the narrow outlook of bourgeois right, and only then will society be able to inscribe on its banners: From each according to his ability, to each according to his needs!

(From *Critique of Gotha Program*, 1825)

20

Epilogue

Western leaders have triumphantly proclaimed the "death of Marxism" We won!" exulted President George Bush in 1990, after the collapse of communism in Eastern Europe and the Soviet Union. The President was declaring the final victory of the "free market" over "big government," savouring the delicious notion that the ideas of the Left, not only in the Eastern bloc but around the globe, were history. Bill Clinton seems to agree that the Left's day is done. Clinton says he has "moved beyond" the old left-right divisions, viewing both Left and Right as Cold War anachronisms and the idea of socialism as a charming relic. As East and West Germans ripped down the Berlin Wall, both liberal and conservative intellectuals were laying the groundwork for this bipartisan burial of the Left. Ralf Dahrendorf, a liberal and one of the most eminent writers about the 1989 "evolution" in Eastern Europe, announces that every form of socialism and "the hundreds of byways of Marxism" are now all ending in the sewers of discarded history". He writes that to speak of "socialism with a human face" is "pathetic" as is the effort by some leftists to construct a "third way" between capitalism and socialism, which Dahrendorf calls "a mirage." After the "double nightmare of Stalin and Brezhnev", and the disenchantment with social democracy in Scandinavia, symbolized by Swedish voters in 1991 throwing out their labour government, the Left is spent. Many commentators have written that the Left has already self-destructed. Neoconservative sociologist Seymour Martin Lipset writes that "in country after country, socialist and other left learning parties have taken the ideological road back to capitalism." The Left is dissolving itself, Lipset suggests, because it is obvious that leftist economics is a disaster and that the electorate will no longer put leftists in power.

Indeed, as the dust clears after the collapse of the Berlin Wall, it is no longer obvious who or what the left is. Fifty years ago, socialists and communist groups constituted a clear "left," as did civil rights and anti-war activists in the 1990s. But today, while there are lots of "progressive" and dissenting groups, from radical feminists to deep ecologists, who makes up the Left? The only people publicly challenging the idea of the death of the Left have been a small number of radical or Marxist intellectuals who have published their own interpretations of the events in Eastern Europe. Their views are unambiguous: that Eastern Europe is no death warrant for the Left. As Michael Lowy wrote in the Marxist journal *Monthly Review*, I cannot die before being born. Communism is not dead it is not yet born. The same applies to socialism.

Lowy believes, like many Western radicals, that Eastern European socialism was "far from socialism. What the conservative or liberal media call 'the death of communism' is in fact the crisis of the authoritarian and bureaucratic system of development first established in the USSR in the 1920s and 1930s on the ashes of the Russian revolution ... What is moribund and dying in Eastern Europe". Lowy concludes, "is not Communism' but its bureaucratic caricature: the monopoly of power by the nomenclature." Marxist historian Eric Hobsbawm also writes that there remains a compelling case for a "socialist agenda of the 21st century" and that socialism will arise again "from the ashes". "The Eastern European and Soviet working classes will be bitterly disillusioned when they see exactly how market economics really works." If we 'have historical imagination and dare to be Marxists," "the so-called death of socialism will one day transform itself, Phonix-like, into a new birth. Perhaps, but there is a knee-jerk quality here, something as ideologically predictable in these Marxists' responses as the mainstream writers who repeat the "death of socialism" like a mantra. The defensiveness of the Marxists is tangible and their almost reflexive call to struggle on for the real socialism bespeaks the angst of the true believer. A Left not able to contemplate the possibility of its own death may be a Left whose survival in the end will not make much difference.

The mainstream is too eager to bid a hasty and final farewell to the Left, too grandiose in its proclamations of the "end of history," and too smugly complacent about the triumph of capitalism. Marxist writers are too quick to gloss over the significance of what has happened in Eastern Europe, too premature in announcing business as usual for the Left, and too facile in their calls for democratic socialism. One finds on both sides some brilliant argumentation and stylish writing but not great wisdom. Remarkably, the "death of the Left" writers, who have written instructively about the decay of civil society in the East, say almost nothing about the crisis in the West. The implicit view is that the collapse of communism proves our own troubles to be pedestrian. In fact, by enthralling themselves and the public with the spectacle of communism's grand collapse, they have obscured the gravity of the West's ills and the need for a new transformative voice.

Western capitalism may have "won," but its problems, as the public has begun to recognize, are not those of ordinary recession nor of traditional political apathy or routine social upheaval. By the early 1990s, a large majority of US citizens told pollsters that they believed the country was fundamentally "off course" and moving in the wrong direction." Alarmed by urban decay, poverty, crime, homelessness, low wages and high unemployment, high medical cost, crumbling public education and many other problems, those polled feared that things would only get worse and sensed that the crisis has a systemic character. Most were pessimistic that any form of mainstream politics could solve the problems.

Indeed, there is a surprising similarity between the problems of Western societies and the disorders of the failed socialist countries. Western economies are not in the same terminal condition as the Eastern ones, but there are overwhelming economic difficulties, even in the most prosperous countries such as the United States. Wages in the United States have declined since 1973, and for the first time children can no longer expect to enjoy a standard of living better than their parents. Productivity and global market share have tumbled in one industry after another. Despite President Clinton's deficit-cutting zeal, the total federal government debt, by 1994, had reached a record $4.6 trillion. None of the conventional fiscal or monetary tools seem to solve the problem-suggesting, as in the East, the need for systemic change. But perhaps the most serious problem facing the West is not economic but social again suggesting surprising parallels with the Eastern bloc failure.

In the United States and other Western countries, similar social and moral although of quite different origins, are spreading. There are endless social statistics that suggest a serious weakening of civil society. We have the highest murder rate in our history. Over fifty million households' stock guns to protect themselves. By one estimate, 135,000 kids bring guns to school on any given day. The social infrastructure is eroding. As affordable housing shrinks, the homeless are multiplying. At least thirty-five million have no health insurance, and 10 percent of the country uses food stamps. Over thirty million are poor, including one out of every five children. Life expectancy of our black urban youth is lower than that of children of the same age in Bangladesh.

Americans of every class are discovering forms of insecurity formerly reserved for the poor. Over one-third of the labour force is disposable workers; these include accountants and middle managers as well as janitors, supermarket cashiers, and factory labourers. As jobs become more contingent for everyone, so do families. Over 50 percent of all marriages break up (75 percent among young married), about 70 percent of children will experience a change, loss, or absence of one parent before age eighteen, and, by the year 2000, over 50 percent of adults are projected to be single or divorced, all suggesting an atomization and family of unprecedented in modern times.' The erosion of civil society is the dark side of what some are calling "postmodern capitalism." Ever since the British enclosures threw the peasantry off the land, as Karl Polanyi described in his epochal book The Great Transformation, the history of capitalism has meant never-ending social dislocation, leaving a trail of broken communities and uprooted workers. But as multinational corporations now shift capital and technology with lightning speed around the globe, they have upped the ante, shredding the fragile social contract.

A healthy civil society is marked by a robust sense of solidarity, in which intact families, neighborhoods, work communities, and other voluntary association cooperate for common ends. A leftist concept of civil 'society envisions democratic communities that meet needs for belonging and meaning while struggling against injustice in all social spheres. This implies, that the Left has not only to pursue a robust agenda of economic democracy but help reshape familial, sexual, ethnic, racial, religious, and other communities so that they create "habits of the heart" consistent with universal ideals of equality and solidarity.

The conservatives argue that the Left is fooling itself; it doesn't exist. Europe is just a sign of that. It wasn't even really the Left, but was something the Left had a relation to. It is more than disillusionment, it is a kind of sudden denuding. "There are two possibilities: either things will get worse, or there will be a catastrophe." The Left is now experiencing a period of profound disillusionment. Although all would agree that the economic and political systems in Eastern Europe and the Soviet Union were not what Marx meant when he referred to communism or even socialism, these were the only countries in the modern world to claim the Marxist tradition as their origin.

The Eastern European and Soviet collapse has precipitated a crisis within Marxism; however, academics are only beginning to fathom its depth. It is hard to identify how Marxism has been challenged by the events. These events won't reduce its usefulness for understanding capitalism. On the other hand, these events could have a debilitating effect on theory in that they will spark changes in the theory and some rethinking on the part of the Left. It is hard to predict exactly how. These events should, but won't necessarily, precipitate a lot of soul-searching on the Left. The idea is that, because this Stalinist socialism has collapsed Marxism is dead. We don't buy that at all, any more than you could claim that capitalism is finished and you will never see it again on the globe. In the short term, I think this is a time when Marxists, socialists, leftists. They are very pessimistic. But I think in the medium-to-long term, there is a possibility that what we're witnessing in the late eighties and early nineties is the fertilizing ideological landscape. Out of the wreckage of Stalinism it may possible to build a democratic socialism.

People are making all of these assumptions about the death of socialism based on the demise of Stalinism – that doesn't make any sense. The demise of Stalinism had nothing to do with the different types of socialism. This was a reflection on Stalinism and not a reflection on socialist countries. Now that the socialist systems of Eastern Europe and the Soviet Union have been discredited. The leftist position at the political and academic levels of has become one of scorn: "If you called someone a communist now, that wouldn't be a way to make people fear them but a way to make them laugh. It would be a form of ridicule". On the other hand, there are some academics who seem to be unconcerned with the implications of these events and who are able to dismiss them in a flippant manner. Marxist theory was already being challenged in major ways from within as much as from without. Since the 1950s and 1960s there has been much critique and revision. In the last ten years – the post - 68 period-there's been an impact on those working within and around Marxism. These revisions have come from poststructuralist and postmodernist arguments. People like Foucault and some of the deconstructionists were part of a broad-sided challcnge to Marxist theory, and then came this total disruption in Eastern Europe and the complete fragmentation of the Soviet empire. So it wasn't as if Marxism in general was sailing smoothly. It was an already embattled and tattered ship.

There are lots of achievements of the intellectual Left and the sixties generation in terms of cultural politics and the way we think about the world. So there have been these developments which are encouraging in one sphere or another, momentary victories which have masked the lingering, long-term crisis of Marxist politics. None of us have quite figured out what we're going to do in America to seriously impact the mainstream politics. Thus, the Left is enveloped in a state of disillusionment, a spiritual crisis, a "dark night of the soul." This position is characterized by moralization, uncertainty, hopelessness, and even denial. After gradually building up over the course of several decades, such sentiments are now at a peak. Knowing that there is a crisis, we may now seek to understand what this state of affairs implies for Marxist theory. The largest single area of disagreement among leftist academics has to do with the relative strengths and weaknesses of Marxist theory within the context of the larger spiritual crisis of a Left bereft of any existing socialist model. Some have cast Marxism aside for theoretical positions that more fully address their concerns. Other cling to the tools Marxism has to offer for the lack of a better alternative. It is over the attractiveness or unattractiveness of Marxist principles in a post-communist world that the debate among progressive intellectuals comes to bear. Marxism continues to present a discriminating critique of power structures within capitalism.

Marxism is extremely relevant for critiquing society, particularly capitalist society. Everything it had to say about how capitalism functioned, who created the wealth versus who benefits, all these basic fundamental

Marxist ideas are applicable today, or twenty years from now. Marxism remains very empowering for the dispossessed within society insofar as it gives them hope for a brighter future.

Marxism is a secular vision of self and word transformation that is incredibly enabling for people who feel themselves to be dispossessed and disenfranchised. In secular terms, Marxism survives for many of the reasons that religions survive, and it will have this type of staying power and also be helped by the dilemmas which capitalism keeps confronting people with. Beyond presenting a critique of the power structures within capitalism, Marxism continues to allow one to understand the actual workings of the capitalist economy. Marxism offers a vision that there was a different way to organize the economy. There were so many ways that Marxism made sense of particular economic problems in western capitalism, and still does make sense of the ups and downs of the economy, the rise and fall of different powers, and so on – all these fronts of critical analysis of the works of capitalism that Marxism seemed to give us still seem to make sense. Although most academics do believe that Marxism is still very important as a critique, point out that Marxism is not a scientific endeavour per se, but a set of tools for looking at social and political phenomena. It remains powerful in that regard. There is a more suitable vocabulary or way of talking about those phenomena. But the Marxisian vocabulary concepts such as class, exploitation, power, etcetera- are the most powerful tools and without some alternative, would result in abandoning the problems in social and political phenomena.

The Failings of Marxism

In the light of collapse of socialism and communism, academic perceptions of the areas in which Marxist theory falls short are much more varied than the areas considered to be its strengths. It must be noted that all of these failings of Marxism leave enough of the theoretical perspectives intact to be worthwhile as a tool for analysis and many theorists argue that some of the assumptions Marxism shares with the Enlightenment are really questionable – the way human beings operate in the world, the emphatically rational nature of human beings, and the Marxist view that if only the working class were "sober" – Marx uses that image a lot. He hopes to make workers sober by ripping off all the drugs and narcotics that lay on people through religion, metaphysics, and so forth. Foucault's view is that Marx has not got the faintest idea of what humans are like – they're much more strange, their relationship to power is so bizarre. [Thus] he focuses on how far out of touch Marx is – that he doesn't comprehend anything. That's why he's so interested in power. And this all comes at a time just when Eastern Europe blows up. Academics argue that Marxism is limited in other ways as well. Marxism, while said to be a theory that is also a form of practice, actually provides little practical guidance for its application beyond calling for a revolution by the proletariat. Once you recognise, say, who your enemies are – and that's what Marxism does, it tells you who your enemies are – how does it distinguish the practice of one group from another, or how does it give more detailed practical guidance for how to pursue environmental struggles, union organizing strategies, or anything like that?

Some argue that Marxism has obscured any viable political strategy because of its romance with revolution. We think that essentially if you feel that most popular mobilizations are very good but limited in that their further development means entering the political system in a serious way, it means you've got to start thinking about what mass-democratic politics is all about-how you influence it. And Marxism isn't a very good guide on that – or at least the kind of Marxism we've had elaborated for us within the academy of socialist parties. This criticism does not stop with the acknowledgment of the role of political structures, but continues with a more direct critique of the Marxist assumptions concerning the economic base.

We agree with Habermas that we have to reconstruct the productive model of Marxism. The emphasis on production is wrong. There is no way to isolate production from social relations. There is no transformation without democratization; so the idea that we could have a higher level of freedom by changing an economy independently of dealing with the democratic structures is absurd. In terms of "keeping the faith," we think that element of Marxian analysis is right. In terms of capitalistic monopoly and its distortions, corruptions, etcetera, Marx is completely right about that; but one does not change that simply by altering the productive mechanism. This is ineffective from the very issue of productive relations themselves because what happens is we tend to destroy economies. Eastern bloc countries could barely provide for their own needs. These were totally repressive societies. Marx had a pretty simplistic notion of economy –

economies require a great deal of direction, and it's not a simple matter of distribution; it's a problem of public wealth and how it's distributed. In the twentieth century, you can't merely take over the means of production; that would never work because whoever takes it over simply controls it – "let's keep it for us." So other mechanisms have to intervene.

It may even be that such a focus on the means of production ultimately proved to be the downfall of the economic systems of the Eastern bloc countries. State central planning apparently is not up to the management of the complexity of a modern technological society. It doesn't seem to be able to generate technical innovation. It did not seem in the Soviet Union and Eastern Europe to properly allocate price mechanisms so that we could evolve successfully from producing goods to consuming goods. It didn't seem to be able to create a set of structures for high-quality production of everyday commodities. Another perceived weakness is that, as "grand theorists" with a very broad focus, Marxists hubris has proven to be the undoing of the Marxist experiment.

On the other hand, there is also the notion that Marxism is too limited in its focus on class. Such a restricted focus on class seems to imply that a single revolution is needed in order to correct the ills of society, a misapprehension borne out by the events in Eastern Europe and the Soviet Union. There is an assumption that there is a revolution which will take place not forty or fifty revolutions taking place at same time – and that revolution will be taking place at the most fundamental point in society. The implication is that changes in all the other point are not fundamental and that focusing on them is a disservice to this fundamental change because once this single change is made, all forms of oppression will be eliminated – including those based on gender, race, and so on. That's hard to accept. However, not everyone agrees that focus on class is a problems with Marxism. Some academics feel that the Left has moved too far away from class issues.

Marx's theory of class stratification, in which he describes the division between the bourgeoisie and the proletariat, is one of the central ideas of Marxism. However, many academics feel that dividing the populace solely on the basis of class blinds Marxists to other divisions within society. The sudden release of ethnic tensions in Eastern Europe and the Soviet Union illustrates the point. The race and ethnicity – and one could also add gender as well as other differences such as sexual orientation – produce equally fundamental divisions and hierarchies within society. This crisis within the Left is also a challenge to Marxist stratification theory, which is based on the primacy of class over race or ethnicity. The alleged primacy of class needs to be either defended or reduced, but it certainly cannot stand unexamined by a seeker after truth.

It's clear from the past events that this theory does not adequately deal with religious and ethnic passions that animate people all the critics point out that the focus of rethinking of Marxian theory will be on the state, state planning, organization, etc. Overall, there is a deeper disenchantment with the state, and attempts have been made to refine the role of the state within Marxian theory, which have been useful but have not really integrated into classical theory of Marx. The model in which the market is completely predominant and the state is weak and reactive is really only true in England and America. In Germany and France, certainly had a state – managed development of capitalism. Those are certainly successful capitalist models in that certainly there's a high- tech, high level of productivity. We are not saying that perfect social justice has been achieved in those societies, but those are certainly models of the state being very proactive in economic development. But then they become unduly burdensome on the economic process. That certainly is from a market point of view with the assumption that getting a market established is a legitimate objective. Any antidemocratic state is clearly a problem. We would not want to lay the Soviet experiment at the feet of Marxism, basically. If we think of the major totalitarian systems which are available to the Eurocentric imagination, there's Russia, Where there is some connection to Marxist theory; Nazi Germany, where there is no connection to Marxist theory; and apartheid in South Africa, where there is also no connection to Marxist theory. The Third Reich and apartheid are conducted in the teeth of Marxism – against Marxism. There's any real correlation between Marxist theory on the one hand and totalitarian political practice on the other. Unfortunately, there are a number of ways to construct totalitarian experiments. Certain variants of Marxism are clearly one of them, but not one out of three. Some would also argue that the problems surrounding a theory of the state are actually greater than those of Marxism in itself. The point is that theories of the state in general are inadequate and need much more attention. One will recall that the Marxist critique and analysis of capitalist systems is regarded as one of its most important assets. However, there is also a point at which this asset becomes a liability in that a critique implies a viable alternative at the risk of losing its credibility. Marxist analysis and critique have been jeopardized. The spiritual crisis facing the Left at this time boils down to the possibilities of finding alternative economic and political structures. Thus, we have arrived at the heart of the predicament in which the Left has become mired.

Capitalism Has Not Won

Although there is much disillusionment among the Left, there is still a general conviction that capitalism is a system with deep problems of its own. Some even see it on the verge of a collapse. We can't speak of the collapse of communism/socialism without wondering about the imminent collapse of capitalism, since capitalism is undergoing more strain now than it has in years. The observable signs of crisis within the capitalist system are many, although not everyone would agree as to what, exactly they are. The bottom line seems to be that, as a system, it is just not working for a significant number of people. While we're talking of the demise of socialism, capitalism is in dire strait. If you look at the strongest capitalist country in the world the standard of living is on the decline, wages are stagnant, unemployment is persistent, there's increasing poverty, and so on. Capitalism is not working for us, and it's getting worse. At the precise moment in world history where people are saying that capitalism is the wave of the future, in every capitalist society there is decline. The decline is faster in communist societies. But capitalist societies are undergoing these crises too. We spent too much on the military just as they have. We haven't trained our civilian sector, we haven't built up our infrastructure, and we haven't delivered the goods to the people who are demanding and need them. This is happening in a lot of places, so we don't think capitalism in its many forms is the wave of the future. Below the surface of concrete indicators, there is the feeling of a global crisis that includes capitalism in its dark embrace. Perhaps there is a more pervasive lack of inspiration which includes capitalist systems since it is even more bankrupt intellectually; it has no ideas. The Left is a mess, but so is conservatism and liberalism-so is capitalism. Thus, while the Left is caught in an ideological mire of its own and the crisis it is experiencing is much more acute, the malaise in which it finds itself may be an indicator of something much more widespread. You look at the reaction to government in the United States – belief structures, the general collapse of the Bush administration, the need to fight wars to keep the thing going the great disaffection that people have. We wonder if there's not some kind of worldwide movement or at least some paralysis that's occurring in Western societies.

Marx and Marxism gives us a heightened awarencss that an ideology is a vital part of any society. As part of his particular ideology, Marx stressed the way in which a society's ethos and values are created by its members. This awareness is now part of our consciousness. Although Marx did not see his own work as ideological, that very work, paradoxically, forces us to recognize it as such. Marx was a great creative battle, always striving for a better world. Nothing was sacred for him, nothing curtailed his desire to perceive the human condition clearly and to act on that perception. The trust honour we can accord him is to carry on in his spirit. Marxism, as a doctrine, an ideology, is outmoded. It is largely irrelevant to our contemporary problems. Its economic analysis is anachronistic, as is its appeal to class conflict. It offers pious simplicities, where our problems are complex.

Marxism, in its various national embodiments, varies greatly: the Yugoslav version is not the same as the Russian, nor is the Chinese the same as the Ethiopian. We have noted the paradox of international Marxism fuelling nationalist revolutions. Marx had correctly called attention to the breakdown of affective ties in economic life under capitalism – the cash nexus was the only one remaining that he recognized – but neglected the other ties that contrived to hold people to gather: religious, ethics, communal, and nationalistic. In fact, Marxism itself as secular or civil religion gave a valid content to new nationalism, supplying a source of unity to former African tribal kingdoms as well as to ancient celestial ones, such as the Chinese. National Marxism's that comprise what we call "Marxism", and which vary so greatly, while still sharing, to greater or lesser degree, the simplicities of the overarching ideology.

There is a slogan current today: "Better dead than Red". For those who hold to this view, Communism is a monstrous evil, a world in the hands of the Devil. Rather than "live" under such conditions, violent anti-Marxists would prefer to bring the world crashing down on all our head I hope that my book helps dispelling such a simple-minded notion. Whatever the flaws in Marxism, it still remains a human, not inhuman, creation, with the potentiality for creating viable cultures. Opposition to it should not cause us to overlook this fact. Marxism is not evil incarnate, but one among a number of current ways of understanding human condition and organizing human societies.

With this said, I can return to my statement that it is outmoded. The fact is that we are confronted with problems that go well beyond the quarrels of capitalism and communism. We appear to have a cluster of world –wide problems that has created a special crisis of human survival: overpopulation, depletion of resources, pollution, and overwhelming all else, nuclear holocaust. Human will, guided by good will, and critical understanding – these are essentials needed to deal with the challenge. Capitalism and communism, locked in ideological conflict, are quite a truly dialectical theory.

Let us perform a thought experiment. Imagine the United State as a communist state. Would this end conflict and solve the problems? Let us imagine the reverse: Russian becomes capitalistic. A glance at history shows that capitalist nations have entered into wars and conflicts with each other, too. There is no simple solution. Capitalism and communism must, for the time being co-exist if humanity is to exist. At some point being confronted to cope with the problems now facing the world, both will fade into some other social system. Mao's comment to Edgar Snow in 1965 is illuminating. A thousand years from now all of us, he said, even Marx, Engels, and Lenin would probably appear rather ridiculous.

Mao, we must cope with our present reality. Détente, co-existence, whatever one may call it, is the order of the day. It should not be grudging, but rather, carried out in a spirit of mutuality, recognizing in the opponent a human quality.

I have written this book in that spirit. Marx's meaning is a human one – his own favourite maxim was that "Nothing human is alien to me"– and calls for a human response. His is a great creative effort, however open to criticism and rejection in its dogmatic form. Marxists and non-Marxist alike need to re-examine Marx in the light of the realities that have been created since his time. We must all recognize the mote in our own eyes and the way it blinds us to "what should be" – that we being to this task. Marx, that great creative spirit with carbuncles, places this enterprise forcefully before us as he wrestles with the tension between his desires for a religious ending and his drive for a critical, or analytic, understanding and solution to the industrial crisis of his time. We, in our time, with our crisis, must wrestle as mightily as he did. This is the final meaning inhering in the life and work of Karl Marx.

Bibliography

Althusser, L. *For Marx*, London, 1977.

Althusser, L. and Balibar, E. *Reading Capital*, London, 1975.

Anderson, P. *Considerations on Western Marxism*, London, 1977.

Arthur, C. *Dialectics of Labour: Marx and his Relation to Hegel*, Oxford, 1986.

Aston, T. and Philpin, C. *The Brenner Debate,* Cambridge, 1985.

Avineri, S. *Social and Political Thought of Karl Marx*, Cambridge, 1968. (see also under ID.)

Barren, M. 'Marxism-feminism and the work of Karl Marx', in B. Matthews (ed.) *Marx: a Hundred Years on*, London, 1983.

Bologh, R. *Dialectical Phenomenology: Marx's Method*, London, 1979.

Bottomore, T. *Marxist Sociology*, London, 1975.

Bottomore, T. (ed.) *Modern Interpretations of Marx*, Oxford, 1981. (see also under IB, 3A.)

Brewer, A. *Guide to Marx's Capital,* Cambridge, 1984.

Buchanan, A. *Marx and Justice*, London, 1982.

Carver, T. *Marx's Social Theory*, Oxford, 1982.

Carver, T. *Marx and Engels: the Intellectual Relationship*, Brighton, 1983. (see also under ID.)

Clarke, S. *Marx, marginalism and modern sociology*, London, 1983.

Cleaver, H. *Reading Capital Politically*, Austin, 1979.

Cohen, G. A. *Karl Marx's Theory of History: a Defence*, Oxford, 1978.

Cohen, M. et al. (eds) *Marx, Justice, and History*, Princeton, 1980.

Colletti, L. (ed.) 'Bernstein and the Marxism of the Second International', in *From Rousseau to Lenin*, London, 1972.

Colletti, L. *Marxism and Hegel*, London, 1973. (See also under ID.)

Collins, H. and Abramski, C. *Karl Marx and the British Labour Movement*, London, 1985.

Corrigan, P. and Sayer, D. 'How the law rules: variations on some themes in Karl Marx', in B. Fryer (ed.) *Law, State and Society,* London, 1981.

Corrigan, P. and Sayer, D. 'Revolution against the stale: context and significance of Marx's later writings', in *Dialectical Anthropology,* 12 (1), 1987.

Corrigan, P., Ramsay, H., and Sayer, D. *Socialist Construction and Marxist Theory*, London/New York, 1978.

Coulter, J. 'Marx and the Engels paradox', *Socialist Register*, 1971.

Cummings, I. *Marx, Engels, and National Movements*, New York, 1980.

Cutler, A., Kindness, B., Hirst, P., and Hussain, *A. Marx's Capital and Capitalism Today, 2 vols*, London, 1978.

de Brunhoff, S. *Marx on Money*, New York, 1976.

Delia Volpe, G. *Rousseau and Marx*, New Jersey, 1979.

Dobb, M. *Studies in the Development of Capitalism*, London, 1946.

Draper, H. *Karl Marx's Theory of Revolution, 2 vols,* New York, 1977-78. (see also under ID, 2, 1871a, 3A.)

Dunayevskaya, R. Rosa Luxemburg, *Women's Liberation, and Marx's Philosophy of Revolution,* New Jersey, 1981.

Durkheim, E. *Professional Ethics and Civic Morals*, London, 1957.

Elson, D. (ed.) *Value: the Representation of Labour in Capitalism*, New Jersey, 1979.

Elster, J. *Making Sense of Marx*, Cambridge, 1985.

Elster, J. *An introduction to Karl Marx*, Cambridge, 19' 5. (see also under IB.)

Evans, M. *Karl Marx,* Bloomington, 1975.

Gandy, D. R. *Marx and History*, Austin, 1979.

Geras, N. *Marx and Human Nature*, London, 1983.

Gilbert, A. *Marx's Politics: Communists and Citizens*, London, 1981.

Godelier, M. *L'ldeel et le Matfriel,* Paris, 1984.

Gould, C. *Marx's Social Ontology*, Cambridge, Mass., 1978.

Harris, L. and Fine, B. *Rereading Capital*, New York, 1979.

Heller, A. *The Theory of Need in Marx,* London, 1976.

Henry, M. Marx: *A Philosophy of Human Reality,* Bloomington, 1983.

Hilton, R. (ed.) *Transition from Feudalism to Capitalist*, London, 1978.

Hodges, D. '*Engels's contribution to Marxism*', Socialist Register, 1965.

Howard, M. and King, J. *Political Economy of Marx*, 2nd edn, London, 1985.

Hunt, R. *Political Ideas of Marx and Engels*, London, 1984.

Hyppolite, J. Studies on Marx and Hegel, London, 1969.

Jones, G. S. 'Engels and the end of classical German philosophy', *New Left Review* 79, 1973.

Jones, G. S. 'Engels and the genesis of Marxism', *New Left Review* 106, 1977.

Kain, P. *Marx's Method, Epistemology, and Humanism*, Sovietica, 1986.

Kolakowski, L. *Main Currents of Marxism, 3 vols*, Oxford, 1978.

Korsch, K. *Marxism and Philosophy*, London, 1971.

Krader, L, 'Works of Marx and Engels in ethnology compared', *International Review of Social History* 18 (2), 1973.

Krader, L. *The Asiatic Mode of Production*, Assen, 1975.

Krader, L. 'Still more on Marx, Engels, and Morgan', *Current Anthropology* 18, 1977. (see also under 2, 1879a, 1881a.)

Larrain, J. *Marxism and Ideology*, London, 1983.

Lefebvre, H. *Sociology of Karl Marx*, London, 1968.

Lichtheim, G. *From Marx to Hegel*, London, 1971.

Lippi, M. *Value and Naturalism in Marx*, New York, 1980.

Lukacs, G. *History and Class Consciousness*, London, 1970.

McBride, W. *Philosophy of Marx*, London, 1977.

McCarthy, T. *Marx and the Proletariat,* Westport, 1978.

McGovern, A. 'Karl Marx's first political writings: the Rheinische Zeitung 1842-3', in F. Adelmann (ed.) *Demythologising Marxism*, Hague, 1969.

McLellan, D. *The Young Hegelians and Karl Marx*, London, 1969.

McLellan, D. *Marx before Marxism*, London, 1970.

McLellan, D. *Marxism after Marx*, London, 1979. (See also under IB, ID, 2, 1858a, and 3B.)

McLellan, D. (ed.) *Marx: the First 100 Years,* London, 1983.

McMurtry, J. *The Structure of Marx's World View*, Princeton, 1978.

McQuarie, D. (ed.) *Marx: Sociology, Social Change, Capitalism*, London, 1978.

Maguire, J. *Marx's Paris Writings*, Dublin, 1972.

Maguire, J. *Marx's Theory of Politics*, Cambridge, 1978.

Mandel, E. *Introduction to Marxist Economic Theory*, New York, 1970.

Mandel, E. *Formation of Marx's Economic Thought*, London, 1971.

Matthews, B. (ed.) *Marx: a Hundred Years On*, London, 1983.

Meek, R. *Studies in the Labour Theory of Value*, 2nd edn, London, 1973.

Melotti, U. *Marx and the 3rd World*, London, 1977.

Mepham, J. "Theory of ideology in Capital', in Mepham and Ruben (eds) *Issues in Marxist Philosophy*, vol. 3, 1979.

Mepharn, J. and Ruben, D. *Issues in Marxist Philosophy, 3 vols*, Brighton, 1979.

Meszaros, I. *Marx's Theory of Alienation,* London, 1970.

Nicolaus, M. 'The unknown Marx', *New Left Review 48*, 1968. (see also under 2, 1858a.)

Oakley, A. *Marx's Critique of Political Economy: Intellectual Sources and Evolution, 2 vols,* London, 1984-85. (see also under 3A.)

Oilman, B. Alienation: *Marx's Critique of Man in Capitalist Society*, 2nd edn, Cambridge, 1976.

Ollman, B. 'Marx's vision of communism', *Critique*, 1978. Pare,

Parekh, B. *Marx's Theory of Ideology*, London, 1982.

Pashukanis, E. *Law and Marxism*, London, 1978.

Paul, D. 'In the interest of civilisation: Marxist views of race and culture in the 19th century'. *Journal of the History of Ideas* 42, 1981.

Perez-Diaz, V. State, *Bureaucracy and Civil Society: a Critical Discussion of the Political Theory of Karl Marx*, London, 1978.

Phillips, P. *Marx and Engels on Law and Laws*, Oxford, 1980.

Pilling, G. *Marx's Capital: Philosophy and Political Economy*, London, 1980.

Prawer, S. *Marx and World Literature*, Oxford, 1976.

Prinz, A. 'Background and ulterior motive to Marx's Preface of 1859', *Journal of the History of Ideas* 30, 1969.

Rader, M. *Marx's Interpretation of History,* Stanford, 1978.

Rattansi, A. *Marx and the Division of Labour*, London, 1983.

Riazanov, D. *Karl Marx: Man, Thinker, Revolutionist,* London, 1927.

Rosdolsky, R. *Making of Marx's Capital*, London, 1968.

Rosen, Z. *Bruno Bauer and Karl Marx,* Hague, 1977.

Roth, M. and Eldred, M. *Guide to Marx's Capital,* London, 1978.

Rubel, M. 'Les cahiers de lecture de Karl Marx. I. 1840-53', *International Review of Social History* 2, 1957.

Rubel, M. 'Les premieres lectures economiques de Karl Marx', *Etudes de Marxologie* 2, 1959.

Rubel, M. *Rubel on Marx: 5 essays*, Cambridge, 1981.

Ruben, D. *Marxism and Materialism*, New Jersey, 1977.

Rubin, I. *Essays on Marx's Theory of Value*, Detroit, 1972.

Sayer, M. *Marxism and the Question of the Asiatic Mode of Production*, Hague, 1978.

Sayer, D. *Marx's Method: Ideology, Science and Critique in Capital*, 2nd edn, Brighton, 1983 [1983a].

Sayer, D. 'Critique of politics and political economy; capitalism, communism and state in Marx's writings of the mid-1840s', *Sociological Review* 33 (2), 1985.

Sayer, D. *The Violence of Abstraction,* Oxford, 1987. (see also under 3A, and 3C, Corrigan.)

Schmidt, A. *Concept of Nature in Marx*, London, 1971.

Seliger, M. *Marxist Conception of Ideology,* Cambridge, 1979.

Shaw, W. *Marx's Theory of History,* London, 1978.

Sherovei Marcuse, E. *Emancipation and Consciousness: Dogmatic and Dialectical Perspectives in the Early Marx*, Oxford, 1986.

Singer, P. *Marx*, London, 1980.

Steedman, I. *Marx after Sraffa*, London, 1977.

Steedman, I. et al. *The Value Controversy*, London, 1981.

Struick, D. 'Marx and mathematics', *Science and Society* 12, 1948.

Suchting, W. *Marx: An Introduction*, New York, 1983.

Sweezy, P. *Theory of Capitalist Development*, New York, 1942.

Teeple, G. *Marx's Critique of Politics 1842-47*, Toronto, 1984.

Thomas, P. *Karl Marx and the Anarchists,* London, 1980.

Thompson, E. P. *Poverty of Theory*, London, 1978.

Tucker, D. F. *Marxism and Individualism*, New York, 1980.

Turner, B. *Marx and the End of Orientalism*, London, 1978.

Walker, A. *Marx: His Theory and its Context,* London, 1978.

Walliman, I. *Estrangement: Marx's Conception of Human Nature and the Division of Labour,* Westport, 1981.

Wolff, R. P. *Understanding Marx: a Reconstruction and Critique of Capital*, Oxford, 1985.

Worsley, P. *Marx and Marxism,* London, 1982.

Zeleny, J. *The Logic of Marx,* London, 1980.

Index